Students' Book

Language Issues

A course for advanced learners

Gillian Porter-Ladousse

Longman

Contents chart

Unit	Topics	Grammar diagnosis	Grammar development
1	How memory functions	Revision	
2	Astrology and sects	Uses of continuous tenses	Other uses of continuous tenses
3	Nostalgia: what it means to you	*Used to* and *would*	Different uses of *would*
4	Language policies and issues	*The*, *a* and *Ø* articles: basic points	*A*, *the*, *Ø*: some guidelines for advanced learners
5	Coincidences	Past tenses	Past perfect and simple past
6	Learning difficulties	Adverbs: word order	Adverbs and adverbials in initial position Adjectives: word order
7	Fakes and forgeries	Present and past participles	Adverbial participle clauses and adverbial clauses Participles after linking words
8	Ways of being successful	Expressing the future	Future continuous tense
9	The film or the book?	*Can* and *be able to* for ability *Can*, *could*, *may* and *might* for possibility	*Could have*, *may have*, *might have*: attitudes Conversational uses of *may*, *might*, *can* and *could*
10	Growing up (reading literature)	Expressing contrast	Contrast: difference or surprise Different uses of *though*
11	The importance of colour	*It* and *there*	*It*, *this* and *that*: referring backwards and forwards Using *it* with delayed subjects
12	Attitudes to animals	Nouns in groups: – the link with *'s* or *s'* – understanding relationships	Other ways of grouping nouns
13	Eccentricity	Link words	Linking ideas: defining and non-defining clauses
14	Education	Ellipsis and substitution	*One* as a substitute word Ellipsis
15	The future	Conditional sentences	Mixed conditionals Modal auxiliaries in conditional sentences Hypothetical situations
16	Creativity	Preferences	Hopes and wishes
17	Differences of age and culture	Comparisons	Comparisons: continuing processes
18	Current affairs and television programmes	Question tags	Focussing on information: – auxiliary verbs – cleft sentences

Language patterns/ About language	Talking effectively	Vocabulary	Writing
	Chief characteristics of English pronunciation Contrastive analysis	Ways of learning vocabulary	The writing process Appropriacy
Jargon	Weak forms and linking	Personality adjectives Dealing with difficult words	Note taking Report writing
	Stressed and unstressed forms of *would*	Describing objects Multi-part verbs: separable and non separable particles	Creating atmosphere
Base forms with and without *to* with active and passive verbs	Stress on nouns and verbs		Report writing: linking and organising ideas
Persuade, remind, require, warn, etc.	The sounds /aɪ/ and /ɪ/	Words often confused	Paragraphing
	Hesitation Stressed and unstressed modifying adverbs	Compound nouns derived from multi-part verbs Scale and limit words Modifying adverbs	A personal letter: being expressive
Verbs with base forms and/or *-ing*	Sounds and spelling	Multi-part verbs: stylistic and grammatical aspects	Smooth sequences of sentences
To be or not to be 'correct'	Focussing on ideas	Multi-part verbs: adverbs and prepositions Idioms	A personal letter: developing an idea
New words	Conversational style Stress and intonation	Inferring meaning Collocation	Dialogue
Verbs with two objects	British and American accents	Idioms British and American vocabulary	Mini sagas: being concise
Verbs followed by *it*	Sounds and spelling	Word formation	Mini-project: descriptions
Euphemisms	Using a wide pitch range to be more expressive	Multi-part verbs: particles and meanings	Expressing a balanced view
	Pauses High and low pitch in relative clauses	Multi-part verbs: jokes and riddles	Narrative points of view
Gender issues		Culture-related vocabulary	Sequencing paragraphs
Verbs with *-ing*, base forms and *should*		Vocabulary and style Cultural allusions	Style
	Varying pace	Collocation Multi-part verbs: collocation	Creative writing
Like, as	Linking	Dealing with difficult words Idioms of comparison	Writing about experiences
No matter, whatever, however, etc.	Sounding interested		A script for a documentary A review

UNIT 1

Down memory's lanes

Section 1

READING AND SPEAKING

1 Look at the questionnaire below. Work in pairs to find out about your memory. Answer the questions yourself and then compare your answers and final analysis with your partner. You can tick more than one answer in some cases.

QUESTIONNAIRE

What kind of MEMORY have you got?

1 [1.1] Listen to the numbers on the tape and try to remember them. What technique did you use?
a) visualising the numbers
b) repeating the numbers to yourself
c) drawing the numbers with your finger
d) something else

2 If you need to remember something very important, do you:
a) tie a knot in your handkerchief?
b) make a note on a piece of paper?
c) write it in your diary?
d) do nothing – you never forget anything?
e) do something else

3 What do you find easiest to remember?
a) numbers
b) diagrams or pictures
c) rhythms and tunes
d) none of these

4 Write four lines about your very first childhood memory. What kind of memory is it?
a) a general impression
b) a visual memory
c) something that you heard
d) an emotional problem
e) a rational problem

5 Do you remember your dreams?
a) often
b) sometimes
c) rarely

6 Take one minute to write down all the numbers that you know (bank account no., national identity no., phone numbers of people you know, birthdays, dates in history, etc.)
How many different sets of numbers did you remember?

7 Look at the geometric drawings on the right for a maximum of one minute. Cover them up and draw them from memory.

Count two points for each correct drawing, and one point for each drawing for which you only got the general idea.

QUESTIONNAIRE

8 Read the following paragraph to yourself slowly and carefully.

> Darwin said that the species that adapts the best to changes survives the best. This has nothing necessarily to do with sharper claws and fangs or, in the business world, lack of morality. In fact evolution shows that the species which cooperates best survives the best.

Now cover it up and write it out from memory.

Correct your answer as follows:
i) Underline words and expressions which give the idea but are not the exact expression, e.g. *sharp teeth* instead of *sharper claws and fangs*, or *that* for *which*, or *a* for *the*.
ii) Write 0 every time an important word is missing completely, e.g. 'sharper 0 fangs' for 'sharper claws and fangs'.

9 An ordinary incident or an everyday object can suddenly call up a whole sequence of extremely vivid memories, e.g. a certain smell can evoke a period of childhood or a taste can recall strong memories of people from your past. Has this happened to you:
a) several times ☐
b) maybe, you're not sure ☐
c) never ☐

10 Think back to the last news bulletin that you heard. Can you remember:
a) the general idea of most of the topics? ☐
b) the facts and figures? ☐
c) very little of any significance? ☐

Analysis

On the table below, circle your answers in the columns which correspond to different characteristics of your memory. You may circle more than one answer in some cases.

Memory type	I	II	III	IV	V	VI	VII	VIII
Question								
1		c)	b)	a)				d)
2					c)		b)	a)	d) e)
3			c)	b)		a)			d)
4		a)	c)	b)	e)			d)	
5							c)	a)	b)
6					more than 10	5 - 9	less than 4	
7				15 or more		5 - 14	less than 4	
8.i					5 or more			less than 5
8.ii			0 - 5					more than 5
9		a)				c)	b)	
10			a) and b)		a)	b)		c)

Are most of your answers in one column? This means you use mostly one form of memory. Are your answers evenly spread over the columns, or some of the columns? This means you use a variety of memory types. Read the descriptions below to find out about the different memory types.

I These answers are signs that your synaesthetic memory, the primitive memory which uses all senses at the same time and which new-born babies have, is still functioning.

II These answers are signs of an auditory memory. We often use this less as we grow to be adults.

III These answers correspond to a visual memory. In some people it is so well developed as to be called a 'photographic memory'.

IV These answers are signs that you retain the general idea of things. You probably understand and retain concepts, but may well find it difficult to recall details.

V These answers indicate your memory is good with figures. It is a rare gift!

VI These answers indicate that your memory finds it easier to cope with concrete facts rather than abstract ideas.

VII These answers indicate an intuitive memory. You probably have no idea how you remember things. You just do!

VIII These answers are common responses but not significant for this particular test.

(Adapted and translated *Des Tests pour Mieux Communiquer* Bourdoiseau et al)

2 When you have read the analysis, discuss the following questions in groups. Exchange as many ideas as you can, without worrying about your language mistakes. One person in the group should make brief notes on the discussion so that you can report back to the whole class.

a) Who has most responses in one column? Who has most responses in different columns?
b) How similar, or how different are the memories of people in your group?
c) To what extent do you agree upon the analysis of your memory? Compare with other people in the group.
d) Were you surprised by anything that you found out about your own memory or about someone else's?
e) Describe to the group ways in which your memory is particularly good. How do you actually set about the process of remembering? Be as detailed as possible.
f) Have you any ideas about improving your memory? Share them with your group.
g) Is it a good or a bad thing that we don't remember everything?
h) Can you imagine what life would be like if you lost your memory?

Unit 1

SPEAKING

In pairs decide on your speaking skills objectives for the course that you are beginning. Choose one of the following statements, or write one of your own.

a) I can express my ideas quite well but I make a lot of mistakes. By the end of the course I want to make fewer mistakes.
b) I find it difficult to express myself because I don't want to make mistakes. I want to become more fluent and worry less about making mistakes.
c) I find it difficult to express my ideas because I can't always find the right word, although I do know quite a lot. Of course I want to learn more vocabulary, but I also want to get better at communicating my ideas with the language that I already know.
d) I . . .

Join up with another pair and discuss the objectives you have decided on. Report back to the whole class. Can you decide on some class objectives for your course?

TALKING EFFECTIVELY

1   [▣ 1.2] Listen to these people talking about experiences of learning a foreign language, and then work with a partner. Look at the speech objectives below and match each objective to one of the speakers.

a) To speak well enough to pass an exam. *Speaker 1*
b) To speak well enough to enjoy the sounds of the language.
c) To speak well enough to be understood without difficulty when participating in quite sophisticated conversations.
d) To speak like a native speaker.
e) To speak well enough to be understood for travelling.

Work with a partner to discuss which of these objectives is closest to your own for the course you are following.

2   Listen again. Note down the particular difficulty each speaker had with the language he or she was trying to learn. Work in groups and compare notes.

3   Have you had similar problems while learning English? Discuss the following questions.

a) Make a list of sounds in English which do not exist in your language(s). For example, /θ/ as in 'thing' does not exist in many languages.
b) Are there any sounds which English people distinguish between, but which sound the same in your language(s)? For example, speakers of many languages would not make a distinction between the vowel in 'pick' [ɪ] and in 'peak' [iː].
c) [▣ 1.3] Listen to the sentence on the tape. Choose the correct 'tune', or intonation pattern.

   i) The Himalayan mountains are the highest in the world.

   ii) The Himalayan mountains are the highest in the world.

   iii) The Himalayan mountains are the highest in the world.

   Are the tunes of your language very similar to English, or very different? Are they more level?

d) [▣ 1.4] Listen to the same sentence said by a German speaker, a French speaker and a Japanese speaker. Are the words stressed more or less than in the English speaker example? Does your language have stress patterns like English? If not, how is it different?
e) [▣ 1.5] Listen to the following sentence. Note the way the words link up to make one utterance.
   My train's late again.

   Does your language link words together in a continuous sound stream like English does? If not, how is it different?
f) Which of the above problems make it difficult for people to understand foreigners speaking English? Which just add to foreigners' charm when they speak English? Which contribute most to the difficulty of understanding spoken English?

Section 2

VOCABULARY

Note

The problem with remembering words is not so much storing them in our minds as recalling them when we want to. Understanding how we store them may help a little. We store words in networks of related words. The more we reinforce the networks, the easier the recall of the words when we need them.

1 Look at the two columns.

a) Write down in column B the first word you think of associated with the word in column A.

      A   B
  i) salt
  ii) thirsty
  iii) green
  iv) beetle
  v) dog
  vi) plate

b) Compare your column B with other people in your class. What kind of words are they?
  i) a word which has the same status in the language, e.g. beetle – fly, red – green. This category often contains words which are thought of as opposites.
  ii) noun groups or adjectives and nouns which often go together, e.g. sea – green, deep – water.
  iii) a word from a more general category covering the stimulus word, e.g. dog – animal, beetle – insect, green – colour.
  iv) a synonym, a word with similar meanings, e.g. plate – dish.

c) Which kind of association occurs most often in your lists? Find examples of types of associations you have not used.

2 Very often we store words by the first and last letters. Work in small groups to find the words which correspond to the following definitions. You can flick through your dictionary for inspiration if you are stuck. The first one has been done for you.

a) Two different choices are two *alternatives*.
b) A good idea that you suddenly have is a b – – – – – – – e.
c) Something that is made much bigger or more important than it is, is e – – – – – – – – – d.
d) To be enthusiastic about something is to be k – – n on it.
e) Somebody who is very tolerant is o – – n m – – – – d.
f) Somebody who believes in chaos rather than law and order is an a – – – – – – – – t.

3 Ask and answer questions with a partner. Example:
What do you call someone who is always happy and looking on the bright side? It begins with an 'o'. (optimist)

4 When we store category words, we decide whether they are 'good' category words or 'not so good' category words. For example, for most English people a robin is a good example of a bird, whereas an ostrich or a penguin is not.

a) In the following groups, circle the word which you think is the best example for each category.

> **Fruit:** orange apple mango banana kiwi melon
>
> **Animals:** bear lion cat dog hyena rabbit
>
> **Colours:** red blue maroon yellow turquoise orange
>
> **Clothes:** swimming costume tie hat gloves pyjamas skirt
>
> **Furniture:** bookshelf stool armchair coffee table chest

b) Compare your choices with a partner. Decide on the characteristics in each category which made you reach a decision.

c) Write two more similar category sets and ask another pair to decide which is the best example.

Unit 1

READING AND SPEAKING

Much of the reading you do in this course book will involve close attention to detail, for you will be looking at strategies for reading, clues about finer points of meaning, and so on. However, you will need to find other reading matter and do as much extensive reading as you can. This section is designed to help you set about this.

1 What do you read? From the catalogue extract below, which works of fiction would you recommend to someone:

a) who likes adventure stories?
b) who wants something humorous to read?
c) who likes a serious novel?
d) who likes tales of far-off places?
e) who likes suspense?
f) who likes science fiction?
g) who hasn't got much time to read?

2 Which non-fiction book(s) would you recommend to someone:

a) who is interested in politics?
b) who is interested in people's lives?
c) who is interested in fashion?
d) who is interested in the cinema?
e) who likes painting?

FICTION

Of Love and Shadows
Isabel Allende
A vivid cast of characters, set in the colourful landscape of Latin America, acts out a tale of youthful love, selfless courage and political betrayal.
☐ BLACK SWAN p304

The Edge
Dick Francis
Most of the action takes place on a train travelling from Toronto to Vancouver with a party of racing enthusiasts. As always, a twist in the tail and a hero to see that justice is done.
☐ MICHAEL JOSEPH p266

Vinegar Soup
Miles Gibson
Fat and 50, Gilbert Firestone's dreams of travel materialise in West Africa. He finds rain, starvation, pygmies and meets the mountainous Charlotte in her brothel on wheels.
☐ BLACK SWAN p286

Those Who Walk Away
Patricia Highsmith
A vengeful father stalks his American son-in-law through the gloomy underside of Venice after the unexplained suicide of his rich, fey daughter. A psychological thriller with the slow Highsmith fuse.
☐ PENGUIN p250

The Playmaker
Thomas Keneally
A Royal Marines Lieutenant in an 18th-century Australian penal colony decides to put on a play, using the convicts as his cast. An astonishing tale based on fact.
☐ SCEPTRE p366

Classic Crime
Edited by Ellery Queen
An assortment of crime novellas that preserve bedrock traditions by McVain, Simenon, Gilbert Stout, Gardener and the indefatigable editor himself.
☐ ROBINSON p327

The World of the Short Story
Selected by Clifton Fadiman
A magnificent collection of the world's best 20th-century short stories, with 62 stories from 16 different countries.
☐ PICADOR p864

Raft
Stephen Baxter
His ingenious and much blurbed *Raft* takes a lost human expedition into a universe where gravity is vastly different and all they have is what they took with them.
☐ GRAFTON 264pp

Only Begotten Daughter
James Morrow
James Morrow's witty and intelligent, if rather preachy, work has always been at the eschatological end of SF. His new *Only Begotten Daughter* gives us a female Messiah, Christ's younger sister, in Atlantic City, learning to walk on water only when no one is looking. *This is the Way the World Ends* deals with the last things of nuclear war.
☐ LEGEND 320pp

This is the Way the World Ends
☐ ARROW 336pp

NON-FICTION

The Keys to Creativity
Peter Evans and Geoff Deehan
What makes some people creative geniuses? Peter Evans and Geoff Deehan try to find out. They give insights into others' creativity, and tell us how to train ourselves to become more creative. Good fun.
☐ GRAFTON p224

Supersense: Perception in the Animal World
John Downer Accompanying a BBC TV series, this book challenges the assumption that man is the most highly evolved form of life. With over 200 colour photographs. *Supersense* opens up hitherto unimagined forms of perception.
☐ BBC p160

The Marco Polo Expedition: A Journey Along the Silk Road
Richard B Fisher:
Photography by Tom Ang
Undertaken at the request of UNESCO to prove that the Silk Road could once more be an important route, the account of this journey is a subtle mix of history and contemporary social comment. It makes riveting reading.
☐ HODDER p224

Paradise Lost
Christopher Wood
The 19th-century English landscape painters yearned after a vanished ideal of rural life, as do we. Their vision was sadly at odds with reality and this paradox is beautifully portrayed here with over 200 pictures.
☐ BARRIE AND JENKINS p224

Fabulous Fakes: This History of Fantasy and Fashion Jewellery
Vivienne Becker
From 18th-century splendour to the 1980s this gloriously illustrated book is the first authoritative and comprehensive study of costume jewellery, set against a background of changing roles and fashion.
☐ GRAFTON p240

'It's Only a Movie, Ingrid'
Alexander Walker
These marvellously entertaining memoirs combine critical comments on the film industry with warm anecdotes of Alexander Walker's encounters with Charlie Chaplin, Grace Kelly, Ken Russell, Alec Guinness...
☐ HEADLINE p336

Reflect on Things Past: The Memoirs of Lord Carrington
A personal record of an immensely varied life from one of the most experienced and respected figures of our time. Lord Carrington discusses his love of liberty, his political beliefs and describes with warmth and humour the people he has met.
☐ COLLINS p400 A102 £17.50

Stalker
John Stalker
In this disturbing book John Stalker tells the hitherto incomplete story of his investigation into the RUCs alleged shoot-to-kill policy in Northern Ireland.
☐ PENGUIN p304 A184 £3.50

3 Roleplay the following situation.

STUDENT A   LIBRARIAN
You are a librarian and are advising a customer about the choice of a book. You will need to ask questions about his or her interests to give the best advice. Recommend books from the catalogue extract above. You may use the language suggested in the box below to help you make your recommendations.

You may/might like to consider this book.
If I may/might make a suggestion, why don't you try this one?
Would you care for some non-fiction?
I was wondering if you'd ever thought of reading something by this author?

STUDENT B   BORROWER
You are looking for a book to read and are giving the librarian some idea of what you would like to read. You politely refuse the librarian's suggestions as none of them appeals to you particularly. Give reasons for your refusals. You may use some of the language in the box below to help you refuse politely.

I'm afraid I'm not too fond of science fiction.
That sounds interesting, but you see, I never read novels.
That's quite a good idea, but what I would really like is some non-fiction.
I wouldn't mind an adventure story, but it must be a good one.

---

4 How do you read?

a) Read the following statements and tick [✓] any of them that apply to you.

How do you read?

What do you usually read in English?
- I only read the kind of books I read in my own language. ☐
- I read anything that interests me. ☐
- I only read books that I am told to read at school. ☐
- I would like to read more books but I find reading a whole book very difficult. ☐
- I often buy English language newspapers or magazines. ☐

What techniques do you use when you read in English?
- I look up every word as I go along. ☐
- I note down or underline the words which prevent me understanding the general idea, and when I get too frustrated I get out the dictionary. ☐
- I never use a dictionary. I understand enough to get the general idea. ☐
- I read to the very end of everything I begin. ☐
- I often read the first thirty to fifty lines of an article or pages of a book and then decide not to continue because I am not enjoying it. ☐

b) In small groups, compare the statements you have ticked and discuss them. Which techniques are the most useful in order to become a fluent reader in English? Has anything else helped you to become a fluent reader in English?

Section 3

LEARNING GRAMMAR

▶ Diagnosis ◀◀◀

This test will tell you how your basic grammar matches up to the grammar presented in this course. Check your answers in the Key to see how you score.

1 Tenses and verb forms. In the sentences below, put the verbs in brackets in an appropriate form.

a) This year we (*have*) a very dry summer. It (*not rain*) since the month of April. If the drought (*continue*), there (*be*) a severe water shortage before the autumn.
b) She says she (*be*) very happy since she (*go*) to university.
c) '. . . and Smith (*pass*) the ball to Green, who (*run*) down the pitch and (*kick*) it straight into the goal, which (*put*) Manchester in the lead by 2 goals to 1.'
d) What can they (*do*)? We (*wait*) for over half an hour!
e) If I (*know*) about his dishonest dealings at the start of our negotiations last year, I (*not invest*) my money in his company three months later.
f) Although the cost of living (*rise*) at the moment, unemployment (*decrease*).
g) You should (*go*) to the doctor immediately. You would be better by now.
h) We hoped we (*be able to*) come to your golden wedding party next month, but unfortunately we both (*be*) away on business.
i) I wanted my daughter (*go*) to dancing classes. I dreamt she (*be*) a star one day.
j) I am used to (*live*) in the big city and I don't mind the dirt and the noise.
k) (*marry*) you me?

2 Complete the following sentences with one of the words in brackets.

a) Elizabeth doesn't like her new school because she has . . . friends than at her last one. (*fewer/less*)
b) Do you know what the . . . fashion is? (*last/latest*)
c) It's not the same . . . in England. (*as/than*)
d) There were 35 . . . in the room. (*persons/people*)
e) She . . . she was not guilty. (*said/told*)

3 What is wrong with the following sentences? Write them out correctly.

a) I don't know where is the treasure.
b) She picked up again the phone and called her parents.
c) You are coming tonight?
d) I would like to explain to you the problem.
e) She's a blues singer very good.

4 Put a preposition in the following sentences where necessary.

a) I am interested . . . going to England.
b) She paid . . . her drink and left.
c) It depends . . . the situation.
d) He asked . . . me where I lived.
e) The Prime Minister answered . . . the President's questions.

5 Articles and nouns. Correct the mistakes in the following sentences.

a) The receptionist gave me a lot of informations about London.
b) The human beings are made that way!
c) There will be the new economic crisis if inflation is not stopped.
d) The government policies on immigration question are becoming more and more strict.
e) My father gave me a lot of advices before I came to London and said studying English was a very hard work.

6 The following sentences contain a variety of common mistakes. Write them out correctly.

a) I am born in Buenos Aires.
b) This friday I am meeting an american business man.
c) I lived in Tokyo during two months.
d) You can to stay longer if you like.
e) My hotel was near from the Tower of London.
f) The people which left the meeting all disagreed with the speaker.
g) I want that we begin the meeting at 8 a.m.
h) You don't have to smoke on the Tube in London. You will be fined £50 if you do.
i) I had dinner before to come here.
j) I am not agreed with you.

WRITING

The writing process

1 There are different stages in preparing a good piece of writing. With a partner, look at the list of stages below and decide which you would do first. You may not want to include all the stages and you may not always agree about the order.

a) editing: checking style and elegance
b) preparing an outline
c) putting ideas in a logical sequence
d) editing: making sure the grammar is correct
e) noting down any relevant idea or key word
f) writing a draft without worrying about grammar or style
g) eliminating repetitions or ideas which are not totally relevant

2 Discuss the following questions.

a) Which of the stages in Exercise 1 is most important in each of the following types of writing?
 i) a postcard to a member of your family
 ii) an academic paper
 iii) a memo to a colleague about a future project
 iv) an entry in your diary
 v) a letter of complaint
 vi) a letter to a friend

b) Think about the types of writing above. When is it important to express your ideas fluently rather than produce a completely accurate text? When is it more important to write without making mistakes?

Appropriacy

1 In certain types of writing, correct grammar is obviously very important. However, appropriacy of style is just as important. There are many errors of appropriacy in letter A above. Underline examples of the following:

a) superfluous expressions
b) expressions that are too informal
c) sentences that mix formal and informal English
d) inappropriate set phrases

2 Read letter B and cross out the alternatives that are not suitable. Pay particular attention to appropriacy of meaning and style.

Letter A

29 September
Corina Bilin
203 Corazon St.
Kalit
Philippines

Application Letter

To the hotel management
TO WHOM IT MAY CONCERN

Dear Sir,
As far as I'm concerned, I'm very glad to inform you that I'm interested in joining your prestigious Five Star Hotel.
 As you wouldn't know, I was previously employed too at Plaza Five Star hotel which, I might say, was good when it comes to hotel experience. Meanwhile with this application letter of mine is included my Personal Data. In order that I may accomplish my goal, it's your turn now to judge me.
 I hope you will extend to me your kind consideration on this matter. And I'll appreciate it a lot.
 Thanks and my warmest regards.
 Very truly yours,

Corina Bilin

Letter B

Dear Sir,

I am a) at present/right now/currently looking for work in Edinburgh and was wondering whether you might have any b) spare jobs/vacancies/employment opportunities.

I am c) shoving in/enclosing/communicating my CV. I would like to d) underline/point out/emphasise that I have had considerable experience as a receptionist in several e) well-known/bloody good/marvellous hotels and can give you the names of f) referees/supporters/friends if you should require them.

I am available for g) a chat/interview/an exchange of views during the coming month. In the hope that you will h) reflect on/consider/grab my application favourably, I look forward to your reply.

Yours faithfully,
Alessandra Tura

Unit 1

3 Work with a partner.

a) Read the advertisements and decide what qualities a successful candidate would need for each of them.

b) Choose one of the advertisements and write a letter of application. Before you begin, imagine an appropriate CV for the job. Note down any points that would be particularly relevant (qualifications, past experience, etc.). Include these points in your letter and a description of any relevant qualities that you possess or imagine you possess.

c) Swap letters with your partner. Suggest improvements, paying attention to grammatical accuracy as well as appropriacy of style.

MANAGER
THE BODYCARE SHOP

Required for our prestigious shop in Hampstead.
If you are a dynamic, energetic person with retail experience at a senior level then this could be the career opportunity that you have been waiting for.
The successful applicant will be aged 25-30, accomplished in all aspects of recruitment, staff motivation, stock control, merchandising and display, and administrative systems.
This is a demanding position requiring a high degree of commitment, initiative and ability.
If you feel that you have the above qualities please apply in writing, with full C.V. to:
Eileen Shawcross The Bodycare Shop
16 Hounslow Road, London SW2 6XP

✚ Internation Aid
NATIONAL STRATEGIC PLANNING OFFICER

Internation Aid is actively reviewing all areas of its work and is in the process of implementing its new Five Year Plan. The Strategic Plan is a central part of this development.

The successful applicant will be the third member of the Strategic Planning Task Force and will, in conjunction with Regional Officers, assist designated Branches in the formulation of Branch Five Year Plans.

Applicants must be able to promote and encourage the management of change, have excellent communication skills and be able to work on their own initiative within agreed guidelines. A thorough understanding of the dynamics of voluntary organisations is highly desirable. The territory to be covered includes Wales, the Border counties and the South West. Residence in this area is desirable.

Starting salary in the range of £15,500 - £19,500 plus car, contributory pension scheme and other benefits.

Please apply in writing with full CV to: John Northcott, Internation Aid, National Headquarters, 9 Brent Crescent, London, N3 1AN.

CURATOR
ITALIAN COLLECTION

You will be responsible for the care and cataloguing of the 17th and 18th century Italian Collection. You will be a member of the Curatorial Department and play a role in its work which includes displays of the collection; exhibition planning; educational activities; representing the Gallery at home and abroad; answering enquiries; accompanying pictures on overseas loans; and assisting in general administration.

You must have a wide knowledge of the history of European art covering the 17th and 18th century. You should also have a relevant degree. A working knowledge of at least two modern foreign European languages is essential.

Salary range for Curator E is £15,200 to £19,665 (including London Weighting). Starting salary according to qualifications and experience.

Please apply in writing with full CV to: Miss Tracey Wall, The London Gallery, 6 Piccadilly, London W1 3TS. Telephone 071-938-2117.

The London Gallery is an Equal Opportunities Employer.

THE **LONDON GALLERY**

Domitat
Display Senior
C £12K + benefits

Creative flair, energy, and commercial acumen are the skills you will need to possess, in order to manage a team providing a quality display service to our Kings Road Store. You will enjoy the challenge of visually promoting the image and style of Domitat, and will have extensive display experience.

Please write with full CV to Graham Smith, Domitat, 208 Queen's Park Road, London, SW3 2NQ. Domitat, a member of the Homelife Group of Companies, is an Equal Opportunities Employer.

CV: curriculum vitae
benefits: anything that brings help, advantage or profit
acumen: the ability to think and judge quickly and well
Equal Opportunities Employer: an employer who does not discriminate against age, race or sex

UNIT 2

Cosmic bodies

Section 1

VOCABULARY AND LISTENING

1 Look briefly at the adjectives in the box below.

a) Do you know which sign of the zodiac any of them are associated with? Does anyone in your class know? If so, write them on the table as in the example.

independent	perfectionist	hardworking
fiery	changeable	proud	anxious
extremist	conservative	sensitive	tolerant
level-headed

Zodiac Sign	Characteristics
Aries (Mar 21–Apr 20)	fiery
Taurus (Apr 21–May 20)	
Gemini (May 21–Jun 20)	
Cancer (Jun 21–Jul 20)	
Leo (Jul 21–Aug 20)	
Virgo (Aug 21–Sep 20)	
Libra (Sep 21–Oct 20)	
Scorpio (Oct 21–Nov 20)	
Sagittarius (Nov 21–Dec 20)	
Capricorn (Dec 21–Jan 19)	
Aquarius (Jan 20–Feb 18)	
Pisces (Feb 19–Mar 20)	

b) [2.1] Listen and complete the table.
c) Do you know any other adjectives associated with the signs? Work in small groups and try to add to the table.

2 In your groups, find out if your personalities match your signs? If you are not typical of your sign, can you suggest reasons for this?

READING AND SPEAKING

1 Work in pairs to find out about how a new zodiac affects you. Read the text below and fill in the quiz on page 14. Then compare your answers with your partner.

THE ONLY TRUE ZODIAC

Our astrological signs have apparently changed. Nowadays not one Geminian was born when the sun was in Gemini, nor one Scorpian when the sun was in Scorpio. The problem is that the sun is terribly late, say the astronomers. This means that most of us were born under a different star sign. And there is even a new sign, Ophiuchus, which is the sign of creativity and interest in the life of the psyche.
But new stars don't replace old ones. Our new signs point to the most creative part in us and tell us not so much 'Who am I?' but 'Where am I going?'
From the table below, you'll be able to find out which of the thirteen signs of the new zodiac your birthdate comes under. The quiz will reveal how much you are influenced by your new sign.

Aries	19 April-13 May
Taurus	14 May-22 June
Gemini	23 June-21 July
Cancer	22 July - 10 August
Leo	11 August-16 September
Virgo	17 September-31 October
Libra	1 November-23 November
Scorpio	24 November-29 November
Ophiuchus	30 November-17 December
Sagittarius	18 December-19 January
Capricorn	20 January-17 February
Aquarius	18 February-12 March
Pisces	13 March-18 April

ARE YOU UNDER THE INFLUENCE?

1 *What do you watch on TV?*
- A Soap operas
- B Nature films
- C Debates
- D Chat shows
- E Ballet

2 *What is your ideal home?*
- A A houseboat or a caravan
- B A flat in the centre of a big city
- C A commune with friends and children
- D A fifteenth century cottage in secluded countryside
- E A folly (= an unusually shaped building without any particular purpose)

3 *Which of the following jobs would you feel happiest in?*
- A Business manager
- B Nurse
- C Literary critic
- D Art gallery director
- E Sculptor

4 *Which quality do you feel is most important in a partner?*
- A Charm
- B Supportiveness
- C Intellectual abilities
- D Fairness
- E Sexual attractiveness

5 *Which of the following would you find most exciting?*
- A Diving into water from a great height
- B Getting undressed
- C Throwing a rotten egg at a politician
- D Taking part in a car race along a winding road
- E Swaying in a very large crowd

6 *What is your greatest ambition?*
- A Having an exciting life
- B Having a successful career
- C Doing something useful/meaningful
- D Learning all there is to know
- E Being all-powerful

7 *If you had to, what would you go without in your life?*
- A Friends
- B Job
- C Music
- D Religion
- E Technology

8 *What would make you the most angry?*
- A Your date standing you up
- B Being sacked
- C New cuts in the health service
- D A friend of yours being mugged
- E Someone reading your secret diary

Scoring

1 A = 2	B = 1	C = 0	D = 1	E = 1
2 A = 1	B = 2	C = 1	D = 0	E = 1
3 A = 2	B = 0	C = 0	D = 2	E = 1
4 A = 0	B = 2	C = 2	D = 1	E = 1
5 A = 0	B = 1	C = 1	D = 2	E = 1
6 A = 2	B = 0	C = 1	D = 0	E = 1
7 A = 0	B = 2	C = 1	D = 2	E = 1
8 A = 1	B = 0	C = 2	D = 2	E = 1

The influence of Ophiuchus on you

If you scored between 0 and 6:
You belong to the old zodiac. You like things that are familiar and you prefer to take a safe path in life rather than to strike out and take dangerous risks. You enjoy life as it is, although sometimes you might wish you had just a bit more ambition! Your new sign probably doesn't tell you much about yourself.

If you scored between 7 and 11:
You are at a crossroad between the old and the new, where you feel you have to reconcile different aspects of your personality, different urges and ambitions. The struggle between the old and the new may be an open conflict, a cold war or a final peace treatise.

If you scored between 12 and 16:
You are a person of this age – the age of Aquarius. Many aspects of your old sign may puzzle you, the more so as you move further from your roots. You are the type to grasp new opportunities, to rely on the future and on yourself, sometimes at the cost of personal security.

How many E answers did you have?
The E answers reflect the way the new sign, Ophiuchus, affects your personality. The fewer E answers you have, the less you are interested in questions of life after death and the paranormal. The more E answers you have, the more fascinated by the occult you are and the more likely you are to have a psychic experience in your life.

---

2 Fill in the table on the right by interviewing people in your class as in the example. Write in their date of birth, their old sign and their new sign. Ask them about their personal characteristics. Which ones belong to their old sign? Which ones to their new sign? Do they agree with the analysis of their personality?

Name	Old sign/characteristics	New sign/characteristics
Tracey b. 22 April	Taurus – hardworking	Aries – fiery, pioneering

Section 2

READING

1 You are going to read an extract from a novel called *Imaginary Friends*.

a) With a partner, imagine briefly what the story might be about if it was:
   i) a science fiction story.
   ii) a story about contemporary society.
   iii) a historical novel.
   Make brief notes on your ideas; you will need them again later in this section.
b) Compare your ideas with another group.

2 Read the first section.

> And if any of us comes to feel an urging to share our great secret with friends, or speak of it to anyone, we must say to ourselves, Stop, and remember that The Time Is Not Now. The time will come later. We know that when we're fully enlightened, many of us will be sent out as teachers of spiritual light all over the world, so that this planet may be freed from its darkness and confusion.'
>
> 'That's right,' several of the group murmured.
>
> 'Now let's go on. Here is our first instruction. PURIFY COSMIC BODIES REREJECT AND AVOID DEAD FOOD MATTER. Have you got that? I'll read it again more

3 Discuss the following questions with a partner. Tick the most probable answer in each case.

a) The person speaking is:
   i) a person with a position of responsibility in an organised religion.
   ii) the leader of an informal religious group.
   iii) a school teacher.
b) 'Us' and 'we' refer to:
   i) a family.
   ii) an educational group.
   iii) a sect.
c) 'Our great secret' is to do with:
   i) the meetings of the group.
   ii) the group's spiritual enlightenment.
   iii) the source of darkness and confusion on the planet.

4 Now read the second section.

'Now let's go on. Here is our first instruction. PURIFY COSMIC BODIES REREJECT AND AVOID DEAD FOOD MATTER. Have you got that? I'll read it again more slowly, so you can take it down.' Verena did so. 'You know we've heard something about this before. We've had leadings that one thing that's holding down our progress here, making us heavy spiritually, is that our earthly bodies are full of so much disintegrating dead food matter; and every day, every breakfast, lunch and supper, we're adding to that heavy weight.'

'Now we can't go without material nourishment completely yet, like our guides on Varna and other fully developed beings do. We're not progressed to anywhere near that level. But we do have to realise that some of the foods we've been taking into our bodies are automatically heavier than others; they drag us down much more. There's other things that aren't so harmful, because they contain natural life vibrations which are still emanating after they're consumed into our bodies. Now I want to go into this in more detail.'

5 Discuss the following questions with a partner. Tick the most probable answer in each case.

a) 'PURIFY COSMIC BODIES REREJECT AND AVOID DEAD FOOD MATTER' is in capital letters because:
   i) the author thinks it is vitally important.
   ii) it is an instruction from the sect's holy book.
   iii) it is the voice of the sect's guide from another planet.
b) Verena is:
   i) the leader of the sect.
   ii) a guide from Varna.
   iii) a member of the sect.
c) 'Natural life vibrations' (line 27) are:
   i) a well-known scientific phenomenon.
   ii) a little-known scientific phenomenon.
   iii) Verena's peculiar jargon for something which is not scientific at all.
d) The aims of the sect are:
   i) eccentric.
   ii) good.
   iii) evil.

6 Read the third section.

While the Seekers scribbled in their notebooks, Verena outlined the rules which were to control our menu during the next ten days. In general, the less we ate the better. Light-coloured foods were preferable to dark ones, and a low specific gravity was good.

All dairy products (milk, butter, cheese) had strong life vibrations, we learned. Fruits and nuts, especially when uncooked, were also excellent. Vegetables that could be eaten raw, like carrots and lettuce, still contained some vital neutrons. Cooked vegetables, and bread, cake and cookies, were less desirable. Eggs were questionable; while steak, chicken, ham and fish were full of heavy, decaying electricity: not only were they dead, they were murdered, food matter. In effect, what Verena now offered the Seekers was the diet of a tame rabbit.

'Are there any questions?' she asked. Voices and hands were raised all round the room. What about coffee and tea? What about baked beans, ice cream, pizza and 7-up? My pen jumped nervously back and forth from the right-hand page of the notebook, on which I was recording the instructions from Varna, to the left, where I was making notes for the study in a kind of shorthand. McMann and I took turns at this; it was supposed to be his turn that evening, but he was recording posture changes again, so I had his heavy, black loose-leaf book.

Coffee, occasionally; tea, no; white bread rather than brown. They were all taking it down carefully. The complicated food phobias which Verena had been developing over the past few weeks were becoming the norm for the group.

Wheaties and other cold cereals, yes; hot cereal and oatmeal, no. I finished the page and turned to the back of McMann's notebook for another, unsnapping the stiff metal rings. Pasted on the inside cover was a dated outline of the Truth Seekers meetings we had attended, from my first trip to Sophis ('Sept 24: welcome to RZ. Present: VR, EN', etc.) to this evening ('Nov. 25: 1st announcement of Coming').

I took out the paper automatically, snapped the rings

7 Discuss the following questions with a partner. Tick the most probable answer in each case.

a) The Seekers' questions about 'baked beans, ice cream, pizza and 7-up' make the passage seem:
   i) comic.
   ii) realistic.
   iii) serious.
b) The narrator is:
   i) a member of the sect.
   ii) an observer of the sect.
   iii) a detective.
c) McMann is:
   i) a member of the sect.
   ii) the narrator's colleague.
   iii) the narrator's boss.
d) Verena's rules about food are:
   i) simply advice about healthy eating.
   ii) for people who want to be vegetarian.
   iii) bizarre and idiosyncratic.
e) The 'announcement of Coming' is to do with:
   i) the coming of a prophet.
   ii) members coming to the meeting.
   iii) McMann's and the narrator's arrival in town.

8 Read the final section.

announcement of Coming').

I took out the paper automatically, snapped the rings together, turned forward, unsnapped them again and paused, holding the sheet suspended. Then I turned back the pages again. All this had taken a couple of seconds at the most, while I went on attending to the meeting. Now there occurred one of those vacuums in time when the hands of the internal clock stick. 'Nov. 25: 1st announcement of Coming.' I couldn't say whether I looked at those words half a second or five minutes. They were a perfectly innocuous and accurate description of this meeting; the only trouble was that they shouldn't have been written yet. Unless McMann was gifted with precognition. He had somehow known in advance what Ro of Varna was going to tell us that Thanksgiving night.

25

9 Discuss the following questions with a partner. Tick the most probable answer in each case.

a) The narrator feels as if time has stopped for him because:
   i) there is a revelation.
   ii) he feels faint.
   iii) he discovers McMann has anticipated what is to happen at the meeting that night.
b) The narrator thinks McMann:
   i) is behaving suspiciously.
   ii) is a good sociologist.
   iii) might be gifted with precognition.

10 In small groups discuss the following questions.

a) Look back at your answers to all four sections. Have you changed your mind about any of them? Check your final answers with your teacher.
b) What do you now think the title of the novel refers to?
c) In the passage there is no explanation for McMann's 'premonition'. Which of the following is the most likely?
   i) McMann is very intuitive and guessed that the Coming would be that night from the way the group was behaving.
   ii) McMann is cynical, an academic who is desperate to publish research findings. He is manipulating Verena to get good results for his research.
   iii) McMann is dishonest – the Truth Seekers were a fake sect and had preplanned the 'Coming' cooperating with McMann.
d) Look at your notes in Exercise 1. Is the novel similar in any way to any of your ideas? If not, how is it different? Which of the adjectives in the box below help you to describe the author's intentions? What other adjectives would you choose to describe it?

satirical	mysterious	technical	amusing
dramatic	comic	farcical	poetical
critical	serious	spiritual	caricatural

(from *Imaginary Friends* by Alison Lurie)

Unit 2

VOCABULARY

Dealing with difficult words

Sometimes there are clues in the text which help you identify the meaning of difficult words. For example, in line 25 'drag' is probably something to do with the effect of carrying something heavy because the word 'heavy' precedes it and the preposition 'down' follows it. These clues can often be enough to get the general meaning of a word.

With a partner, look back at the text and work out the meanings of any of these words that you do not already know. Underline the clues.

a) scribbled (line 30)
b) shorthand (line 51)
c) loose-leaf book (line 54)
d) snapped (line 68)
e) Thanksgiving (line 81)

WRITING

1 The narrator in the reading text is a sociologist who is studying the group and making detailed notes on their behaviour. His note-pad might have looked like this.

> Verena → group:
> keep secret for
> a while

a) With a partner, choose one section of the passage and make notes in the same way.
b) Use your notes to write a report in a neutral and objective way. Before you begin make a list of useful reporting verbs, and check you know their patterns. You may begin like this:
Verena told the group that they should keep their secret for a while . . .

2 Imagine you and a partner are sociologists from another planet. Discuss and note down the different stages in the lesson you have been having. Write up your notes as a sociologist's report.

Section 3

ABOUT LANGUAGE

Jargon

> **jargon** /ˈdʒɑːgən‖ ˈdʒɑːrgən, -gɑːn/ *n* [C;U] *often derog* difficult or strange language which uses words known only to the members of a certain group: *computer jargon/the jargon of the advertising business*

1 Alison Lurie makes fun of the sect by inventing jargon they might use, such as *natural life vibrations* and *decaying electricity*. Can you find any other examples of such jargon in the text?

2 The following jargon comes from the worlds of advertising, medicine, law, business and computers.

bail	jingle	homicide	corporate ladder
lacerations	software	brand loyalty	
headhunter	bug	haemorrhage	

Work with a partner to decide which category each word belongs to. Use a dictionary to help you. Then write sentences using the words.
Example:
bail = law
The accused was released on bail of £2,000.

LEARNING GRAMMAR

▶Diagnosis ◀◀◀

Continuous tenses

1 Study these sentences from the reading text (pages 15–17) which all contain a verb in the continuous tense.
  i) Every day . . . we're *adding* to that heavy weight. (lines 18–19)
  ii) Some of the foods we *have been taking* into our bodies are automatically heavier than others. (lines 23–25)
  iii) Natural life vibrations . . . *are* still *emanating* after they're consumed into our bodies. (lines 27–28)
  iv) The complicated food phobias which Verena *had been developing* over the last few weeks were becoming the norm for the group. (lines 56–59)
  v) My pen jumped nervously back and forth from the right-hand page of the notebook, on which I *was recording* the instructions from Varna, to the left, where I *was making* notes for the study in a kind of shorthand. (lines 48–51)

a) Wherever grammatically correct and appropriate in the context, write the sentences out with a simple tense. Refer back to the text.
b) Work with a partner. Compare your sentences, and then decide if the change of tense affects the meaning of the sentence or not. Check your answers in the Key.

2 In these sentences from the text, can you turn any of the simple tenses which are underlined into continuous forms? If so, how does it affect the meaning? Refer back to the text.

a) While the Seekers scribbled in their notebooks, Verena outlined the rules . . . (lines 30–31)
b) We've had leadings that one thing that's holding down our progress here . . . is that our earthly bodies are full of so much . . . dead food matter. (lines 14–18)
c) All dairy products . . . had strong life vibrations, we learned. (lines 35–36)
d) What Verena now offered the Seekers was the diet of a tame rabbit. (lines 43–44)

3 Look back at both exercises. When the meaning does not really differ in the two forms, what do you think governs the author's choice of tense? Use the guidelines in the Key if necessary.

▶Development ◀◀◀

Other uses of continuous tenses

Repeated actions
Adverbs such as *always* (in the sense of 'frequently'), *constantly, continually* and *forever* can be used with the present and past continuous tenses to describe repeated actions. Examples:
They are always hearing strange noises. They say their house is haunted.
Our neighbours were very friendly. They were constantly inviting us over for drinks.
This use of the continuous tense can imply that something is happening too often and be a form of complaint. Examples:
The neighbours are forever having noisy parties.
The car was very old. It was constantly breaking down.

The future continuous for arrangements and plans
The future continuous can be used as an alternative to the present simple to talk about arrangements and plans. Examples:
We'll be leaving on Friday, and we'll be spending two nights in Paris, two nights in Rome and two nights in Madrid.
Sarah Santos will be giving a concert at the Palladium on March 23rd.

Practice

1 Put the verbs in brackets into a continuous tense wherever possible. More than one tense is possible in some cases.

a) The guests (*arrive*) at eight o'clock.
b) She (*complain*) about her job every time the boss refuses to raise her salary.
c) Jack, (*take down*) the minutes for the meeting, please? (a request)
d) What (*do*) you this time next year?
e) Sarah's nose (*stream*) constantly – she must have an allergy.
f) The new supermarket (*not open*) for another week or two.
g) When she began to drive, Jane (*have*) always accidents.
h) The weather (*be*) fine tomorrow.

2 Role play. Work with a partner to ask and answer questions about holiday plans, using the itineraries below.

STUDENT A
You are telling a friend about your plans for a holiday in Egypt. The itinerary is outlined below. Example:
We'll be leaving on 9th March and we'll be flying directly to Luxor. We won't be going to Alexandria this time . . .
Your friend is planning a holiday in the United States. You should ask him/her questions about his/her plans. Example:
Will you be visiting Universal Studios?

STUDENT B
You are telling a friend about your plans for a holiday in the United States. The itinerary is outlined below. Example:
I'll be leaving on 6th June. I'll be taking a direct flight to Los Angeles. I won't be taking much luggage because we'll be moving around a lot.
Your friend is planning a holiday in Egypt. You should ask him/her questions about his/her plans. Example:
Will you be visiting Cairo?

Itinerary for Mr/Ms C Logan

Thu 09 Mar	London to Luxor Accommodation on board the Nile Queen Spacious air-conditioned cabins
Fri 10 Mar	Visits to Thebes, the Valley of the Kings
Sat 11 Mar	Tour of Luxor temple. Departure up river for Aswan
Sun 12 Mar	Plane trip to Abu Simbel
Mon 13 Mar	Trip on Nile in a felucca (small local sailing boat)
Tues 14 Mar	*Morning:* Flight to Cairo. Visit Memphis. Lunch near the Pyramids. *Afternoon:* the Oasis Hotel
Wed 15 Mar	Free day in Cairo
Thurs 16 Mar	Return to London

ITINERARY FOR MS/MR P WALTON

SUN 06 JUN	DEPARTURE FROM LONDON TO LOS ANGELES ARRIVAL 6 P.M. LOCAL TIME. ACCOMMODATION: HOTEL FIGUEROA
MON 07 JUN	FREE DAY. EARLY EVENING HELICOPTER FLIGHT OVER BEVERLY HILLS, HOLLYWOOD, SUNSET BOULEVARD, ETC. CANDLELIGHT DINNER IN THE LANDINGS RESTAURANT
TUE 08 JUN	VISIT UNIVERSAL STUDIOS
WED 09 JUN	VISIT TO DISNEYLAND
THU 10 JUN	FLIGHT TO LAS VEGAS. ACCOMMODATION: CAESARS PALACE
FRI 11 JUN	FLIGHT TO GRAND CANYON. EXCURSION AND PACKED LUNCH
SAT 12 JUN	FLIGHT TO SAN FRANCISCO. ACCOMMODATION: HOTEL PAN PACIFIC AFTERNOON AND EVENING FREE
SUN 13 JUN MORNING: AFTERNOON:	 VISIT MUIR WOODS AND SEE MAGNIFICENT REDWOOD TREES. VISIT PICTURESQUE SAUSALITO
MON 14 JUN	RETURN FLIGHT TO LONDON

3 In small groups talk about your real or imaginary holiday plans in the same way.

TALKING EFFECTIVELY

Study this sentence from Practice, Exercise 1 on page 19. It has been written out with the weak forms /ə/ and the linking marks.
The guests wəll be arriving ət eight ə 'clock.

a) Write out the other sentences which contain continuous tenses in the same way. Which types of words are pronounced with a weak form? When are they used in their weak form and when in their strong form?

b) [🖵 2.2] Listen to the recording and practise saying them.

Practice

The future perfect continuous game: Secret destinations
Work in groups of three. Write down the name of a country and three things that you *will be doing* on holiday in that country. The things you choose should be probable but not too obvious. *Do not* show your notes to the other people in your group.

> EGYPT
> riding a camel
> going on a boat trip on the Nile
> sleeping in an air-conditioned room

Students A and B ask student C twenty questions in order to find out his or her destination. Try to pay attention to the use of weak forms and linking as you play the game. Example:
A: *Will you be sitting in the sun?*
C: *No, I won't.*
B: *Will you be driving long distances?*
C: *No, I won't.*
A: *Will you be visiting museums?*
C: *Yes, I will.*
B: *Will you be going to Rome?*

If students A and B guess the destination and the three activities on student C's paper in less than twenty questions, they score a point each. If not, student C scores two points. Take it in turns to be student C.

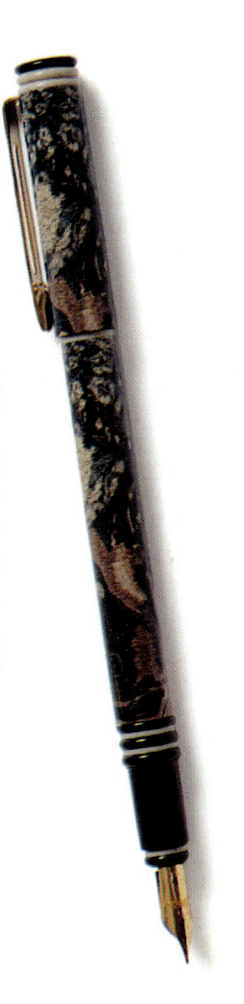

UNIT 3

Magic moments

Section 1

LISTENING AND SPEAKING

1 [■ 3.1] Listen to people saying what the word nostalgia means to them.

a) Do you agree with any of them?
b) Write down your definition of nostalgia in not more than one sentence and list several things you are nostalgic about. Compare your definition and your list with other students.

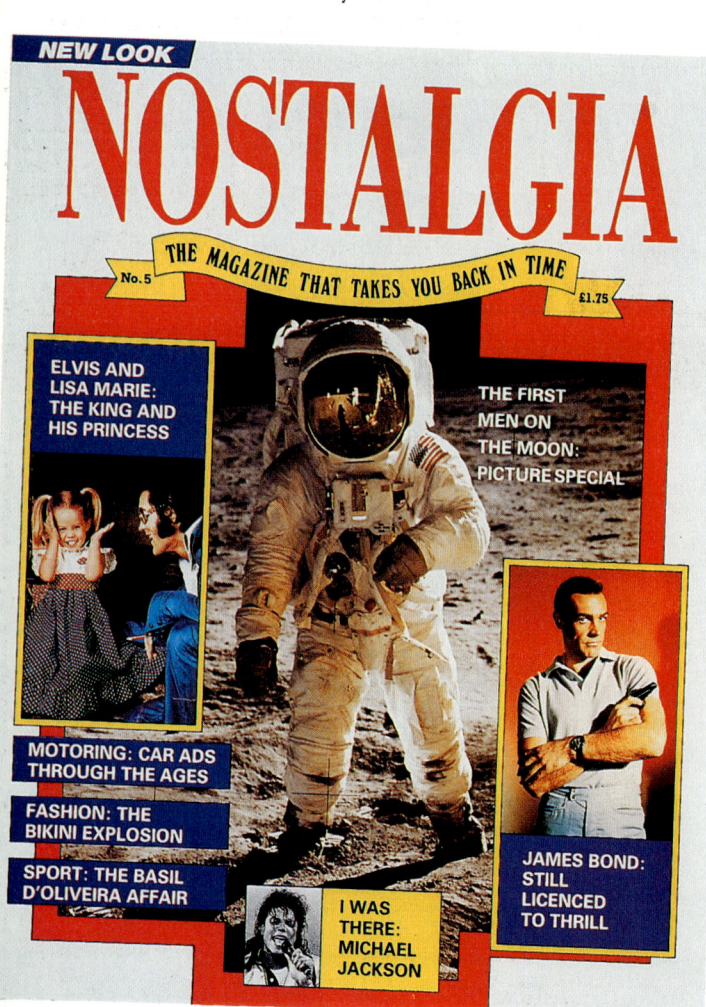

2 The picture on the left is the front cover of a British magazine called *Nostalgia*. Look at the topics and work in groups to decide which is the most and the least nostalgic. Number them from 1 to 6.

a) Elvis ☐
b) The first men on the moon ☐
c) James Bond ☐
d) Motoring through the ages ☐
e) Michael Jackson ☐
f) The bikini explosion ☐

3 Role play the following situation. A meeting of the editorial board of the magazine *Nostalgia*. Work in groups of four or five students. You are the editors of the magazine and are planning the next issue.

a) Decide on interesting topics for the four or five main articles you would like to publish.
b) Each member of the group chooses an idea for an article and jots down ideas about it to present to the others. Think of a topic which can be presented from an interesting angle, e.g. a dramatic or memorable scene or event, a memory which is full of emotion, etc.

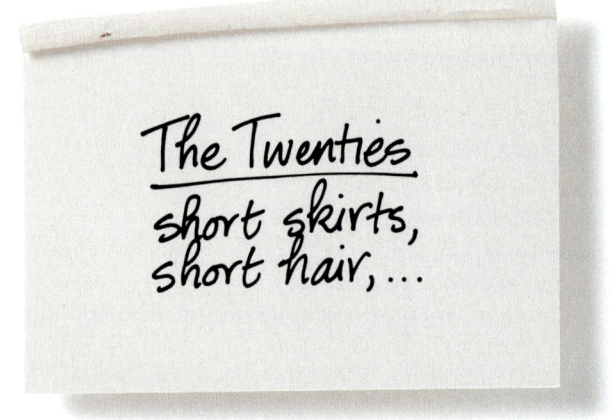

The Twenties
short skirts,
short hair,...

The Wild West
in America
excitement,
discovery,...

c) [▣ 3.2] Before you present your suggestion to your group, listen to the tape. Speaker A makes suggestions and speaker B tactfully disagrees in order to present alternative suggestions. On the list below, tick the strategies each speaker uses. An example has been done for you.

	A	B
Affirmative question tags, e.g. *do you?*		✓
Negative question tags, e.g. *don't you think?*		
Yes/No questions, e.g. *do you like . . . ?*		
Wh- questions, e.g. *What do you like?*		
Negative questions, e.g. *Don't you think . . . ?*		
Genuine agreement, e.g. *That's a great idea!*		
Apparent agreement, e.g. *That's a great idea, but . . .*		

4 Now present your suggestions for articles to the group using the same strategies as the speakers on the tape.

a) The group selects the most interesting articles to present to the whole class.
b) The class listens to the presentations and makes a final, well-balanced choice of topics for the magazine.

READING

The Nostalgia Shop Quiz

How fast can you answer the following questions by skimming through the advert?

a) A Charlie Chaplin fan wants to order a video. What must he or she do?
b) Your best friend wants to know who her great-great-grandmother was. How can she find out?
c) You are looking for a present for a friend who is a clothes designer. Can you find anything suitable?
d) A friend of yours is looking for an appropriate birthday present for his grandfather, who was born on 6th August 1898. Can you give him some advice?
e) Your grandmother cannot remember the words of a song she used to sing in her youth. How can you help her?
f) An aunt of yours who is a history teacher is looking for an interesting way of presenting contemporary history to her class. What could you suggest?
g) Some friends of yours have just moved house and are decorating their new home in a nineteenth-century style. What could you give them for a house-warming present?

Compare your answers with a partner.

NOSTALGIA SHOP

1 Pam Gulliver (Mrs). **Anything Nostalgic.** Looking for Something — old books; sheet music; magazines (a speciality)? Let The People Who Never Give Up help you. Anything Nostalgic, 35 Northcourt Avenue, Reading RG2 7HE. Tel: (0734) 871479.

2 ANCESTRY **Debrett**
Were your ancestors labourers or lords? Debrett will trace them whoever they were and provide a report as a family heirloom or unique gift. *For free booklet*: Debrett Ancestry Research Ltd, Dept NA Gordon Road, Winchester SO23 7DD Tel: (0962) 69067

3 Classical Victorian Lamp-posts and Lighting
From £189.00
Tel: 09544 637
Pastures Drive, Caxton Cambridgeshire CB3 8PF

4 Banner Headlines
Thirty large cards carry these original newspaper headlines spanning the years 1914-1950. The pack traces major political, social, sporting and royal landmarks — from the *Daily Mirror's* front-page headline of 5 August 1914 declaring World War 1, to the *News Chronicle's* 25 February 1950 headline declaring the result of the general election.
Contents: 30 large cards size 290 x 210 mm and a manual in a storage box. ISBN 0 86388 016 9
Write to: Banner Headlines, Winslow Press, Telford Road, Bicester Oxon OX6 0TS or phone (0868) 244644 (Access/Visa accepted) £17.85

5 BORN 1890-1980?
Order an **original** London **Times** newspaper for birthdates, anniversary/retirement etc., in attractive presentation wallet, £13.95 inc. P&P (UK); 3 for £36. Access, Visa.
Free details from **Bygone News**, 56 Hill Road, Weston-super-Mare, Avon. Tel: 0934 412844 (24 hours)

6 THE STORY OF YOUR LIFE ... A way to build it up, with pictures, into a real treasure by the year 2000. The **Half Century Diary** is a big looseleaf album arranged in years, (so you can start with Sarah's wedding, or anywhere...) It runs from 1950-2001 with brief notes to capture the essence of each year and prompt your memory, perhaps your father's too. *Details:* 20th Century Diaries, Severels, Runction, Chichester PO20 6PS.

7 Fan Clubs
The official Kenneth Williams, Sid James British Comedy magazine — *Stop Messin' About!* Patron: Nicholas Parsons. £8 subscription. Carl St. John, 27 Brookmead Way, Orpington, Kent

8 We buy and sell dated and beaded clothes, Victorian – 1950.
(Shop)
Wardrobe:
10 Glebe Avenue Ickenham, Hillingdon, Middlesex UB10 8QU or Tel: Ruislip 633795 (evenings)

9 COMEDY VIDEO CLASSICS
Charlie Chaplin: The Pawnshop, The Rink, One a.m.
Buster Keaton: Balloonatic, The Blacksmith, Coney Island.
Buster Keaton: Cops, Harry Langdon: All Night Long, Harold Lloyd: Cinema Director.
Ford Sterling: A Bedroom Blunder, Our Dare-Devil Chief, A Desperate Scoundrel.
Laurel & Hardy: Musical Moments.

For all videos, send your order + remittance to: Nostalgia, 29 Enford Street, London W1H 1DG. Overseas postage rates on request.

VOCABULARY

1 [▭ 3.3] Work with a partner to describe the objects in the pictures. Do you know, or can you imagine what purpose they served? Listen to the tape to find out if you were right.

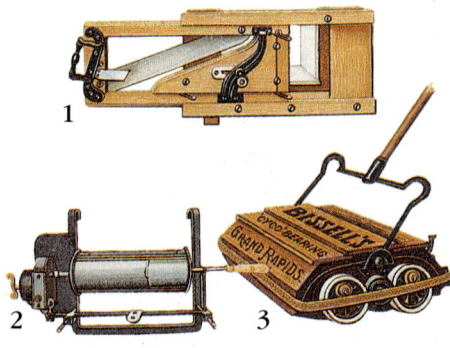

2 Think of other objects that are obsolete or which have changed beyond recognition. Describe one of them to a partner without naming it. Can your partner guess what the object is?

Section 2

LEARNING GRAMMAR

► Diagnosis ◄ ◄ ◄

Used to and *Would*

Answer the following questions with a partner. Check the guidelines in the Key.

a) Which of the following forms is incorrect?
   i) Jane was used to have long curly hair.
   ii) Jane used to have long curly hair.
b) Which of the following forms is fairly formal? Which is usually used only in spoken English?
   i) Graham didn't use to have car.
   ii) Graham used not to have a car.
c) Which of the following sentences is incorrect if the speaker is talking about the past? Why?
   i) There would be a cinema in the centre of town.
   ii) There used to be a cinema in the centre of town.
d) Which of these sentences about the past can only be understood if you add more details?
   i) I used to smoke.
   ii) I would smoke.

Practice

1 Correct the following sentences where necessary so that they all make sense about the past. The first one has been done for you.

a) There would be a statue on the corner, but they took it away last week. *used to*
b) Jane was used to buy a new car every two years.
c) We would go dancing every Saturday night.
d) Sally would have a dog when she was little.
e) People do not work as hard as they would.
f) The whole village would go to church on Christmas morning.

2 Using *used to* and *would* appropriately can help add variety, elegance and style to your English. Study the following paragraph which shows how *used to* and *would* can be used in sequence. Note that repetition of *used to* is clumsy and usually avoided. *Would*, however can easily be repeated once or twice.

> When I was at school I wanted to be an actress. I used to spend my whole time dreaming about movie stars. I'd go to the cinema twice a week and I'd read any movie magazine that I could lay my hands on.

3 Write a short paragraph about yourself, using the same sequence. Read out your paragraph to a partner.

Development

Different uses of *would*

Study the different uses of *would* below.
a) past habit
b) characteristic behaviour
c) expression of strong will, determination
d) probability, making a deduction from clues or evidence presented
e) the future in the past, referring to events that are destined to happen
f) being more polite through being tentative

1 [▣ 3.4] Listen and read the following remarks which all contain the modal auxiliary *would*. With a partner, match the remarks to the meanings above. What is the context for each of them? The first one has been done for you.

a) She loved staying on the farm. Every morning, she would help her uncle milk the cows.
   Context: someone is talking about childhood holidays
   Meaning a), past habit
b) That would be Julie, from your description. She is very tall with long fair hair and she often goes to the *Calypso*.
c) I don't like the first proposal, or the second one, so I think the third one would be the best solution.
d) The boss said that she would not tolerate such behaviour.
e) John would make a mess of things. You should never have asked him to help in the first place.
f) Mary would be sorry for that later, but at the time she couldn't know that things would turn out as they did.
g) Although Chris Bonington didn't get to the top of Everest the first time he tried, he wouldn't give up and made several more attempts.

2 Which of the sentences in Exercise 1 refer to the present, which to the past and which to the future? Fill in the grid below. The first one has been done for you.

	a)	b)	c)	d)	e)	f)	g)
Past	✓						
Present							
Future							

Would and the future-in-the-past

1 *Would* and *Going to* are used in narratives in the following ways:

a) to predict the future or to talk about probability from a point in the past (see example 1f). Example:

Sally	would / was going to	see Bill at work the next day.

b) to express an intention at a moment in the past. Example:

John	would / was going to	do everything he could to succeed in his new venture.

Would is probably more common in written narrative and *going to* in spoken narrative.

c) If the prediction, probability or intention turns out to be unfulfilled, or if we do not know the outcome, only *going to* is possible. For example, you can say:
Sally was going to see Bill at work tomorrow, but the next day she woke up with 'flu and couldn't get out of bed.
Last time I saw you, you were going to move.
You cannot say:
~~Sally would see Bill at work tomorrow, but the next day she woke up with 'flu and couldn't get out of bed.~~
~~Last time I saw you, you would move.~~

2 In the negative form *would* and *going to* express intention or unwillingness or refusal. For example, in the following sentence *would* might mean intention or refusal.

Stephanie	wouldn't / wasn't going to	leave home before she had enough money to buy a flat.

3 The *past continuous* is used to talk about events that are planned for the future at a point in the past. *Would* is not used in this sense. Example:
I had to go shopping because the Smiths were coming to dinner that night.
You cannot say:
~~I had to go shopping because the Smiths would come to dinner that night.~~

4 *Was/were to* or *going to* may also be used to present an event as a plan for the future at a point in the past. *Was/were to* may appear slightly more formal or literary. Example:

| Her daughter | was going to / was to | spend the summer with friends. |

Going to may appear a little heavy stylistically. Example:
I had to go shopping because the Smiths were going to come to dinner.

5 We are more likely to use *was/were to* or *going to* than the *past continuous* in the following cases:

a) if it is uncertain whether the planned event took place. Examples:
 i) *I had to go shopping because the Smiths were to come to dinner that night.* (We do not know whether the Smiths came or not.)
b) if the event did not take place. Examples:
 i) *I was to leave the next day, but in the end I changed my mind.*
 ii) *I was going to leave the next day, but in the end I changed my mind.*
 iii) *I was leaving the next day, but in the end I changed my mind.* (just possible if *was* is stressed)

6 When we want to talk about a future event from a point in the past and make it very clear that the event did in fact happen, for example in order to give a future perspective to historical fact, we use *was/were to* or *would*. The style is formal and literary. Example:
Napoleon was to lose the Battle of Waterloo and would spend the rest of his life in exile in Saint Helena.

Practice

1 Correct the mistakes in the following sentences where necessary. There may be more than one answer. The first one has been done for you. Check your answers with a partner.

a) Jenny would be a lawyer when she grew up but later she changed her mind and became a doctor.   *was going to (intention)/was to (planning)*
b) The first issue of the new magazine would come out last Sunday, but the printers went on strike.
c) The time was coming when he was regretting his decision.
d) Brian Smith was leaving CNA television at the end of the week to join a new team at CBS.
e) The meeting would be held the following week, but in the end it was cancelled.
f) That year the winter would be a hard one.
g) After his first trip in 1492, Christopher Columbus was making three more voyages of discovery to South America.
h) When Tracy learnt how to drive, she was being much more independent.
i) The Martins were in a hurry because they would leave in two hours time.
j) When we last met, you would start a new job.

2 Make the following statements less definite and more polite by using *would*. The first one has been done for you.

a) Will you give me a hand for the party tomorrow?
 Would you give me a hand for the party tomorrow?
b) Open the window, will you?
c) If you will wait here a moment, I'll see if Mr Smith can see you now.
d) Will you carry my suitcase for me, please?
e) I don't agree with that at all.
f) I think the third candidate we interviewed will be the best person for the job.
d) Wait a moment, please.
h) Do you mind posting this letter for me?

TALKING EFFECTIVELY

[▣ 3.5] Listen to the tape again.

a) In which cases is *would* stressed? In which cases is it reduced to its weak unstressed form?
b) Which of the following statements is true?
   i) *Would* can be stressed or unstressed in any context.
   ii) Some meanings of *would* are always stressed.
c) Complete the rule below.
   The following two meanings of *would* are always stressed:
   i) . . .
   ii) . . .

Practice

1 [▣ 3.6] Study the following mini-dialogue, which is an example of use d) on page 25. Improvise similar mini-dialogues with a partner about people or things that you have seen.

A: There was this lovely painting, full of bright colours and Polynesian women.
B: Ah, yes, that would be a Gauguin.

2 Read the following remarks and work with a partner to decide how *would* is being used in each case, and whether it is stressed or unstressed. Then choose three of the remarks and put them into a short paragraph or dialogue. Read out what you have written to another group. Refer back to the uses on page 25 if necessary.

a) He'd always talk for hours if you gave him a chance.
b) That would be her mother.
c) It's your own fault. You would take the baby with you.
d) It would be a long time before she saw him again.
e) Next weekend would be better for me.
f) We would go for the most wonderful drives along the coast.

Section 3

LISTENING

1 [▣ 3.7] Listen to the three speakers. Which one is speaking about which period in history?

2 Listen to the tape again and make notes under the different headings for each speaker.

- Entertainment and leisure
- Food
- Clothes
- Atmosphere
- Work
- Homes
- Ideas

3 In groups, discuss some of the advantages and disadvantages of the periods the speakers were talking about. Which period of history would you most like to have lived in? Give your reasons.

VOCABULARY

Multi-part verbs: adverbial particles

1 Using the dictionary entry to help you, fill in the gaps with a suitable multi-part verb. Separate the verb from the particle whenever possible. The first one has been done for you.

> actually removing it: *to take down one's trousers*
> **take** sbdy./sthg. ↔ **in** *phr v* [T] **1** to receive into one's home; provide lodgings for (a person): *He had nowhere to sleep so we offered to take him in.* **2** to understand fully; GRASP: *It took me a long time to take in what you were saying.* **3** to deceive: *Don't be taken in by his promises.*
> **take on** *phr v* **1** [T] (**take** sbdy.↔**on**) to start to employ: *We've decided to take on a new clerk in the accounts department.* **2** [T] (**take on** sthg.) to begin to have (a quality or appearance); ASSUME (3): *These insects can take on the colour of their surroundings.* | *His face took on a worried expression.*
> **take to** sbdy./sthg. *phr v* [T] **1** to feel a liking for, esp. at once: *I took to Paul as soon as we met.* | *I'm not sure if he'll take to the idea.* **2** to begin as a practice, habit, etc.: *All this gloomy news is enough to make you take to drink.* [+v-ing] *Just lately he's taken to hiding his socks under the carpet.*
> **take** sbdy./sthg. ↔ **up** *phr v* [T] **1** to begin to spend time

a) 'What did the doctor say?'
   'Well, it was all so complicated that I only *took* half of it *in*.'
b) He lied so skilfully. I was completely . . .
c) You're busy enough already. I don't think you should . . . any more work.
d) We have a whole fortnight after all. Let's . . . Paris, Rome, London and Berlin, and Amsterdam.
e) When they cleaned up the city centre, it . . . a new look.
f) I'm glad Karen joined the staff. I . . . her right from the start.

2 Use your dictionary to help you write similar sentences to test your partner. Student A writes sentences with the verb *put*. Student B writes sentences with the verb *break*.

A: I'm sorry, I can't put you . . . this weekend, as my parents are coming to stay and the house is full.
B: I'm sorry, I can't *put you up* this weekend, as my parents are coming to stay and the house is full.
B: However did the burglars break . . . without being disturbed?
A: However did the burglars *break in* without being disturbed?

WRITING

1 In this short passage from a nostalgic book, *Period Piece*, Gwen Raverat writes about her childhood. Seven adjectives or adjectival phrases, which help the writer create atmosphere, have been removed and are listed in the box below. Put them back into the passage in an appropriate place.

| great | red | the most romantic | steep |
| legendary | strangely shaped | sudden | |

Every day at Down my father used to take us for walks, telling us stories about the places as we went: up the hill to Cudham church; or to look for orchids at Orchis Bank, or along the smuggler's track, or to the Big Woods where Uncle William had been lost as a child. The valleys, the red earth full of flints, the lonely woods, the sense of remoteness, made it different from any other place we knew. We were only sixteen miles from London Bridge, and yet it was so quiet that if a cart came down our lane we all rushed to look over the orchard wall to see it go by.

2 Check your version with a partner and then with the original. Which version do you prefer? Why?

3 Write your own 'period piece'.

a) Write about a period in history or about your own childhood. Before you begin, write down a list of adjectives that you would like to include in your writing.
b) Read out your 'period piece' to other people in your class.

UNIT 4

What language do you speak?

Section 1

READING AND SPEAKING

1 Do you know the answers to the following questions? Discuss them in small groups.

a) How many languages are spoken in your country?
b) If there is more than one, are they all equally important?
c) Can you take school exams in more than one language?
d) Is there an 'official' language which is used for administrative purposes (on passports etc.)?
e) Should there be laws imposing the use of one language in preference to others in your country, in the United States or in the EC?

2 Report back your group's discussion to the whole class.

3 Work in pairs. Half the class read text A on the right and half the class read text B on page 30. Make notes on the topic headings after each text.

Text A

OUR NATION Must Have an Official Language

For decades, our official policy was to encourage the desire of immigrants to learn the language of their new country. But in the last few years, our government officials seem to be doing everything they can to downplay the importance of retaining that common bond of language.

We now have laws that require federal election ballots and other voting materials to be printed in languages other than English. We have laws that require that children from non-English-speaking backgrounds are taught in their native languages, sometimes for several years, while they acquire English. Federal, state and local governments print information in half a dozen languages on everything from preparing income taxes to creating nutritious meals. Several states provide exams in dozens of languages for licenses for driving cars to cutting hair. These laws and programs, which allow immigrants and their children to continue to function in their native languages, may actually serve as a disincentive to their learning English.

Immigrants come here seeking economic opportunity and democratic freedom. Learning the language of their new society will help them achieve those aims. Elected leaders who devise ways to keep people functioning outside the mainstream of this English-speaking society are harming the very people they claim to be helping.

The English Language Amendment will ensure our heritage as a nation with a diverse population bound by a common language. Most importantly, it will guarantee that our government continues to protect that heritage.

Linda Chavez, President of US English

(from *USA Today*)

The English Language Amendment: a proposal to introduce a change in the American constitution making English the official language of the United States.
US English: an association which wishes to see English adopted as the official and legal language of the United States.

Topic headings: Current Situation; Educational opportunities; Participation in American society; Attitudes to an English language policy

Text B

OUR NATION Doesn't Need an 'Official' Language

In California, English-only advocates tried to ban Chinese signs on restaurants and protested publication of Spanish-language Yellow Pages. In Florida, they challenged housing ads in Spanish.

That sort of intolerance should not be tolerated. From this nation's earliest days, many of those who arrived here spoke no English. But most soon learned. In the process, they enriched our language – and our way of life. In some areas, such as South Florida, there are enclaves where Spanish is dominant. That trend disturbs the official-English advocates. They say it could weaken the national unity. Their solution is to enshrine English in the lawbooks. So far, 14 states have accepted that approach. But 19 other states wisely rejected such proposals last year.

Supporters of official-English laws say they clarify public policy and give English legal protection. They are wrong. At best, such laws will have a negligible effect. At worst they could result in the banning of bilingual ballots and bilingual education programs and deprive non-English speakers of vital services by eliminating government translators. That won't help English. That won't help this nation. But it will hurt the people who don't speak English.

English has always been the ticket to educational, social and economic success in the USA, and it will continue to be. We don't need laws or constitutional amendments to guarantee that. We do need a commitment to provide the learning opportunities – for adults as well as children. That's the right approach: Teach the language; don't try to ram it down people's throats.

(from *USA Today*)

Yellow pages: a reference book of professional phone numbers.

Topic headings: Current situation; Historical aspects; Linguistic variety; Participation in American society; Attitudes to an English language policy

4 Find another pair who has read the other text. Find out about their text by asking them questions.

5 With your partner, do the following role play. If you read text A, read role card A. If you read text B, read role card B.

STUDENT A (TEXT A)
You are a member of U.S. English. You are for the English Language Amendment. You are trying to convince a member of your community to sign a petition for your cause. You may use some of the suggested language in the box below to help you convince your partner.

- Wouldn't you agree that an official policy is justified?
- Surely you agree that children would have better opportunities.
- If we take race relations into account, it's obvious that we need an official language.
- Let's not forget that everyone needs English.
- Everyone know that equal opportunities will not exist until English is the official language.

STUDENT B (TEXT B)
You have been approached by a member of US English and asked to sign a petition supporting the English Language Amendment. You are basically against the amendment, but you are prepared to listen to the arguments and discuss the matter. You might even be persuaded to change your mind! You may use some of the language in the box below to help you express your disagreement.

- That's not really how I see it.
- I'm not entirely convinced that you are right about that.
- I can't say that I share your views on that.
- I can't help thinking that things aren't exactly as you say.

6 Report back to the class on your discussion in the role play.

Section 2

LEARNING GRAMMAR

▶ Diagnosis ◀◀◀

***The, a,* or ∅ zero article:** basic points

1 Work with a partner to correct the mistakes in the following sentences where necessary. Check your answers in the Key.

a) The apples are my favourite fruit.
b) I love travelling by the plane.
c) I used to play the violin. (British English)
d) Himalayas are higher than any other mountains in the world.
e) What beautiful view!
f) I have never been to the South America.
g) Bill is an engineer.

2 With your partner, complete the following sentences with *a, the* or ∅ (nothing). Check your answers in the Key.

a) . . . jazz is not usually my favourite music, but I'll come to the concert tonight if you like.
b) I came home by . . . car.
c) I'm learning to play . . . piano. (Br English)
d) She wants to be . . . doctor.
e) Photos of . . . Venus are now being analysed by scientists.
f) . . . Indian Ocean is the most beautiful in the world.
g) . . . Toyota's chairman congratulated the employees on . . . company's excellent results.
h) 'Which one do you like?' 'I like . . . both of them.'
i) . . . most birds can fly.

3 Look at the examples in Exercises 1 and 2.

a) What rules can you note down about the use of the article with:
  i) countable and uncountable nouns?
  ii) geographical place names?
  iii) musical instruments?
  iv) people's professions?
  Refer to the Key if you are not sure.
b) In a small group, brainstorm common expressions of transport and of places which do not have an article.
  Examples: *by car, at school.*
  Are your examples the same as the ones in the Key?

▶ Development ◀◀◀

***A, the* or ∅ *zero article*:** some guidelines

a) *The* is used to talk about people or things when it is obvious what is being talked about to both the speaker and the listener, whether there is any other reference in the sentence or not. Examples:
I found the book I lost last week. (the book is defined in the next bit of the sentence)
Give me the book. (the book is visible)
I loved the book. (we have been talking about a book or I have been given a book)

b) Although no article is used to talk about things in general, it is used to talk about things in particular. This distinction is sometimes not easy to see and not very important for the general meaning of the sentence. For example, it is difficult to find any significant difference of meaning between the following examples:
Cars in Brazil cause a lot of pollution.
The cars in Brazil cause a lot of pollution.

c) Although *the* is not usually used with an uncountable noun, it must be used if it is related to a specific person or thing. Examples:
We must fight for freedom.
We must fight for the freedom of every single human being.

d) Some nouns can be both countable and uncountable nouns and the use of *the* must take this into account. Examples:
Young people lack opportunity. (this refers to the idea of opportunity in general)
It was a wonderful opportunity. (this refers to a particular opportunity for a particular person)

Unit 4

Practice

1 With a partner complete the following extract from the reading texts in Section 1 with *a, the* or Ø *(zero article)*. Then look at pages 29–30 and compare your version to the original. If your version is different, use the guide lines on page 31 to say if it is an acceptable alternative or a mistake.

> ..(a).. immigrants come here seeking ..(b).. economic opportunity and ..(c).. democratic freedom. Learning ..(d).. language of their new society will help them achieve those aims. ..(e).. elected leaders who devise ways to keep ..(f).. people functioning outside the mainstream of this English-speaking society are harming the very people they claim to be helping.

> In California, ..(g).. English-only advocates tried to ban ..(h).. Chinese signs on ..(i).. restaurants and protested about ..(j).. publication of ..(k).. Spanish-language Yellow Pages. In Florida, they challenged ..(l).. housing ads in Spanish.

2 The same or different?

a) Read the following pairs of sentences with a partner and find the only pair in which the presence or absence of the article radically affects the context and meaning.
  i) Students at the technical college often eat here.
  The students at the technical college often eat here.
  ii) Economy could be the answer.
  The economy could be the answer.
  iii) Evidence presented at the trial was later found to be inaccurate.
  The evidence presented at the trial was later found to be inaccurate.
  iv) Women I saw in India were dressed in saris.
  The women I saw in India were dressed in saris.

b) With a partner, compare the following pairs of sentences. Which pair means the same thing, which pair could mean the same thing in a specific context and which pair has two different meanings?
  i) Books are expensive.
  The books are expensive.
  ii) I hate the telephone.
  I hate telephones.
  iii) He invented telescopes.
  He invented the telescope.

3 Say whether the following statements are true.

a) Sometimes the presence or absence of an article can make almost no difference to the meaning of a sentence.
b) There are definite, fixed rules about the use of the article in every context.
c) Sometimes the presence or absence of the article makes a significant difference to the meaning of a sentence.
d) In English it does not matter whether you use an article or not.

4 There are particular cases in which the use of the article changes the meaning of the sentence. Study the difference of meaning between the following two sentences.

a) She went to prison. (She had been sent to prison for committing a crime.)
b) She went to the prison. (She went to visit the prison but was not an inmate.)

5 With a partner, say what the context could be for each sentence below and add another remark which would be appropriate in the context. The first one has been done for you. Use your dictionary if necessary.

a) She went to prison *for robbing a bank*.
  She went to the prison to *visit her uncle*.
b) I dislike painting.
  I dislike the painting.
c) I read the literature.
  I read literature.
d) I love life.
  I love the life.

LANGUAGE PATTERNS

1 In the following set of sentences, write a tick [✓] against the sentence in which there is a base form with *to* and a cross [✗] against the sentence in which there is a base form without *to*.

  a) i) I heard someone give a very good speech last night.
    ii) We chose Bill to give the speech at the wedding.
    iii) We made her talk.
    iv) We encouraged her to talk.
    v) Kim saw a tiny bird fly away.

vi) Kim expected the tiny bird to fly away.
vii) I watched her drink a cup of tea.
viii) I invited her to drink a cup of tea.

b) Look back at the examples in a) and complete the following statement.
The following verbs are followed by the base form of the verb without *to*: . . .

2 Look at the following sentences.

a) Write *P* against sentences which are in the passive and *A* against the sentences which are in the active form.
i) I saw him leave in a hurry. *A*
ii) Justice must be done, but it must also be seen to be done.
iii) He was heard to speak very highly of the Prime Minister.
iv) I heard you come in very late last night.
v) The boss made me stay late.
vi) I was made to stay late.

b) Look back at the examples in a) and complete the following statement.
In the passive form all verbs are followed by...

Practice

1 Write sentences using the elements below, and adding *to* where necessary.

a) the teacher/the homework/the pupil/again/do/made
The teacher made the pupil do the homework again.
b) hide/seen/the man/in his pocket/three packets of biscuits/was
c) heard/in the lock/the key/turn/I
d) a kind word/the miserable old man/say/was/never/about anyone/heard
e) will/the greatest actress/she/seen/of our time/be/be

2 Write sentences using *make* with or without *to* to describe your childhood at home and at school. Examples:
I was/wasn't made to go to bed early.
When I was a child I was never made to help in the house.
My teachers often made me do my homework again.
I was made to play football in the freezing cold and I hated it.
Read other people's sentences. Find out more about their experiences.

Section 3

LISTENING

1 You are going to listen to an interview with a lexicographer (a person who compiles dictionaries) about a new approach to dictionary making. Before you listen, discuss the following questions with a partner and guess the answers.

a) How many words do you think there are in the English language?
b) How many new words get invented in English in a year?
c) Where do new words come from?
d) What sources do lexicographers use to find new words?
e) How do lexicographers decide which words to put in a dictionary and which words to leave out?
f) How long have people been using new words before they are included in a dictionary?

Report back your guesses to the whole class.

2 [📼 4.1] Listen to the tape. Are the speaker's answers to the questions above the same as your own, or are they different? What are the differences?

Unit 4

LONGMAN WORDWATCH

Word *goldfished*
Citation

Just after lunch the Labour conference was plunged into gloom, and the funny thing is that it cheered most of the delegates up.
  Gerald Kaufman had just opened the afternoon's debate, saying "the British people are preparing to give Labour power", when there was an electricity cut.
  The lights were going out all over the Brighton conference centre, and it was not at all clear whether we would see them lit again.
  "Hang on," said the conference chairman as a delegate goldfished into a silent microphone. "It looks like there's been something of a power failure." Just the sort of thing Labour is supposed to have put behind it.

Source of citation *The Guardian 4/10/91*

3 Listen to the tape again and work with a partner to take down notes and answer the following questions on the Wordwatch project.

a) Who contributes to the Wordwatch scheme? How do they do this?
b) In what ways is it different from other dictionary compilation schemes?
c) What are the two reasons for the existence of this scheme?

4 Can you match the words mentioned by Brian O'Kill, listed in Column A, to their probable origin in column B?

A	B
1 perestroika	a) made up from two separate words
2 derbrain	b) an existing word which has taken on a new, completely different meaning
3 wicked	c) a foreign language
4 gongoozler	d) regional dialect
5 polac	e) children's jargon

5 Why does Brian O'Kill use words like *nice*, *lovely*, and *interesting* to describe new words?

a) What do you think is 'nice' about them?
b) Can you think of some new words in your own language? Where do they come from? What do they mean?
c) Tell other people in your class about them.

TALKING EFFECTIVELY

Stress on nouns and verbs

1 Some words can be used as both nouns and verbs. Example:
Wordwatch provides a record of the living language.
I recorded a wonderful concert last night.
In this case, the stress is placed differently according to their function.

[▶ 4.2] Listen to the sentences below and mark in the two stress patterns for each word.

a) ADDICT
   i) He's a drug-addict.
   ii) I'm addicted to chocolate.
b) CONTENT
   i) Nothing would content her.
   ii) The content of this magazine is very interesting.

What is the rule? Where does the stress go on the noun? Where does it go on the verb?

2 With a partner, mark in the stress patterns on the following sentences and practise saying them.

a) DICTATE
   i) The teacher dictated the questions.
   ii) You must respect the dictates of your own conscience.
b) ESCORT
   i) Presidents always need a police escort.
   ii) John refused to escort me home last night.
c) INSULT
   i) I didn't mean to insult him.
   ii) Don't take any notice of his insults.

[▶ 4.3] Listen to the tape to check.

3 Choose one or two of the words from the box. Use them in two contrasting sentences as a noun and a verb. Read out your sentences to a partner.

permit	protest	prospect	reprint	reject
survey	contrast			

34

WRITING

Report writing: linking and organising ideas

1 A foreign publisher is thinking of starting a Wordwatch scheme for your language and needs a report on the Wordwatch scheme. Here is the beginning of the report in its rough draft and in its final form. Underline the words in the final version which help to link up and organise the ideas. Two examples have been done for you.

a) First draft

```
A great variety of people from
the general public contribute to
the scheme. People contribute
new or unfamiliar words which
they come across either in the
written language or in speech.
The words are sometimes foreign,
sometimes from regional dialects
and sometimes invented.
```

b) Final version

```
The first thing to note is that
a great variety of people from
the general public contribute to
the scheme. They do this by
sending in new or unfamiliar
words which they come across
either in the written language
or in speech. These reported
items are sometimes foreign,
sometimes from regional dialects
and sometimes invented.
```

(The first thing to note and this are underlined.)

2 Study the following pairs of sentences. In each case choose the sentence which continues the report most clearly and smoothly, linking the ideas to the previous sentence and avoiding repetition. Underline the words that do the linking.

a) i) The result is a kind of dictionary which is very different from any other because members of the public contribute as well as lexicographers.
   ii) The dictionary is different from others because members of the public contribute as well as lexicographers.

b) i) The dictionary deals with words that have appeared recently and which may only stay in the language temporarily.
   ii) Moreover, it deals with words that have appeared recently and which may only stay in the language temporarily.

c) i) A reference work such as this has two vital functions.
   ii) The dictionary has two vital functions.

d) i) Its most important function is to provide a record of the language.
   ii) First and above all, it provides a record of the language.

e) i) Secondly it can be used as an up-to-date guide to the language, which is not possible in a traditional dictionary.
   ii) It provides an up-to-date guide to the language, which is not possible in a traditional dictionary.

f) i) Wordwatch is a very worthwhile project.
   ii) All these factors contribute to making Wordwatch a very worthwhile project.

3 Look back at the words and expressions you have underlined.

a) Which ones help to organise the ideas in the report? Which ones simply refer back to earlier ideas?
b) What do the expressions 'These reported items' in 1b) and 'a reference work' in 2c) refer to? What strategy is the writer using in order to avoid repetition?

4 Use your notes from the texts in Section 1 to write a report on the question of an official language in the United States. Write about either the advantages or the disadvantages. Remember to link each sentence to the previous one and to avoid repetition as in the examples in Exercise 2 above.

5 Read some other people's reports. How are they similar to yours? How are they different?

UNIT 5

What a coincidence!

Section 1

SPEAKING

1 Work with a partner you do not know very well, and discuss briefly the following topics to see if you can find something you have in common. For example, do you have a similar number of brothers and sisters?

a) families   d) homes
b) travels   e) hobbies and interests
c) school   f) likes and dislikes

2 Discuss the same topics with other pairs.

a) Has anyone found coincidences between his or her life and someone else's? When does something people 'have in common' become a coincidence?
b) Discuss with a partner how your life has been affected by coincidences. Talk about your relationships, your job, etc.
c) Report back to the rest of the class.

READING

1 Do you agree with the following statements? Write *T* (*True*), *F* (*False*) or *?* (*Don't know*) in column A against each one. Compare your list with a partner's.

	A	B
a) Coincidences are merely a matter of chance.		
b) Coincidences often have some rational or scientific explanation.		
c) Coincidences are a proof that telepathy and other paranormal phenomena really exist.		
d) Identical twins who are not brought up together are liable to have very many coincidences in their lives.		

2 Read the following text.

a) Write *T* (*True*), *F* (*False*) or *?* (*Don't know*) in column B in the table in Exercise 1 according to what the author thinks. Check your answers with a partner. Are the author's views different from your own?

b) What have you learnt from the passage about the link between coincidences and the laws of nature? With your partner, list any other mysteries of nature that you know which may be explained by science one day.

The Coincidence Factor

Barbara Herbert met her twin sister Daphne Goodship when they were 39. They had been brought up in different towns and in different social classes, but they arrived wearing practically the same clothes. They were both local government workers; both had met their husbands at a dance when they were 16 and married in their early twenties; both had fallen downstairs when they were 15 and had weak ankles as a result; both had miscarriages with their first pregnancy, then went on to have two boys followed by a girl.

Jim Lewis started to search for his twin brother when he was 39. When they met (they were both called Jim), they discovered a mind-boggling string of coincidences.

They both married women called Linda, divorced, then married women called Betty; they called their sons James Alan, owned dogs called Toy, spent their holidays in Florida and used the same short beach; both had a tree in the garden with a white bench around it, and they had each put on ten pounds at the same age and then lost them again.

Identical twins who had been brought up separately became the focus of a study by American psychologist Tim Bouchard and a British social worker, John Stroud. They found that these kinds of coincidences were the rule. *They* are surely the clearest demonstration of meaningful coincidence in all its forms. The twins' identical health patterns would be explained by the fact that they grew from one egg. But the same jobs, dates and clothes cannot be explained by inherited genetic patterns. Could there be telepathic or precognitive phenomena? Even more mysterious is the incidence of identical accidents, births and miscarriages.

Baffling the boffins

It is the world of science, not the paranormal, that offers the explanation for *this*. Experiments with sub-atomic particles called electrons have baffled scientists because the behaviour of these particles does not correspond with the prescribed laws of science. When two electrons are fired from an electron gun, they demonstrate telepathic behaviour. No matter how far they fly apart, an alteration in the direction of one causes a similar alteration in the direction of the other.

The particular experiments prove a connection between 'identical-twin electrons', so the odd coincidences that befall twins may not be a violation of the laws of common sense but the expression of some basic law of nature. *It is in this framework* of immeasurable connection between the entire human race that the conundrum of coincidence operates.

(from *She*)

Unit 5

Text organisation

3 Each of the following sentences summarises a paragraph from the passage.

a) Match each sentence to the right paragraph.
  i) There must be some significant pattern behind coincidences.
  ii) A pair of identical twins who had been brought up separately discovered that their lives were very similar.
  iii) A basic law of nature, as yet undiscovered, may explain both coincidences and the electron phenomenon.
  iv) The details of the lives of two identical twins, raised apart, were quite amazing.
  v) Two electrons fired from an electron gun behave in an identical manner, thus defying the laws of nature as they are understood at present.

b) Each of the headings in the list below describes the function of one of the paragraphs from the passage. Match each heading to one of the sentences in Exercise 3a).
  i) a logical conclusion drawn from a comparison of two different problems.
  ii) the main question raised in the article.
  iii) an example.
  iv) an example.
  v) the introduction of information from a different branch of knowledge to back the argument.

c) Discuss the following questions briefly.
  i) Do you think the paragraphs are organised in an effective way?
  ii) Could you put them in any other order?
  iii) How do you usually organise your main points and examples in a short essay?

Linking ideas

4 What do the following words in the passage refer to?

a) They (line 29)   c) It (line 53)
b) this (line 40)   d) this framework (line 53)

Dealing with difficult words

5 Look back at the passage and decide what the following words mean in their context. Use your dictionary if necessary.

a) 'mind-boggling' (line 15) means:
  i) completely crazy
  ii) surprisingly unusual
  iii) very mysterious

b) 'baffled' (line 41) means:
  i) puzzled
  ii) interested
  iii) challenged

c) 'befall' (line 51) means:
  i) fall on
  ii) surprise
  iii) happen to

d) 'conundrum' (line 55) means:
  i) a problem
  ii) a question
  iii) a solution

Put a tick against any of the words above that you think it would be a good idea to try and remember. Compare your list with a partner's.

VOCABULARY

Words which are often confused

1 Choose the most probable word in brackets to complete the following sentences, and then write a second sentence to illustrate the meaning of the word you have not used. Use your dictionary to help you clarify the meanings you are not sure of. The first one has been done for you.

a) My handbag has been (robbed/*stolen*).
   I was robbed by a man wearing a black raincoat.
b) In order to buy a new car, I had to (borrow/lend) quite a lot of money.
c) I had been working very (hard/hardly).
d) Some writers are very (sensitive/sensible) to criticism.
e) The (notorious/famous) criminal spent many years in hiding.
f) Many people volunteered to take part in the medical (experiment/experience).
g) It was impossible to avoid hitting the man who walked out from behind a (stationery/stationary) car.
h) The police have carried out an (exhausting/exhaustive) enquiry.

2 Think of some other English words that you have sometimes confused. They may be similar pairs of words, as in Exercise 1, or 'false friends' (words which look the same as words in your language but have a different meaning). Write sentences to illustrate clearly the right meanings. Make your sentences as memorable or as funny as possible.

38

Section 2

LEARNING GRAMMAR

▶ Diagnosis ◀◀◀

Past tenses

1 Work with a partner.

a) Correct the following sentences where necessary. Check your answers in the Key.
  i) We had lived in Hong Kong when I was a child.
  ii) We had never tasted crab before we went to Hong Kong.
  iii) When Noah had set sail on the ark, he had taken every kind of living creature with him.
  iv) King Solomon had never had such a difficult decision to make.
  v) By the time I got there the room was empty and everyone left.
  vi) I had left my shoes to be repaired on Monday. Are they ready yet?
  vii) When I finished my speech, I sat down.

b) With your partner, note down any rules you know about using the past perfect tense. Refer to the guidelines in the Key if you need help.

2 Complete the text below. Put the verb in the past simple or continuous or the past perfect simple or continuous. The first one has been done for you.

> We a) (wait) *had been waiting* for the train for ages when, at last, it b) *(arrive)* a whole hour late. Most of the other passengers c) *(left)* the station by the time Harry finally d) *(appear)*. He e) *(explain)* that he f) *(look)* for his suitcase, which he couldn't find anywhere. He knew he g) *(put)* it in the luggage rack when he h) *(get)* on the train and i) *(think)* it would be safe, even while he j) *(be)* in the restaurant. Now he was sure it must have been stolen while he k) *(eat)* his lunch.

▶ Development ◀◀◀

The past perfect and the simple past

The meaning of a sentence changes according to whether you use the simple past or past perfect.

I knew Sally was poor. (Sally was poor at the time of speaking)
I knew Sally had been poor. (Sally had been poor at some time in the past)

Practice

1 Answer the questions about the following pairs of sentences.

a) In which sentence did Jane not see Bill?
  i) Jane left when Bill arrived.
  ii) Jane had left when Bill arrived.
b) In which sentence is it certain that Megan is working for Margaret Jones at the time of speaking?
  i) I knew Megan worked for Margaret Jones.
  ii) I knew Megan had worked for Margaret Jones.
c) In which sentence has Kevin only been stupid on one particular occasion?
  i) Kevin realised he was careless.
  ii) Kevin realised he had been careless.

2 Look back at the sentences in Exercise 1 and add a remark to each sentence which would be appropriate in the context. The first one has been done for you.

a) i) Jane left when Bill arrived – *I think they've had a quarrel.*
   ii) Jane had left when Bill arrived – *I think she'd given up waiting for him.*

The past perfect for explanations

We sometimes use the past perfect to explain a situation. Examples:
I felt exhausted. I hadn't slept a wink the night before.
The car broke down this morning. I had completely forgotten to take it to the garage to be serviced last month.

Practice

In groups, respond to the following prompts giving as many different reasons as you can think of. The first one has been done for you.

a) There was no food in the house.
   I hadn't been shopping that week.
   We had just got back from holiday.
   The dog had eaten everything.
b) We came back home feeling exhilarated.
c) Our phone was disconnected yesterday.
d) I was so hungry!
e) I was so happy!
f) We came back home and there was water everywhere!

LANGUAGE PATTERNS

Persuade, remind, require, warn

Basic pattern

SUBJECT + VERB		NOUN	+ base form of verb with *to*
I	persuaded	her	to take me home.

Examples:
I reminded him to go to the dentist.
The school requires students to attend all classes.
The ski instructor warned us not to go too fast.

Practice

Combine what the speaker is saying using the prompts in brackets. The first one has been done for you.

a) I am surprised to see you! I thought you hated parties. (*Who/persuade/come?*)
   Who persuaded you to come?
b) Look at you! You're covered in blood! (*I/warn/not get in a fight.*)
c) I never remember appointments. (*Can/you/remind/go to the doctor's on Thursday?*)
d) In England, young men are lucky. (*The army/not require/do national service.*)
e) I never wanted an animal in the house. However, (*my children/persuade/get a dog.*)

Other patterns

These verbs can also be used with *that* clauses. However, *persuade* and *remind* always have a noun or pronoun between the verb and the *that* clause, whereas *require* does not. Study the following examples.
She persuaded ME that her idea was better.
He reminded HER that she was supposed to be at the meeting.
The regulations require that all students attend at least 80% of the courses.

Warn can also be used with either a base form or a *that* clause. However, after *warn* a noun or pronoun is optional before a *that* clause. Compare these two examples:
The police warned that a dangerous criminal was at large.
The police warned the local population that a dangerous criminal was at large.

Practice

1 Your boss has left these notes on the word processor. They are part of a letter to Despatch Services about a recent order. You, the secretary, must type them up into complete sentences. Add any other words you need. Begin like this:
We would like to remind . . .

> Remind/delivery date for our recent order/1st March. As you know, we require/suppliers/deliver promptly. If we can persuade/deliver goods early, prepared/pay cash. We/warn however/late delivery/mean/take our custom elsewhere.

2 Make a list of all the things you have to do or want to do in the next few weeks such as going to the dentist or seeing a film that has just come out. Ask different people in your class to remind you to do each of the different things you have listed. Example:
Ah, Fernando, could you remind me to call my grandmother on Saturday?

3 Game: Chinese whispers. The whole class sits in a circle or in several circles of eight to ten students. Every second student imagines that the person on their right is going on a dangerous journey. He or she whispers a warning to that person, e.g. *Be careful of the snakes* or *Do not go out by yourself at night*. The student who receives the warning transforms it into indirect speech and whispers it to the next person: e.g. *S/he warned me to be careful of the snakes.* or *S/he warned me that it was dangerous to go out by myself.*

The whispers travel round the circle in this way until they return to their sender. Is the message still the same? Compare the messages that were sent with the messages that were received.

Section 3

TALKING EFFECTIVELY

1 [🖻 5.1] Work with a partner to decide whether the underlined syllable in each of the words below is pronounced /aɪ/ as in 'five' or /ɪ/ as in 'skill'. Put them in the right column and check your answers on the tape if you are not sure.

A	B
/aɪ/	/ɪ/
five	skill

defi<u>ni</u>tion	ex<u>pli</u>cit	<u>li</u>nen
<u>mind</u>-boggling	lat<u>tice</u>	mi<u>nute</u>
coin<u>cide</u>	en<u>tire</u>	<u>ri</u>val
coin<u>ci</u>dence	exa<u>mine</u>	<u>slice</u>
deter<u>mine</u>	<u>live</u>	fi<u>nally</u>
accom<u>plice</u>	<u>wind</u>	<u>ti</u>tle

2 Which of the words can go in either column with a different meaning? Use them to complete the following sentences, and put the right symbol /aɪ/ or /ɪ/ next to them.

a) The . . . blew my hat off.
b) I have been given an old-fashioned watch that I have to . . . up every evening.
c) The laboratory was accused of doing experiments on . . . animals.
d) We . . . in London.
e) We were so far from the stage that the actors looked . . . .
f) You cook a soft-boiled egg for four . . . s.

3 Discuss the following questions with a partner.

a) Does the spelling of a word tell you to pronounce it with the /aɪ/ and /ɪ/ sound always, often, or never?
What are the guidelines that can help you? Think of other words you know with similar spellings.
b) Which of the following ideas will you find most useful for learning the sounds of new words like the ones in this activity?
  i) Keep a special page in your notebook with two columns for [aɪ] and [ɪ] sounds.
  ii) Write in the phonetic symbol every time you write a new word down in your notebook.
  iii) Write the new word down with a word that rhymes with it.
  iv) Something else . . .

LISTENING AND SPEAKING

1 [🖻 5.2] Listen to people talking about coincidences that have happened to them.

2 Have any similar incidents happened to you? Relate your coincidences in small groups.

3 Report your discussion to the class.

WRITING

Paragraphs

1 What makes a paragraph? The following passage has been written out without any paragraph breaks. Read the passage and mark in where each new paragraph should begin. Compare your marks with a partner's. Explain the reasons for your choices.

Just writing about these things makes me feel somewhat superstitious, as I believe it is possible to create reality out of thought. Edgar Allan Poe wrote a story about three shipwrecked sailors and a cabin boy adrift in a boat. After many days the sailors killed and ate the cabin boy whose name was Richard Parker. Fifty years later, the incident actually happened, just as in Poe's story - and the cabin boy was called Richard Parker. The sinking of the *Titanic* was preceded by a novel in 1898 called *The Wreck of the Titan*. The parallels with the real event were uncanny in their accuracy, right down to the fact that there were an inadequate number of lifeboats. Would the real ship's fate have been any different had its name not been so close to the fictional one? Several other authors have been shocked by the appearance of characters they have created. In a novel called *Ladies Only*, the three co-authors enjoyed the creation of a homeless old Hungarian tramp in Hyde Park. 'Give him some unpronounceable name,' one of them said. 'Nadoly ... Horvath Nadoly.' A couple of days later, a newspaper carried a report of a homeless old foreigner in Hyde Park called Horvath Nadoly. Many writers of fiction will be familiar with the sensation of characters of fiction who seem to take on a life of their own. When writing a story or a novel, a different kind of consciousness takes over and often the story 'writes itself'. It is highly possible that at this level of consciousness the mind is receptive to psychic suggestion. Welsh writer Alice Thomas Ellis was once asked in an interview if she based her characters on people she knew. She replied that she did not; they were her own creation, but she inevitably met them in real life once she put them down on paper. So how do we distinguish between precognition, clairvoyance, telepathy and coincidence? The answer seems to be that they are all part of the same higher consciousness which we all possess and that coincidence is the result of the linking of individuals at an unconscious level. In other words we cause it to happen without knowing how.

2 Putting paragraphs together coherently.

a) Write a short paragraph, in rough draft form, on one particular aspect of 'paranormal' phenomena and coincidences. For example, you could write about one of the stories you heard or told in *Listening and Speaking* on page 41 or you could give your opinion about coincidences, telepathy, etc., or write a story to do with the topic. Make sure you write a paragraph which matches the criteria you discussed in Exercise 1.

b) Join up with three other people in your class and look at what you have all written. Choose a title which covers the areas that all four of you have written about and discuss how to make your four paragraphs form a well-constructed essay. Decide what order they should go in and how they will have to be adapted, what you should add or leave out and what words and expressions you should add to make the transitions from one paragraph to the next.

c) Rewrite your paragraphs with the necessary alterations so that you produce a group essay. Read other groups' essays. How well do their paragraphs fit together?

UNIT 6

Susan's story

Section 1

SPEAKING AND READING

1 Read the passage below and discuss the questions with a partner.

a) Are Susan Hampshire's bad days different from yours?
b) What specific problem does she have?
c) Do you know people who have similar problems?
d) How do they manage their lives?

> A 'bad day' for me is a day when I have spent hours carefully embroidering 'Passionetly lovd' instead of 'passionately loved' on a corner of my husband's handkerchief. Or a day when I have taken two right turns instead of two left turns on my way to Bermans, the theatrical costumiers, and become helplessly lost in the maze beyond Camden Town, finally arriving three-quarters of an hour late. Or when I find I have agreed to do a sixteen-week instead of six-week tour, having read six for sixteen in the contract. Or when I have forgotten how to spell 'phenomenon', 'psychology', 'pharmacy', and 'disciple', and can't think of any way of looking them up in the dictionary. Or when I have made five attempts at writing a simple thank-you letter and have ended up with:
>
> Thank you it was a ~~delieghtfull deleightfull deleightful~~ — it was lovely!
>
> Love,
> S.

2 Susan Hampshire, the actress who wrote this, is dyslexic. Find out what people in your class know about dyslexia, or any other learning difficulty, by answering the following questions. Work in small groups and then report back to your class.

a) Do you know anyone who has a learning difficulty? What problems do/did they have at school?
b) What kind of treatment can be offered to people with learning difficulties?
c) Are all learning difficulties related to psychological problems? If so, what kind of problems? If not, can there be a medical explanation?
d) Do learning disabilities get better or worse as people grow older?

LISTENING

1 [6.1] Listen to the interview with Susan Hampshire and add more information to your answers in Exercise 2. Check with a partner.

2 Listen to the tape again and write *T* (*True*) or *F* (*False*) against the following statements. The information is not stated directly on the tape so you will have to infer the answers. Check your answers with a partner, giving your reasons.

a) Dyslexics have reading and writing problems.
b) There is no medical or physical cause for dyslexia.
c) Medical proof of the existence of dyslexia has always existed.
d) All dyslexics can learn to spell with a special method.
e) Education authorities have usually made provision for special help for dyslexic children.
f) Remedial help was not available for Susan Hampshire when she was a child.

43

Unit 6

TALKING EFFECTIVELY

Hesitation

1 Look at the following list of hesitation markers and other devices which give people time to formulate their ideas as they speak.

a) Listen to the interview with Susan Hampshire again and tick the two that she uses.
  i) saying 'you know' ☐
  ii) repeating one or two words several times ☐
  iii) saying 'uhm' ☐
  iv) saying 'well' ☐
  v) saying 'and so' ☐
  vi) saying 'I mean . . .' ☐
  vii) saying 'now . . .' ☐
  viii) stopping in the middle of a sentence and starting a different sentence ☐

b) Check your answers with a partner. Do speech devices like this make it easier or more difficult to understand the speaker?

2 Work in small groups. Think about your own language, and describe any similar speech techniques that are used. Practise using some of the English hesitation markers above as you talk.

SPEAKING

Susan Hampshire speaks of 'tricks' in the interview.

a) Look at the page of a play that she has annotated in order to learn it. What are some of the techniques she uses?

> ANN [*rising in sudden enlightenment*]: ⌐O-o-o-o-oh! now I understand why you warned Tavy that I am a ⌐boa constrictor.⌐ Granny told me.⌐ [*She laughs and throws her boa round his neck.*] Doesn't it feel nice and soft, Jack?
> TANNER [*in the toils*]: You scandalous woman, will you throw away even your hypocrisy?
> ANN: I am never ⌐hypocritical⌐ with you, Jack. Are you angry? [*She withdraws the boa and throws it on chair.*] ⌐Perhaps I shouldn't/have done that.

☐☐ — I underline all the words of my part
— words that are unusual and that I need to watch out for
<u>you</u> — words that I need to stress to get the sense
p.p. — softly
~ — boa constrictor
☺ — Granny
⌐ — pause
// — breaks between words to help me see them more clearly

b) Most people have some special techniques to help them learn. Think of different situations in which you have been a learner, and note down any technique(s) that helped you.

c) Work in a small group and describe your techniques to one another.

Section 2

LEARNING GRAMMAR

▶ Diagnosis ◀◀◀

Adverbs: word order

1 In the following sets of sentences the adverbs are in wrong or unusual places. With a partner, decide what the most usual place for the adverb is in each sentence. Check in the Key.

a) i) Frequently I go to the cinema. *I frequently go to the cinema.*
   ii) Jane visits often her parents.
   iii) Sharon works always on Sundays.
b) i) The postman delivers the mail at noon.
   ii) We yesterday celebrated Jacky's birthday.
   iii) The committee monthly meets to discuss general business.
c) i) The policewoman examined carefully the evidence.
   ii) Elegantly Rosie walked through the room.
   iii) Badly Joe failed his exam.
d) i) Nearly we missed the bus.
   ii) They had an accident almost.
   iii) She smiled hardly the whole evening.
e) i) Southwards we drove yesterday.
   ii) After the party we home went.
   iii) There I have never been.

2 Work with a partner.

a) Match each of the sets in Exercise 1 to the type of adverb in the box below.

> manner (adverbs which answer the question 'how?')
> frequency (adverbs which answer the question 'how often?')
> degree (adverbs which answer the question 'how much?/to what extent?')
> place (adverbs which answer the question 'where?')
> time (adverbs which answer the question 'when?')

Example: *set a) = frequency adverbs*

b) Decide whether the most usual place for each adverb is mid-position or end-position. Use the guidelines in the Key. Example:
   a) Frequency adverbs usually go in mid-position.

3 Look at the sentences below.

a) With your partner find the three incorrect sentences. Check your answers in the Key.
   i) Yesterday the weather was lovely.
   ii) Late the plane was.
   iii) Once I was top of the class.
   iv) Always I make the same mistake.
   v) Sometimes we get really bored.
   vi) Fortunately the burglar didn't find my jewellery.
   vii) Frankly, that's very kind of you but I've already eaten.
   viii) Suddenly the dog leapt up and bit me.
   ix) Badly Ben plays the piano.

b) Cross out the incorrect information in the following sentences. Compare your answers with your partner's and check in the Key.
   i) The place of an adverb always/sometimes depends on fixed rules.
   ii) The place of an adverb always/sometimes depends on the emphasis the speaker wants to give.
   iii) Some/all adverbs of time can go in initial position.
   iv) Adverbs of manner often/rarely go in initial position.
   v) Adverbs expressing attitude, comment or viewpoint can always/sometimes go in initial position.

4 Put the adverbs in brackets in an appropriate place in the sentences below. There may be more than one solution. The first one has been done for you. Check your answers in the Key.

a) Bob was driving when the accident happened. (*carelessly*)
   Bob was driving carelessly when the accident happened.
b) I may have been a little harsh with my children. (*sometimes*)
c) Karen walked into the room. (*backwards*)
d) I know the area. (*well*)
e) I don't know. (*honestly*)
f) She hurt her arm. (*badly*)
g) Although I have broken a leg three times, I like skiing. (*still*)
h) You have designed this interior. (*well*)
i) I knew Kate. (*hardly*)

Development

Adverbs and adverbials in initial position: special cases

You can use some adverbs and adverbial expressions in initial position for stylistic effect. When you do this you must pay special attention to the word order and invert the subject and the verb. Study the most common usages below.

Negative and near-negative adverbials in formal speaking (for example speeches) and writing

a) The adverbials in the box below can be used at the beginning of a sentence for special emphasis.

> *Never, only, seldom, rarely, little*, expressions with NO and NOT such as *under no circumstances, not until*, etc.

b) Note the inversion of the subject and verb in the examples:

NEGATIVE ADVERB	AUXILIARY VERB (*be, do, have, can, must*, etc.)	SUBJECT	+ the rest of the sentence
Only then	did	I	realise my luck.
Rarely	has	she	been to a meeting.

Adverbs of place used for dramatic or colloquial* effect

a) Adverbs such as *here, there, up, down, back, off,* etc. can be used in initial position for emphasis and effect.
b) Note the inversion of subject and object in the examples:

ADVERB +	VERB +	SUBJECT
There	's	Granny!
Down	came	the rain.
Up	jumped	Jimmy!

Adverbials of place used for formal, literary, descriptive effect

a) With verbs of movement (*come, go, rise, fall*, etc.) or with verbs of position (*lie, live, sit, stand*, etc.), adverbial expressions of place can come in initial position to create a special effect.
b) Note the inversion of subject and object in the examples:

ADVERBIAL EXPRESSION +	VERB +	SUBJECT
Out of the jungle	came	a strange-looking man.
Into the distance	sailed	the solitary vessel.

Practice

Rewrite the sentences below beginning with the words or expressions that are underlined. Before you begin, decide with a partner whether or not you will need to change the word order of the rest of the sentence for any of the reasons described above. You may need to make other minor changes or add a word and there may be more than one way of changing the sentences. The first one has been done for you.

a) I have <u>never in my life</u> seen such disgraceful behaviour.
   Never in my life have I seen such disgraceful behaviour.
b) A bedraggled figure struggled <u>out of the swirling water</u>.
c) You have been to Venice already, <u>perhaps</u>.
d) She didn't say <u>a single word all evening</u>.
e) Billy leapt <u>up</u> and gave her mother a kiss.
f) She wouldn't like the play, <u>anyway</u>.
g) Virginia Woolf is <u>undoubtedly</u> one of the most famous British novelists.
h) The actress had <u>seldom</u> met with such enthusiasm.
i) I did not realise what was going on <u>until the noise stopped</u>.
j) The little dog ran <u>onto the beach</u>.

Adjectives: word order

1 Different types of adjectives are listed in column A. Work with a partner to match them with an example in column B.

A	B
1 origin	a) round
2 adjectival past participle	b) young
3 material	c) superb
4 size	d) fragrant
5 colour	e) Australian
6 quality (subjective judgement)	f) painted
7 shape	g) stainless steel
8 purpose or use	h) small
9 age	i) summer
10 taste, smell, etc.	j) pink

2 Study the order of the adjectives in the examples below.

i) An interesting small green insect.
ii) A pretty new blue woollen scarf.
iii) An excellent mature Scottish whisky.
iv) A Persian silk carpet.
v) A large smelly half-eaten lump of cheese.
vi) A beautiful fragrant red rose.
vii) A fragrant beautiful red rose.
viii) An exciting new Ford model.
ix) Small round black beads.
x) An attractive old mahogany dining-room table.
xi) A big old house.

In the box below, write the different kinds of adjectives in the order which appears to be most common. Write in some examples next to each type. Some examples have been done for you. Check your answers with a partner.

Quality	interesting	. . . .
. . . .	. . . .	. . . .
Age	. . . .	. . . .
. . . .	round	. . . .
Taste/smell	. . . .	. . . .
. . . .	. . . .	. . . .
. . . .	Persian	. . . .
Past participle	. . . .	. . . .
. . . .	woollen	. . . .
Purpose/use	. . . .	. . . .

3 Write *T* (*True*) or *F* (*False*) against the statements below. Check your answers with a partner.

a) Particular qualities go before general qualities.
b) Adjectives defining quality do not usually go in initial position.
c) Colour adjectives usually come before size, shape or age adjectives.
d) Nouns used adjectivally to describe material, purpose or function are not separated from the main noun by other adjectives.
e) The order of adjectives always depends on fixed rules.
f) The place of the adjective depends to some extent on the emphasis the speaker wishes to give.

Practice

1 Put the adjectives in the following examples in a more usual order. Check your answers with a partner. The first one has been done for you.

a) A cloudless blue vast sky.
   A vast cloudless blue sky.
b) An expensive return second-class ticket.
c) A white bright light.
d) A dark long frightening tunnel.
e) A metal bent spoon.

2 Put the following adjectives into an appropriate order. The first one has been done for you.

a) An green/short/attractive/skirt
   An attractive short green skirt.
b) A kitchen/large/useful/cupboard
c) A well-fed/lively/adorable/young/cat
d) A silk/handwoven/magnificent/carpet
e) A Japanese/electronic/new/interesting/invention

3 With a partner, take it in turns to describe objects in the room without naming them. Guess what your partner is talking about. Make sure you use adjectives in the right order. Study the example below before you begin. Example:
A: *It's a useful flat-topped wooden object.*
B: *It is a table?*

Unit 6

Adjective order: special cases

Some adjectives can change the meaning of a sentence if they come before or after a noun. Note that when these adjectives follow the noun, a relative clause is usually implied and has been elided. Examples:

The concerned (=worried) parents took their child to the doctor.

The parents concerned (=who are concerned, i.e. to whom this statement applies) should make an appointment to see the headmistress.

Practice

Work with a partner, using a dictionary, to find out the different meanings of the words in italics.

a) i) I was given a very long and *involved* explanation.
   ii) None of the people *involved* in the accident was hurt.
b) i) *Present* numbers are high, and an increase is expected.
   ii) The people *present* at the party noticed nothing strange.
c) i) You can trust Jimmy. He's a very *responsible* person.
   ii) The person *responsible* for the accident was sent to prison.
d) i) Not everybody approved of the solution *adopted*.
   ii) An *adopted* child can be just as happy as any other child.

Section 3

VOCABULARY

Compound nouns derived from multi-part verbs

Compound nouns are often derived from multi-part verbs. They are formed either:
– by reversing the order of the verb and the adverbial particle
Examples:
break out – outbreak, take in – intake.
or
– simply using the two words together in one of the following ways:
– two words run together: *to put out/an output*
– two words hyphenated: *to send off/a send-off*

There are no rules for the formation of these words and you must check their meaning and their form in the dictionary. Native speakers often create new compounds spontaneously but for the moment you should be cautious about inventing compound words yourself, as they may not always sound quite English.

Practice

1 Sometimes the noun has the same meaning as the verb from which it is derived. Examples:
He was born just when war broke out.
He was born at the outbreak of war.

The school took in two hundred new pupils last year.
There was an intake of two hundred new pupils last year.

Other examples:

VERB	NOUN
break through	breakthrough
slip up	slip-up
tip off	tip-off
back up	back-up

Use a dictionary to help you find a compound noun similar in meaning to the multi-part verb in each of the sentences below. You will have to look up the verb itself or the particle. Rewrite the sentences with the noun instead of the verb, but without changing the meaning. Make any grammatical changes that are necessary. The first one has been done for you.

a) The car was so badly damaged in the accident that we had to write it off.
   The car was so badly damaged in the accident that it was a write-off.
b) Costs have been cut back considerably this year.
c) The factory puts out 5 million bottles of beer a month.
d) The factory men walked out after the tea-break.
e) We can't afford to keep up the castle in its present state.

2 Use your dictionary to help you find compound nouns which are related in a limited way to the verbs in the box and which match the definitions below. The first one has been done for you.

| fall down | come out | come back |
| come in | look out | turn over |

a) A sudden loss of a high position. *downfall*
b) Money received regularly from one's employer or one's investments.
c) A prediction.
d) An effect, a result.
e) An amount of business done in a given period measured in money.
f) A return to a former position of strength after an absence.

Use the nouns in sentences of your own.

Scale and limit words

Scale words describe a degree of quality which can be put on a scale of temperature, size, distance, intensity, etc. For example, heat can be measured on a scale of degrees centigrade.

Limit words describe the absolute quality at the end of a scale. For example, 'boiling' is normally the hottest point on a scale of heat.

Study the scale below, which contains hot and non-hot words.

Limit words   BOILING, SCALDING +++
              hot ++
              warm +
Scale words   tepid -
              cool --
              cold ---
Limit words   FREEZING, GLACIAL ----

Practice

1 With a partner, decide which are the scale words and which are the limit words in the following list of words relating to size. Build a scale with the words similar to the one above.

large   minute   gigantic   small   average
tiny   enormous

2 Look at the words in the box below.

a) Which of the words are scale words and which are limit words?

stationary	fast	slow	light	short
full-length	interminable	impossible
new-born	young	ordinary	perfect
rare	unique	good	intelligent	dark
old	tired	exhausted

b) In small groups, choose at least one word from the box and use your dictionary to help you build a scale similar to the one in Exercise 1. Look at the scales that other groups have built.

Modifying adverbs with scale and limit words

Modifiers are adverbs which change the meaning of other words. For example: *very, rather, completely*. The modifiers we use with scale words are different to the modifiers we use with limit words.

Modifying adverbs with scale words

These can modify meaning in one of the following ways:

a) a high degree of quality. Examples:
very poor, extremely long, considerably wealthy
b) a moderate or small degree of quality. Examples:
rather hot, fairly rich, slightly dazed, a little strange, somewhat puzzled, pretty mad (informal)

Modifying adverbs with limit words

These can modify meaning in one of the following ways:

a) the highest or lowest degree of quality. Examples:
absolutely boiling, altogether unique, completely exhausted, entirely true, totally deaf, utterly marvellous
b) a point which is close to the highest or lowest degree of quality. Examples:
almost boiling, nearly deaf, practically empty

Unit 6

Notes

1 With some words you can use either scale or limit modifiers.

a) Words expressing strong emotional intensity like *amazing, wonderful, marvellous, terrified* and *disgusted* are mostly used as limit words, although there are obviously different degrees of *wonderful* or *terrified* so they are sometimes used with scale words as well. Examples:
utterly amazing, completely disgusted, pretty marvellous (informal), *fairly terrified*
However, these words cannot usually be used like other limit words with modifiers indicating a point near the end of the scale. For example, you cannot say:
~~The party was almost marvellous. I was nearly amazed.~~

b) Some words have both scale meanings and limit meanings. Examples:
full (completely full or relatively full), *empty* (completely empty or relatively empty), *new* (brand new or just recent), *black* (relatively black or pitch-black). Whether you use scale modifiers or limit modifiers will depend on the meaning of the sentence. For example, you can say:
The boot is absolutely full. We can't put another thing in.
The boot is very full. We can't get much more in.

2 Not all modifiers go with all scale and limit words. For example, we usually say *you are absolutely right* and not *you are utterly right*. We usually say *the bottle is completely empty* rather than *the bottle is altogether empty*. As you listen to and read English, you can pay special attention to the collocations that occur.

A special case: *quite*

a) *Quite* has two uses. When used with scale words it usually means *fairly*. When used with limit words it means *absolutely*.
Examples:
The weather was quite wonderful. (absolutely)
The weather was quite sunny. (fairly)

b) With some words, it is difficult to tell whether *quite* means fairly or absolutely and you can only tell from the context or the intonation. Examples:
I feel quite healthy. I don't need to take extra vitamins. (absolutely)
I feel quite healthy. But I think I need more exercise. (fairly)

Practice

1 Complete the sentences below with the more appropriate of the remarks that follow. The first one has been done for you. Check your answers with a partner.

a) You are quite right
 i) –I couldn't agree with you more.
 ii) . . . though not completely.
I couldn't agree with you more.
b) I'm quite warm,
 i) . . . it's stifling in here.
 ii) but I could do with another pullover.
c) The statue was quite perfect,
 i) I'd never seen anything like it before.
 ii) and the clever lighting hid the few flaws.
d) The task is quite impossible
 i) . . . I wouldn't consider it.
 ii) . . . it would be difficult.

2 Correct the following sentences where necessary. The first one has been done for you. Check your answers with a partner.

a) John is an absolutely clever pupil.
John is a very clever pupil.
b) You should wash pure wool in altogether tepid water.
c) Although this exercise seems very impossible, I'm sure it is utterly useful.
d) That's a totally young baby, isn't it?
e) Grandma was utterly delighted with her present.
f) The piece of furniture was handcrafted and a little unique.
g) I was absolutely pleased with the result.
h) Jenny was entirely satisfied with her progress.
i) Bill was nearly amazed at his daughter's progress.

3 With a partner, write three short dialogues. Each dialogue should contain at least one expression with one modifier and one scale or limit word from the boxes on page 51. Check your sentences with your teacher. Read out your dialogues to another pair in your class. For example:

A: *Did you have a good holiday?*
B: *Yes, not bad. But the house we rented wasn't very modern and the beds were rather uncomfortable.*
A: *What about the area? Was that nice?*
B: *The countryside was absolutely wonderful, and we had some quite amazing walks.*

Unit 6

Box 1 Modifying adverbs

| absolutely | quite | entirely | extremely |
| fairly | rather | very | slightly |

Box 2

poor	wonderful	amazing	true
impossible	useful	empty	pleasant
uncomfortable	outstanding	modern
enjoyable	full	new

4 Work with a partner. Student A thinks of an object which is known to both of you. Do not say the name of the object. Student B tries to guess what the object is by asking twenty questions. Example:
B: *Is it unique?*
A: *I wouldn't say it's unique, but it's quite rare.*

TALKING EFFECTIVELY

1 Modifiers with scale words are usually unstressed and said with low pitch. Practise saying the following example:
The film was quite good.

2 Modifiers with limit words are stressed and are usually said with higher pitch. Practise saying the following example:
The film was quite marvellous.

3 [📼 6.2] Underline the modifiers in the following passage. Listen to the tape and write *S* (*Stressed*) or *U* (*Unstressed*) for each one. An example has been done for you.

We were visiting a museum in Athens, and it was you know, well, rather[U] interesting but nothing special, and we had this utterly boring guide when all of a sudden I saw this absolutely marvellous statue. It was quite perfect. The friend I was with was pretty surprised to see me so altogether overwhelmed as I'm not usually like that, but I stood rooted to the spot for five minutes at least. When I got back home, I told a friend who's a specialist in Greek antiquity all about it, and he said yes, he thought it was rather nice but it was a fairly common sort of statue. I was somewhat put out, and my wonderful experience was quite spoiled by his comments.

WRITING

Writing a personal letter

1 The tone of the letter below, written by a young person to an older aunt who is in hospital, is very flat. Make it more lively by:

a) adding one of the modifiers from the box in the gaps provided. You can use each modifier more than once, although you should aim to use as many different ones as possible for the sake of variety.
b) giving more emphasis by making any possible inversions of word order.

utterly	rather	absolutely	quite
completely	almost	entirely	fairly
altogether	really

4 Brent Drive
Colchester
Essex
6th June

Dear Aunt Lily,
I was ___(a)___ delighted to receive your letter and hear that you are ___(b)___ better after your operation. I gather that it was ___(c)___ successful, although the hospital food was ___(d)___ disgusting!
Life for us has been ___(e)___ hectic. I have been ___(f)___ busy and Richard has been away. Last weekend we were both ___(g)___ exhausted. In fact we, the ___(h)___ perfect love birds, almost had a row! There was a flower show in Cambridge and I wanted to see it but Richard said he wanted to watch the golf on TV. He sulked all evening, but I got my own way and he had to admit afterwards that we had an ___(i)___ marvellous time.
Something ___(j)___ dreadful happened on the way home. We were driving along when suddenly a maniac driver came out from a side road. He drove straight into us. Fortunately, nobody was hurt but the car is a write-off.
I hope you'll be able to visit us very soon.
Love,
Sarah

Compare your version with other people's in your class and with the one in the Key.

2 Write a similar letter giving your real or imaginary news to a person in your class, relative or a friend. Use modifiers to make it more vivid and interesting. In small groups, read out your letters.

51

UNIT 7

Believe it or not . . .

Section 1

READING AND SPEAKING

1 Work with a partner and discuss the questions below.

a) What do the pictures show?
b) What might they have in common?
c) Do you know any stories of famous fakes?
d) List the professions in which people sometimes produce fakes. What are the reasons they do this?
e) In what professions do people practise other kinds of deception? What do they do? Why do they do it?
f) Is deception always punished? Can it and should it be punished?

2 Read the passage below quickly. With a partner, decide which of the following headings best sums up the author's general idea in the passage.

a) Fakes are immoral.
b) There is a strong link between fakes and fashions in art.
c) Aesthetic judgement is subjective and unreliable.
d) Fakes are often as good as the original.

Will the Real Vermeer Please Stand Up?

Van Meegeren was a Dutch art dealer and a minor artist, who remained in the Netherlands throughout the Second World War and German Occupation, following his trade
5 as best he could. After the war, he was prosecuted as a collaborator, the evidence being that he had sold to Goering a masterpiece by Vermeer, a huge 'Christ at Emmaus'. The picture was undoubtedly among Goering's loot and it had certainly been
10 sold to him or his agents by van Meegeren, so the case looked black. The dealer, however, pleaded not guilty, and his defence caused a considerable sensation. He claimed that instead of being condemned for collaboration with the enemy he
15 should be commended for making fools of them, for, so far from the picture being painted by Vermeer, he had painted it himself.

His claim was greeted with considerable scepticism; the picture had been vouched for by leading
20 art experts. Whereupon, van Meegeren caused an even greater sensation; he announced that if the court would order him to be provided in his prison with canvas, brushes, paint and a sufficiency of north light, he would be pleased to
25 match the customer's sample by turning out another Vermeer on the same scale and with the same apparent authenticity. And this is precisely what he did.

This brings me to van Meegeren's question which
30 has haunted me for decades. As it happens, he did not ask the question himself, though it enshrined what was obviously his view; it occurred in a play about the case, at one point at which van Meegeren is reflecting on the fact that his 'Christ
35 at Emmaus' was universally accepted as genuine until he himself proved that it was a fake. I quote van Meegeren's question from memory, but it went something like this:

'Yesterday this picture was worth millions of
40 guilders, and experts and art lovers would come from all over the world and pay money to see it. Today it is worth nothing, and nobody would

52

3 Read the passage again. Each sentence below summarises one of the paragraphs. Match the sentences to the paragraphs. Check your answers with a partner.

a) The author tries to analyse why our judgement of a painting varies according to who we think painted it.
b) The story of a forger who confessed his crime to save himself in the face of accusations of a greater crime.
c) The author expresses scepticism about the difference in artistic value that people think exists between good fakes and their originals.
d) The story of how a forger demonstrated that the experts can be wrong.

(from *The Times*)

cross the street to see it free. But the picture has not changed. What has?'
45 The price of a picture is determined by supply and demand, so there is no clue there; certainly people will go and see a picture that has been sold for a record sum just because of the money it fetched, but they would go and see, for the same
50 reason, a giant uncut diamond or for that matter a very large pile of bank notes. The beauty of a picture ought not to be in the eye of the beholder but that 'ought' is a fat lot of use in the face of van Meegeren's success. If we stood in front of his
55 Vermeer and felt profoundly affected by the majesty and power of the scene, just why would we stop feeling such things if a newsboy rushed into the gallery shouting that it had just been proved a fake?
60 It is no use saying that there is a vast gulf between any masterpiece and any imitation of it, however meticulous. I have no doubt there is, but if we cannot see the difference - and successful art forgery would not exist if we could - what exactly
65 does the difference consist of, apart from the fact that there must be one? Suppose the four-million-dollar Manet sold at Christie's last week turned out to be a fake: the buyer could get his money back from Christie's, of course, but questions of
70 legal liability plainly have nothing to do with artistic validity, so what then would be the standing of the oohs and ahs - quite genuine ones, I am sure - heard in the saleroom when it was held up before the bidding started?

loot: goods which are stolen or obtained illegally
vouched for: declared authentic
enshrined: contained
Christie's: a well-known London firm of art dealers
bidding: offering a price

4 Look at the context of these sentences in the passage. Study the alternatives. In pairs, decide which could replace the original sentence. The meaning does not have to be exactly the same, but the alternative must make sense in the passage *and* match its style.

a) The picture was undoubtedly among Goering's loot and it had certainly been sold to him or his agents by van Meegeren, so the case looked black. (lines 8–11)
   i) Goering was guilty of being in possession of the painting and there was definitely a case against him. (*Does not make sense in this context.*)
   ii) The fact that it was proven that the painting was in Goering's possession provided a strong case against van Meegeren. (*Similar meaning but not the same style.*)
   iii) The painting was, for sure, part of Goering's swag, a fact which made van Meegeren look pretty guilty. (*Similar meaning, same style.*)

b) His claim was greeted with considerable scepticism; the picture had been vouched for by leading art experts. (lines 18–20)
   i) As respected members of the art world had been taken in by his fake, most people thought van Meegeren was lying.
   ii) His claim to have taken in the enemy and respected members of the art world was considered exaggerated.
   iii) The substance of his utterances was received with a high degree of doubt: eminent art professionals had declared their firm belief in its authenticity.

c) And this is precisely what he did. (lines 27–28)
   i) He pursued his goal to its successful completion.
   ii) And just such a painting was what he produced.
   iii) And he painted another copy precisely.

d) It is no use saying that there is a vast gulf between any masterpiece and any imitation of it. (lines 60–61)
   i) To say that there is no difference between any masterpiece and the very best copy is beside the point.
   ii) To say that a copy can never be more than a pale imitation of a masterpiece is beside the point.
   iii) It's daft to say that there is a whole load of difference between a masterpiece and a copy, even when the copy is pretty good.

Unit 7

Section 2

LEARNING GRAMMAR

▶ Diagnosis ◀◀◀

Participles: adjectives/adjectival clauses

1 With a partner, decide which sentence in each of the following pairs is correct and which is incorrect or very strange. Use the guidelines in the Key to help you if you are not sure.

a) i) No one talked to me at the party so I was very boring.
   ii) The party was very boring as no one talked to me.
b) i) I am very interested in this subject.
   ii) I am very interesting in this subject.
c) i) I was exhausting so I went to bed early.
   ii) It was an exhausting journey, so I went to bed early.
d) i) Look! There's a man climbing that cliff.
   ii) Look! There's a climbing man on that cliff.
e) i) Those are very pretty climbing plants on the wall.
   ii) Those are very pretty plants climbing the wall.
f) i) Anyone holding a winning ticket should come to the office now.
   ii) Anyone having bought a faulty machine will be refunded immediately.
g) i) The person teaching our class is sick today.
   ii) The person teaching in room 3 is new today.

2 Some of the participles in the following passage are in the wrong form. A present participle may appear instead of a past participle and vice versa. Work with a partner to correct them.

> I was very exciting at the prospect of going on holiday to China. I packed a very small bag with only a very few toiletries and a spare set of clothes. At first, the flight seemed very long and I was very boring. I couldn't sleep, for the man sat next to me snored all night and the book I bought at the airport turned out to be one I had already read. Suddenly, the slept passengers were woken up by the captain's voice. Two hi-jackers worn balaclavas and carried guns were in the cockpit threatened him. He explained the situation and told us to keep calm. Everyone was very frightening, but the flight personnel were very good and calmed most of the passengers down. However, one person spent the rest of the flight screaming. We landed somewhere in Malaysia. Most of us were allowed off the plane almost immediately and I was very relieving. The army soon arrived and encircled the plane. The hi-jackers seemed discouraged and soon gave up their fight. Police took the capturing hi-jackers off the plane. That was the last I heard of them. I never found out what happened afterwards.

▶ Development ◀◀◀

Adverbial participle clauses and adverbial clauses

1 Adverbial participle clauses are used to give more information about the action of a verb or the idea expressed in a whole sentence. They are like adverbial clauses without the linking word, the subject and the main verb form. They are used mostly in written English. Study the following examples.

Being out of work at the moment, I need to find cheaper accommodation.
As I am out of work at the moment, I need to find cheaper accommodation.

Having understood your point of view, I am willing to compromise.
Now that I have understood your point of view, I am willing to compromise.

Warned of bad weather, the mountaineers decided to rest for the day.
The mountaineers had been warned of bad weather, so they decided to rest for the day.

2 The different meaning relationships of a participle clause with the main part of the sentences are:

a) time (*at the same time as, after, now that, once, as, while*)
b) reason (*because, as, since, seeing that*)
c) result or consequence (*so that, with the result that, so*)
d) condition (*if*)

Practice

1 Match one of the meanings on page 54 to the following participle clauses. The first one has been done for you.

i) Living in a small village, we don't see a lot of people. (*Reason*)
ii) Kept in a cool dark place, the product will conserve its full strength for many months.
iii) She entered the room, greeting everyone warmly.
iv) Having finished our meal, we asked for the bill.
v) She fell down the stairs, breaking her ankle.
vi) Having phoned for a taxi, we went downstairs to wait.
vii) Having gone to bed early, I was not pleased when the phone rang at midnight.
viii) Placed in a warm light room, this plant needs very little care.
ix) Having attempted every possible solution, I simply gave up.
x) She knocked over the bottle of milk, spilling it all over the carpet.

2 Look at the sentences below.

a) Put the most appropriate word from the box into each gap. Use each word only once. There may be more than one answer.

| now that   seeing that   so   once |
| since   as |

i) We had better not make a hasty decision, *since* the committee is not sure of the outcome.
ii) Bill was able to do the exercise easily . . . he had understood the problem.
iii) . . . the board has reached a decision, we must act swiftly.
iv) . . . escape was impossible, we settled down to wait to be rescued.
v) I was an only child, . . . I had nobody to turn to when my parents died.
vi) . . . Jane has finished her exams, she intends to have a complete rest.

b) Rewrite the sentences in **a)** with participle clauses. Make any other changes that are necessary. For example, you may need to change the order of the clauses or the position of the subject word.
i) *Not being sure of the outcome, the committee had better not make a hasty decision.*

Participles after linking words

Participle clauses can be used after linking words such as: *while, when, after, before, since, once, as, although, if.* These clauses are like adverbial clauses in which the subject and main verb form have been omitted. Compare the following examples.

a) i) *While travelling through Italy, we visited many beautiful churches.*
   ii) *While we were travelling through Italy, we visited many beautiful churches.*
b) i) *I have enjoyed every moment of my life since leaving school.*
   ii) *I have enjoyed every moment of my life since I left school.*
c) i) *If given a chance, she would do the job very well.*
   ii) *If she was given a chance, she would do the job very well.*

Note

In most cases, the participle construction must be related to the subject of the main clause. If not, the sentence will not make sense. Example:
Coming from Brazil, Mrs Smith, the landlady, thought Maria could probably dance the lambada.

a) Is it the landlady or Maria who is from Brazil? The sentence would make more sense if it was written:
   Mrs Smith, the landlady, thought that Maria, who came/coming from Brazil, could probably dance the lambada.
b) Note that certain verbs do not follow this rule when the subject of the participle is felt to be an indefinite pronoun, such as 'one'.
   Examples:
   Judging from results, it looks as if government policy has been successful. (= *If one judges from results, . . .*)
   All things taken into consideration, she did quite well in her exams. (*If one takes all things into consideration, . . .*)

Unit 7

Practice

1 Link the following sentences with a participle construction and the word in brackets. Make any changes that are necessary. One example has been done for you.

a) Claire crossed the Atlantic single-handed. She never slept more than four hours at a time. (while)
While crossing the Atlantic single-handed, Claire never slept more than four hours at a time.
b) They found the remains of a Roman villa. They were laying the foundations of the new building. (while)
c) I'll not be working for the firm any more. I shall continue to take an interest in it. (although)
d) He should be able to do the job. That is, provided that he is properly trained. (if)
e) The opera was performed. It took on a new meaning. (once)
f) The judge delivered the sentence. He stood up and left the courtroom. (after)

2 Write *S* (*Strange*) against the sentences in which the meaning is not clear.
Rewrite the strange sentences so that they make more sense. Make any changes that are necessary. The first one has been done for you.

a) While riding across the Nevada desert, the scenery looked magnificent in the setting sun. *S*
While riding across the Nevada desert, we thought the scenery looked magnificent in the setting sun.
b) Seen from a different angle, the problem does not seem so difficult to solve.
c) Stretching as far as the eye could see, I contemplated with dismay the urban landscape.
d) Judging from the market research, the company is bound to make enormous profits from its new line of products.
e) Considered to be an extremely dangerous kind of snake, I ran in the opposite direction.
f) Considering recent events, several undesirable pupils are likely to be expelled.
g) Since coming back from America, the job has been more interesting.

LANGUAGE PATTERNS

Some verbs can be followed by the base form or an *-ing* form. With verbs such as *love*, *hate* and *prefer*, there is very little difference in meaning.

Some verbs, however, have different meanings in each case. Example:
I tried to send her some flowers (but the shop was closed).
I tried sending her some flowers (but she refused to accept them).

1 In your dictionary, check how the meaning of each verb below changes according to whether it is followed by a base form or an *-ing* form.

| try | remember | forget | regret | stop |

Complete the sentences below with the right form of the verb.

a) Of course I remembered (post) the letter – I know it was important.
b) I tried (sail) but I didn't like it.
c) I stopped (smoke) last year and I haven't touched a cigarette since.
d) I regret (inform) you that your membership has expired.
e) I regret (say) that – can you ever forgive me?
f) I'll never forget (meet) such a kind person!

2 Write a list of the things that you sometimes forget to do, e.g. turn off the gas when you leave home, keep an eye on the milk when it's being heated, etc. Discuss your lists in small groups.

3 Complete the following list with any information about yourself that you like.

I remember travelling . . .   I remember disliking . . .
I remember going . . .   I remember enjoying . . .
I remember seeing . . .   I remember hating . . .
I remember liking . . .

Work in small groups. Tell your group about the things you remember.

Section 3

LISTENING AND SPEAKING

1 [📻 7.1] Adults sometimes tell children things that are just not true. For example:
If you make a face and the wind changes you will be stuck like that.
If you swallow a cherry stone, a cherry tree will grow out of your mouth.

Listen to the tape and note down some of the things that the speakers were told as children.

2 Discuss the following questions in small groups.

a) Do you think any of the statements are true?
b) Why do adults tell children such things?
c) Do adults tell children similar things in your country?
d) What untrue things were you told as a child? Make a class collection of such sayings.

TALKING EFFECTIVELY

Sounds and spelling

1 Sounds are not always reflected in English spelling in a systematic way. One of the chief difficulties is the fact that many letters used in spelling are not pronounced. This may make it difficult for you to look up words that you only hear and do not see in a dictionary.

Compare the words and expressions below with their phonetic transcriptions. Underline the letters which are not pronounced.

raw carrots   the wind blows
rɔː kærəts   ðə wɪnd bləʊs

2 [📻 7.2] Listen to the tape and fill in the gaps in the sentences below with the missing words. Spell them as best you can for the moment. The first one has been done for you.

a) I saw a *ghastly* accident on the way home, and there were all these people standing around taking a *ghoulish* delight in the scene.
b) I sat reading a book under the . . . old oak tree in the garden, with the dog at my feet, . . . his bone as usual. The sun went down and the . . . came out and started biting, so I went back into the house.
c) The beads of dew were . . . in the sunshine.
d) I knocked on the door sharply with my . . . . The door opened and I caught sight of the baker's wife . . . tomorrow's bread.
e) I was . . . when she said that there was only a very . . . difference between an argument and a difference of opinion.

3 Compare your spelling with a partner. Each of the words should have one of the following silent letters in it somewhere: b, k, g, t, h. Check the words you are not sure about in your dictionary.

4 What other words do you know which have a silent b, k, g, t or h?

VOCABULARY

Multi-part verbs

1 Work with a partner. Underline the expressions in the following passage which do not seem to be in the same style as the rest of the passage. The first one has been done for you.

> Jimmy was a nice lad but he often <u>became acquainted</u> with a rough lot who used to spend their Saturday evenings doing I don't know what. They even did some forged bank notes once but they were so bad they wouldn't have been a source of deception to anyone. Anyway, one Saturday, he became involved in something pretty awful, even worse than usual. He and his pals removed by illegal means a large sum of money from a bank. They made their escape in a waiting car, but somehow the police learned something about who was involved and came along to see me, Jimmy's Mum, thinking I would reveal their whereabouts. The fuzz were sure he was concealing himself somewhere in the neighbourhood, but I wasn't going to inform against him, was I? I just told them to depart.

fuzz: slang for police

2 Look at the verbs in the box below.

a) Use your dictionary to find out which of the verbs corresponds to each of the expressions you have underlined in the passage.

make off with something   get away
get mixed up in something   lie up
get onto someone   tell on someone
fall in with someone   clear off
take someone in   give someone away

b) Which of the above verbs:
   i) take a direct object? Example: *fall in with someone*
   ii) are intransitive and take no object? Example: *get away*
   iii) have particles which can be separated from the verb? Example: *line it up*

c) Write out the passage replacing the underlined expressions with a multi-part verb, making any other changes that are necessary.

WRITING

Sequences of sentences

1 The second sentence in the following sequence of three is missing. Write in the one from the box below which makes the smoothest transition of thought. Pay attention to coherence of meaning and discourse. Check your answer with a partner.

a) Another deceptive practice is the art of the inflated recommendation.
b) . . . . .
c) Yet it obviously injures those who do not benefit from this kind of assistance for they are at an unfair advantage when looking for jobs.

i) It seems morally wrong.
ii) Inflated recommendations are not dishonest.
iii) It seems a harmless enough practice.

2 With a partner, use the same sentence b) and write another sequence of three sentences on a different aspect of dishonesty. Look at the examples before you begin.

A
a) *Many excellent painters copy the works of old masters.*
b) *It seems a harmless enough practice.*
c) *The only problem occurs when they try to pass off their works as the real thing.*

B
a) *Parents often tell children popular sayings which aren't true.*
b) *It seems a harmless enough practice.*
c) *However, when children later find out the truth, they may never believe their parents again.*

Read out your sequence to other groups.

3 Work with a partner.

a) Your teacher will give you other short passages containing three sentences which make up a similar thought unit. Do not show your three sentences to other students. Keeping the original sentence b), write a sentence a) and sentence c) of your own so that they make up a well-connected sequence of ideas like the original passage. Copy out your sequence and the original sequence.

b) Join up with another pair. Read out the original version and your own version in whichever order you like. Can the others guess which version was the original passage? Do the same with other pairs.

4 Write a paragraph of your own giving your view on a particular aspect of dishonesty. You may choose some of the ideas covered in this unit or write about a completely different kind of dishonesty. Pay particular attention to the smooth sequencing of your ideas. Read out your paragraph to other people in your class.

5 Write an essay on one of the following topics:

a) 'Honesty is the best policy.' (Sixteenth century proverb) Discuss.
b) Describe the most honest/dishonest person you have ever met.
c) Describe an occasion on which you told a white lie in order not to offend someone.

UNIT 8

Fame and fortune

Section 1

LISTENING

1 You are going to listen to an interview with Sir Richard Branson, a successful businessman, the founder of Virgin Records. He is talking about how he began his career. Before you listen, discuss these questions with a partner.

a) What kind of family and educational background do most successful business people have?
b) Think of a successful businessperson in your country. What questions would you ask if you were a journalist interviewing him or her?

2 [8.1] Listen to the tape. Were the questions the same as yours? Is Richard Branson similar to the type of businessperson you were thinking of or is he very different?

3 Read the following statements. Which are true and which are false? Listen to the tape again to check your answers.

a) Richard Branson was not yet 17 when he started his first magazine.
b) He had been given some money to help him start the magazine.
c) In order to be taken seriously, he asked a friend to act as his secretary.
d) He was able to publish the magazine when people promised him £5000 in advertising.
e) The interviewer is surprised that such well-known people wrote for the magazine.
f) Richard Branson sold cut-price records through the magazine.
g) All the company's income was originally from the mail order business.
h) Richard Branson went bankrupt because of a postal strike.
i) He started his record company by selling records in a shoe store.

4 What kind of person is he? With a partner, choose one or two of the words in the box and add one or two of your own to describe your impression.

| modest   self-satisfied   self-deprecating |
| confident   warm   cold   direct   evasive |
| defensive   genuine   enthusiastic |
| serious-minded   humorous |

Compare your words with another group. Can you all agree on the most appropriate? Listen to the tape again to check your impressions.

5 In small groups, imagine that you are going to try and start a successful business somewhere in the world today. To plan your business, discuss the following questions.

a) What would you sell? Something practical? Something for people's pleasure?
b) Would you sell through mail-order or in a high street store or in another way?

The interviewer mentions several famous people who contributed to Richard Branson's magazine:
Gerald Scarfe: a well-known cartoonist
David Hockney: a famous painter
John Le Carré: a writer of best-selling spy stories
The Dean of Liverpool: an important figure in the Anglican church

Unit 8

VOCABULARY

Multi-part verbs: adverbs and prepositions

1 Work with a partner to complete the sentences with the correct adverb or preposition.

a) I was brought *up* in a very small village.
b) My father would never tell me . . . for anything.
c) He is someone I can always turn . . . .
d) How does a young boy set . . . a magazine?
e) I put . . . a false voice to pretend I had a secretary.
f) I didn't want to let . . . that I was only fifteen.
g) So it worked well and the money was rolling . . . .
h) Tom Jackson stepped . . . and led a postal strike.
i) We faced going . . . of business.
j) We headed . . . down Oxford St.

2 [▣ 8.2] Listen and check your answers.

a) As you listen, mark in whether the intonation on the preposition or adverb goes up (stressed) or goes down (unstressed). For example:
I was brought up in a very small village.

b) Note that the particles which are stressed and have rising intonation follow one of the following patterns:

   i)   VERB + ADVERB
       The money rolled   in.
   ii)   VERB + ADVERB + OBJECT
       The father brought up   the children.
   iii)   VERB + OBJECT + ADVERB
       The father brought the children up.

In transitive sentences the particles can be separated from the verbs.

c) Note that the particles which are not stressed and have falling intonation are prepositions and follow the pattern below.

      VERB   +   PREPOSITION + OBJECT
  I can turn   to   my father.
  He faced going   out of   business.

The preposition can never be separated from the verb.

3 Choose three of the verbs and use them in sentences of your own. Read out your sentences to a partner, making sure you use the appropriate stress and intonation.

TALKING EFFECTIVELY

Focussing on ideas

When we speak or read aloud in English, we stress the words which express the most important ideas. Different people will think that different ideas are important. This does not matter. The main thing to remember is that some idea words must be emphasised for your message to be clearly understood.

a) [▣ 8.3] Listen to the examples on the tape and underline in different colours the words that are stressed in the two examples. With a partner decide whether the differences of meaning in the two versions are significant. Example:
Some people say that staying on at school after the age of sixteen is a waste of time.

b) Read the following extract from a radio programme giving advice to young people about staying on at school. Work with a partner to decide which words you would stress if you were reading it aloud. You do not have to agree.

> Some people say that staying on at school after the age of sixteen is a waste of time. But there are a lot of good reasons why you should. First of all, schools today do not simply offer academic courses, which are irrelevant to the world of work that you are about to enter. They also offer vocational courses which can help you get a better start on the career ladder. Secondly, it is becoming more and more difficult to actually get a job at sixteen because of rising unemployment, a problem which is unlikely to be resolved in the near future. If you do get a job, you will probably not get rapid promotion because so many people with better educational qualifications will be entering the job market at a higher rung of the career ladder, and because companies can no longer afford training programmes for their own employees. So stay on that extra year or so and get yourself a good education!

c) [▣ 8.4] Listen to the two recordings of the passage and underline in different colours the words that are stressed. Discuss with a partner how similar or how different the recordings are to your own versions. Are the differences significant?

SPEAKING

A debate

A debate is a formal speaking activity in which people may participate to explore the arguments for and against a particular motion. Quite often the audience votes at the beginning and again at the end to see if the speakers have made them change their minds. You are going to debate the following motion:

8 p.m. tonight
Debate
The motion –
Too much education is a bad thing
Come along and listen!

Expressing personal opinions

For
In my view, Richard Branson would probably not have been so successful if he hadn't left school at sixteen.
I must say, I think people who leave school young get a better start in life.
I'd just like to say that all the successful people I know left school very young . . .

Against
As far as I'm concerned, education is about learning and the more you learn the more equipped for life you are.
It seems to me most people get better jobs if they are educated.
Personally, I believe/feel education equips you for life.

a) Your teacher will help you to divide into two equal teams. Team A will prepare arguments to support the motion and team B arguments which oppose it. Work in small groups and prepare your arguments as in the examples. Make notes, but also practise saying your ideas aloud, making sure you focus clearly on the important ideas (see *Talking Effectively*). Use the ideas in the language box to help you. Decide if your arguments will be serious, humorous, dramatic, emotional, etc. and prepare some anecdotes, examples and factual information.

b) Each team chooses two members to present its arguments to the whole class. The speakers present their arguments in turn for a maximum of three minutes each.

c) The rest of the class may then contribute other arguments. A speaker from team A always follows a speaker from team B and vice versa.

d) Your teacher will end the debate after the time limit is up and ask you to vote. Have some of you changed your minds after listening to strong arguments from the other team?

A debate in the Cambridge University Students' Union

Unit 8

Section 2

LEARNING GRAMMAR

▶ Diagnosis ◀◀◀

Ways of expressing the future

1 The pictures on the right show situations using the future. The remarks in each situation use one of the ways we talk about the future in English. However, each remark is incorrect or inappropriate in the context. Rewrite the remarks in the appropriate form, using the guidelines in the Key to help you if necessary.

2 Put the verbs in brackets into an appropriate way of expressing the future. There may be more than one answer. The first one has been done for you.

a) You (*succeed*) never. Climbing Everest is far too difficult for an amateur like you.
   You'll never succeed. Climbing Everest is far too difficult for an amateur like you.
b) I'm sorry I can't come to the party on Saturday. We (*spend*) the weekend with my parents.
c) I don't expect we (*be*) back before 9 this evening, so don't wait for us for dinner.
d) Now everybody, the coach (*leave*) at 5p.m. promptly, so everybody must be back here by then.
e) On our next wedding anniversary we (*be married*) for forty years.
f) I'm going to have a nice hot bath as soon as I (*get*) home.
g) The team (*train*) really seriously for the next four weeks so that we have a maximum chance of winning the competition.
h) By the year 2000 doctors (*find*) cures for many more serious diseases.

a) *[I'm afraid I can't see you for lunch on Friday. I will have lunch with James.]*

b) *[Oh look! The train is running over him!]*

c) *[You meet a tall, handsome stranger. You win a lot of money.]*

d) *[You can have it when you will say please.]*

e) *[In the year 2016, Shakespeare will be dead for 400 years.]*

Development

Future continuous tense: uses

1 To describe actions which are seen to be in progress at a particular time in the future. For example:

a) *She says she'll be wearing a red dress and carrying a copy of* Time *magazine so that you'll be able to recognise her easily when you meet her tomorrow.*
b) *We leave for the country on Saturday, so this time next week I'll be relaxing in the garden.*

2 To talk about the future when it is already planned or arrangements have been made. It is a more neutral way of talking about the future than *will* as meanings of intention, prediction, promising, etc. are absent. Compare the following examples:
 i) *I'll be staying at home tomorrow morning, so you can make the delivery at any time.* (I had already planned to stay at home for another reason.)
 ii) *I'll stay at home tomorrow so you can make the delivery, but come as early as you can.* (I am deciding to stay at home on purpose as I say this.)

The difference is all the more obvious in the negative form:
 i) *I won't see him tomorrow.* (I don't intend to, or I refuse to, or There is very little probability of my seeing him.)
 ii) *I won't be seeing him tomorrow.* (I am doing something else.)

This form is often used as an alternative to the present continuous, and is often used to talk about travel plans. (See Unit 2) You could say either of the following:
 i) *I'll be staying at home tomorrow.*
 ii) *I am staying at home tomorrow.*

3 In questions, to sound more polite and less direct. Compare the following examples.

a) i) *Will you pay the bill yourself?*
 ii) *Will you be paying the bill yourself?*
b) i) *When will you arrive?*
 ii) *When will you be arriving?*

4 The future perfect continuous is normally used when we want to focus on the continuity of time up till a moment in the future. For example:
In half an hour's time I will have been working for 5 hours without a break.
If you stay on the beach till tea time, you'll have been lying in the hot sun for far too long!

Note

1 The future progressive does not have the functional meaning of an invitation or a request. Compare the following examples:

a) i) *Will you come with me?*
 ii) *Will you be coming with me?*
b) i) *Won't you come to stay for a while?*
 ii) *Won't you be coming to stay for a while?*

2 In many contexts, the choice of one form or the other is not significant. For example:

I'll see Sarah at the meeting on Saturday, I'll be seeing Sarah at the meeting on Saturday, I am seeing Sarah on Saturday	so I'll tell her the good news then.

Practice

1 Working with a partner, contrast the following dialogue and answer the questions.

a) i) Can you give this package to Jane?
 Okay. I'll see her tomorrow and give it to her.
 ii) Can you give this package to Jane?
 Yes, I'll be seeing her tomorrow anyway, so it's no trouble.

In which sentence is a meeting between Jane and speaker B already planned at the time of speaking? In which sentence does speaker B decide to see Jane at the time of speaking?

b) i) Have you finished decorating your bedroom yet?
 No, but if everything goes according to plan I'll be finishing on Friday.
 ii) Have you finished decorating your bedroom yet?
 No, but I'll finish on Friday. I have to, I'm going away on Saturday and I don't want to leave everything in a mess.

Which sentence expresses strong intention? Which sentence talks about the way the work is planned?

c) i) I love that record. Will you play it again?
    ii) I love that record. Will you be playing it again this evening?
   Which remark could be addressed to a disc jockey who has already planned an evening's music? Which is a request to hear some music?

2 Correct the following sentences where necessary. Check your answers with a partner.

a) Thanks for lending me the book. I'll be giving it back to you next week, I promise.
   Thanks for lending me the book. I'll give it back to you next week, I promise.
b) I'll go to the supermarket to do my own shopping anyway, so it's no trouble to pick up some milk for you.
c) We'll be giving a party next month.
d) Why won't you be answering my question?
e) I can't come next weekend as Tracy and Kevin will be getting married and I promised to go to the wedding.
f) Will you be holding the door open for me, please?
g) Oh dear, we'll never be getting there in time.
h) Let me have the bill. I'll be paying.
i) Don't call tomorrow evening as we'll have a family party and I won't be able to talk to you.

3 [8.5] Listen to the three people on the tape. Note down the present situation of each speaker and their plans as in the example below.

	Present situation	Plans
A	at school	study law . . .
B		
C		

From your notes, write out what the speakers said as accurately as possible. Listen to the tape again to check.

4 You are going to interview someone about what they will be doing, will have done or will have been doing in one, two and ten years' time. Think about how to phrase your questions and write them down. Then work with a partner. Report back to the whole class and decide who has the most exciting plans.

VOCABULARY

Idioms

1 In these sentences the underlined words and expressions are idioms or colloquial expressions to do with succeeding or failing. Look at the context and write *S* (*Success*) or *F* (*Failure*) against each one.

a) He was born with a silver spoon in his mouth – he always got his own way and was given anything he asked for.
b) The play was a complete flop and only lasted a week.
c) We went on a wild goose chase – we got lost six times and never managed to find that wonderful restaurant you told us about.
d) His getting that wonderful job was a complete fluke – he hasn't got the qualifications and he isn't even competent.
e) She may still make the deal – she hasn't played her last trump-card yet.
f) Even if you only come second in the national championship, it'll still be quite a feather in your cap.
g) Jim completely bungled the job; he stuck the chair legs on the wrong way round.
h) She's intelligent and hard-working so she passed her exam with flying colours.

2 Complete the gaps with the most appropriate idiom. The first one has been done for you.

a) Don't let Harry repair your radio. He's hopeless and will only *bungle* the job.
b) I wouldn't go so far as to say the concert was a . . . . ., but it certainly didn't sell out.
c) It wasn't as if she had been . . . . . . She had worked her way up from absolutely nothing.
d) Her . . . . . was to threaten to resign if they refused to agree to her request.
e) There wasn't another competitor in sight when they crossed the finishing line, winning . . . . . .

3 Look again at the idioms in Exercises 1 and 2.

a) Choose three idioms and use them in sentences of your own after checking them in a dictionary. Read them out to other people in your class.

b) With a partner, decide which of the following statements you agree with.
  i) I enjoy learning and using idioms in English very much.
  ii) I find it difficult to use idioms in English, as I'm sure I get them wrong and they sound silly.
  iii) I need to understand idioms because native speakers use them all the time, but I don't need to use them myself.

ABOUT LANGUAGE

Correct my English!

1 Read the following incorrect sentences. Some of them contain errors that native speakers often make. Some contain errors that native speakers do not usually make. In pairs, write *NS* (*Native speaker*) against any errors you have heard native speakers make or that you guess they might make. Check your answers in the Key.

a) I'll phone when I'll get there.
b) I can't get no satisfaction.
c) Last week I have a party.
d) She was a Jack's friend.
e) I'll do it on me own.
f) If I would be rich, I wouldn't bother to work.
g) I sees the policeman comin', and I runs down the road and disappears as fast as I can.

2 In small groups, discuss the errors that native speakers make in your own language(s).

Section 3

SPEAKING

1 Work with a partner to match the headlines to the pictures. Explain the situation in each picture.

A **Top Grin ...**

B **She won, but the war goes on**

C **New Orleans Beats James Madison**

D **A RECORD IN SLED DOG RACING**

2 [🔊 8.6] Listen to the tape.

a) Note down who the speakers say are successful and why.

b) Add two more names of people you consider to be successful and your reasons for thinking them to be successful and then discuss the following questions with a partner.
  i) Do you agree that the people talked about on the tape are successful?
  ii) Do you agree that the people your partner has added to his or her list are successful?
  iii) Why do you consider the people to be successful?
  iv) Do you know how the people became successful?
  v) What qualities did they need?
  vi) What help did they have from their families or their friends?
  vii) Is a successful person always famous – and vice versa?

Unit 8

Dear Xavier,
   I must send you a short letter of congratulation. This must be the first you have ever had (I don't fancy there are any pre-natal ones). You seem to have timed your arrival most cunningly. I am very proud to think that after tomorrow, I shall have some claims on your personality and productivity as part (a very tiny one I know) of the famous Common Market. Perhaps I shall survive to see you as a lycéen and it will be nice to think that you may spend a holiday on the moon.
   You have chosen two delightful parents. Please be terribly kind to them and make them enormously proud of you. I mean, in your own way, of course. No surrender to their prejudices or plans unless they suit you. Indeed not. But if you could fit in very snugly, I think that would be most enjoyable. You're probably going to have a marvellous life. Very nice food, all sorts of sports, much better clothes and housing than the older generation, a world of gorgeous girls and boys. (The present lot I don't think can really last much longer.)
   Don't bother writing back, not for a few years anyhow.
   Much love to the three of you,
      Lionel

WRITING

Letter from a godparent

1 Read this extract from a letter of advice written from a godparent to his godson. Work with a partner to answer the questions below.

a) On what occasion was it written?
b) How old is the writer?
c) What might the parents' 'prejudices' be? (paragraph 2)
d) Is the writer optimistic or pessimistic about the future? How do you know?
e) Which of the following adjectives would you use to describe the style? Justify your answer with examples.

distant	warm
humorous	serious
light-hearted	

f) What is the godparent's message to the godson? Write it in one sentence. Compare with other pairs. Do you agree?

2 Imagine some friends of yours have asked you to be godparent to their new-born child or that you have a special nephew or niece. Write a letter to him or her giving advice about how to lead a successful life. First write your message in one sentence, and use your one sentence as the basis of your letter. Add details about what you hope for, what the future will be like and what you think your godchild should or shouldn't do with his or her life. Write in a light and informal style as in the example. Read out your letter to other people in your class.

UNIT 9

The film or the book?

Section 1

READING AND SPEAKING

1 Discuss the following questions in small groups. One of you should take notes of your discussion and be prepared to report back to the whole class.

a) Have you ever seen a film of a book after you have read the book itself?
b) What did you think of it?
c) Have you ever read a book after you have seen the film of it? If so, what did you think of it?
d) What is special about a novel that you do not find in a film?
e) What is special about a film that you do not find in a novel?
f) If you had written a novel and it was being made into a film, what would your attitude be?

Text A

Fay Weldon's literary career now spans at least three media and must be one of the most prolific in Britain. So far it adds up to eleven theatrical plays, twenty-two TV plays and seventeen novels, the most famous of which is *The Life and Loves of a She-Devil*. This is the story of a betrayed wife, who instead of taking a knife to her husband has herself carved up by a plastic surgeon into a clone of her husband's 'mistress'.

This torrid tale was later turned into a major Hollywood movie by Susan Seidelman, starring Meryl Streep and Roseanne Barr. Was Weldon's Hollywood sale of She-Devil dependent on having Susan Seidelman, director of *Desperately Seeking Susan,* as director? 'Yes,' she said emphatically, in an interview about the making of the film. 'I could have sold it to John Huston, which gave me a choice between a more traditional Hollywood approach or having a new and different look.'

Though Weldon did not write the script, she was invited to visit the New York set. 'They were nervous in case I rushed round the set screaming 'That's not what I wrote!' or 'Why are her shoes pink instead of green?' But I know enough not to do that. My theory is that the role of the adaptee is to rise from the grave every now and then crying 'Wonderful, wonderful.' Then to sink back again only coming out for the première.'

But she does have one niggling doubt. 'I suspect they're only filming half the book. It stops when the She-Devil has put her husband in prison, confounded his mistress and is running a successful business.' In the novel, the bad woman (i.e. the mistress) becomes good and the effort of being virtuous kills her, whereas the good woman (i.e. the wife) becomes bad, yet is saved. The film has an old-fashioned moral to it: 'You can do it sister — but without the devil's assistance.' Fay Weldon's habitual cynicism has given place to something that is 'very warm to the heart'.

But does Fay Weldon think there's enough material left to make a good film? A brief hesitation, then: 'No. If it was me and the film came to an end halfway through the original story, it would need some other inner purpose. Narrative has to be more than mere progression and I suspect that this film will be just that. The bad mistress just gets her comeuppance.'

So is this a case of take the money and run? 'No,' Weldon firmly replies. 'I don't think you can do that anymore. In the days when Hollywood was run by producers with no taste or judgement that was possible, but since those people are now extremely intelligent and versatile you can't look at it like that. You have to respect their decisions.' ■

Text B

GRAHAM GREENE, the well-known author of more than thirty novels, had already made one film with director Carol Reed when film magnate Sir Alexander Korda asked him to do another set in Vienna during the four-power occupation after the Second World War. The story is about Harry Lime living in this 'smashed and dreary city' where everyone had a racket. Lime, however, was in the particularly dirty business of penicillin, which, diluted for better profit, caused many deaths. At the end of the book, Lime's girlfriend walks away from his graveside with another man. This is what Graham Greene had to say about the making of the film in the preface to the book.

'To me is it almost impossible to write a film play without first writing the story. Even a film depends on more than plot, on a certain measure of characterization, on mood and atmosphere; and these seem to me almost impossible to capture for the first time in the dull shorthand of a script. *The Third Man*, therefore, had to start as a story before those apparently interminable transformations from one treatment to another.'

'On these treatments Carol Reed and I worked closely together, covering so many feet of carpet a day, acting scenes at each other. No third ever joined our conferences; so much value lies in the clear cut-and-thrust of argument between two people.' To the novelist, of course, his novel is the best he can do with a particular subject; he cannot help resenting many of the changes necessary for turning it into a film or a play; but *The Third Man* was never intended to be more than the raw material for a picture. The reader will notice many differences between the story and the film, and he should not imagine that these changes were forced on an unwilling author: as likely or not they were suggested by the author. The film is in fact better than the story because it is in this case the finished state of the story.'

'One of the major disputes between Carol Reed and myself concerned the ending and he has been proved triumphantly right. I held the view that an entertainment of this kind was too light an affair to carry the weight of an unhappy ending. Reed on his side felt that my ending – indeterminate though it was, with no words spoken, would strike the audience who had just seen Harry die, as unpleasantly cynical. I admit I was only half convinced; I was afraid few people would wait in their seat during the girl's long walk from the graveside and they would leave the cinema under the impression that the ending was as conventional as mine and more drawn-out. I had not given enough consideration to the mastery of Reed's direction and at that stage, of course, neither of us could have anticipated Reed's brilliant discovery of Mr. Karas, the zither player.'

zither: a flat, stringed musical instrument

2 The class divides into two groups of equal size.

a) Group A reads text A and Group B reads text B. Both groups should read the questions below briefly before they begin.

b) Note down your answers to the questions, without using a dictionary. Group A answers the questions about text A, Group B about text B.
  i) Was the story originally meant to be a book or a film?
  ii) Did the author write the actual script?
  iii) Did the author decide on the changes from the book to the film?
  iv) Did the author visit the film set?
  v) What does the author think of the way the book has been changed?
  vi) What is the attitude of the author to the film director?
  vii) What does the author say about the ending?
  viii) Are any of the changes made specifically on account of audience sensibility?
  ix) Is the author satisfied with the final product?
  x) Write one sentence describing the author's attitude to the making of the film.

3 Work in pairs, a student from Group A with a student from group B. Swap information about the two authors by comparing your answers to the questions above. Which questions had similar answers? Which were completely different?

4 Quickly read the text you have not yet looked at and discuss with your partner what is meant by the words and phrases below in their contexts. What impression are they trying to create? How do they contribute to the style of each passage?

Text A
a) rise from the grave (line 23)
b) sister (line 34)
c) take the money and run (line 44)

Text B
d) dull shorthand of a script (line 19)
e) covering so many feet of carpet (line 24)
f) the clear cut-and-thrust of argument (lines 26–27)
g) an entertainment (lines 41–42)

5 Work with a partner to decide which pair of adjectives in the box below best describes the style of each text. You may choose other adjectives of your own if you prefer. Give examples to illustrate your choice. Do you and your partner agree?

> popular and journalistic   fairly literary and polished   exaggerated and dramatic
> light-hearted and conversational
> serious and reflective

6 Where do you and your partner think each text came from – a popular magazine? A specialist cinema review? A biography? A publicity blurb? A newspaper article? Give your reasons. Report your discussion back to the whole class.

VOCABULARY

Inferring meaning

1 Work with a partner to scan the texts for a word or expression that gives the meaning of one of the following definitions.

Text A
a) a very accurate copy or reproduction
b) defeated

Text B
c) basic ingredients
d) very probably

How did you find the word? Was it one that you noticed when you first read the passage and half-understood? Did you work it out from the context? Discuss any other strategies you used.

2 Now work out the meanings of the following words:

Text A
a) torrid (line 9)
b) niggling (line 26)
c) comeuppance (line 43)

Text B
d) smashed and dreary (lines 6–7)
e) drawn-out (line 52)

Unit 9

Collocation

1 Each word in column A goes with all the words beside it in column B except one. Which is the odd one out in each case? The first one has been done for you.

	A	B
a)	niggling	doubt, pain, worry, (relation)
b)	raw	nerve, material, meal, egg
c)	far-reaching	implications, survey, question, reply
d)	carve	a joint, a pencil, a statue, an initial

2 In groups of three, play the word game shown in the examples below. Student A produces a three-word sentence which contains a subject, an intransitive verb and an adverb. For example: *Rivers flow fast*. Students B then changes one of the words, for example: *Rivers flow swiftly*, or *Rivers run fast*. or *The tide flows fast*. No part of the sentence may stay for more than three turns and a different part of the sentence must change each time. Read the example before you start. Example:

Student A: *Rivers flow fast.*
Student B: *Rivers flow swiftly.*
Student C: *Rivers move swiftly.*
Student A: *The wind moves swiftly.*
Student B: *The wind moves invisibly.*
Student C: *The wind whispers invisibly.*
Student A: *Ghosts whisper invisibly.*
Student B: *Ghosts whisper quietly.*
Student C: *Ghosts talk quietly, etc.*

ABOUT LANGUAGE

New words

Fay Weldon invents the word *adaptee*. You will find *adapter* in the dictionary but not *adaptee*. To work out what it means you must use your knowledge of word formation in English. Compare *employer* and *employee*. It becomes obvious that *adaptee* means 'the person whose work is being adapted'.

Work with a partner. Check in a dictionary any words in column B that you do not know. Match each word in column A to its 'original' in column B and decide what you think the invented words mean. Example:

g) megabucks = 6 megatons
   Meaning = lots of dollars

	A		B
a)	womanslaughter	1	Chinese, journalese
b)	person Friday	2	freedom
c)	computerate	3	telegram
d)	yuppiedom	4	Man Friday
e)	computerese	5	manslaughter
f)	kissagram	6	megatons
g)	megabucks	7	literate

Wanted— Person Friday to work in busy office

70

Section 2

LEARNING GRAMMAR

▶ Diagnosis ◀ ◀ ◀

Can and *be able to* for ability

1 Work with a partner to correct the mistakes in the following sentences where necessary. Check your answers in the Key. The first one has been done for you.

a) I'd like to can talk Spanish more fluently.
   I'd like to be able to talk Spanish more fluently.
b) I can come on Thursday or Friday but not on Saturday.
c) In two months' time, you can drive really well.
d) She could play the piano brilliantly when she was only six.
e) She was a very strong swimmer and could save the drowning man.
f) I cannot get any more information about the case so far, but I'll keep trying.
g) The vet said afterwards that he could give the dog an injection which would have saved his life.

2 Work with a partner to look back at the examples and complete the following list. The first one has been done for you. Use the guidelines in the Key to help you if necessary.

You must use *be able to* instead of *can*:
a) in the infinitive form.
b) . . .
c) . . .
d) . . .

3 Complete the gaps with the correct form of *can* (*can, could, could have*) wherever possible and the verb in brackets. Use the correct form of *be able to* where *can* is not possible.

a) Although she was guarded carefully, the hostage (*escape*) . . . .
b) If the traffic hadn't been so heavy, we (*get*) . . . there on time.
c) I (*not swim*) . . . when I was a child.
d) I (*not come*) . . . next week.
e) In time, she'll get better and (*walk*) . . . again.

Can, could, may and *might* for possibility

1 Work with a partner to decide which of the following pairs of sentences mean almost the same thing and which mean something completely different. The first one has been done for you.

a) i) We can go for a picnic on Saturday.
   ii) We may go for a picnic on Saturday.
   Completely different. In i), the speaker makes a suggestion about something to do. In ii), the speaker has already envisaged the event and is talking about the chances of it happening.
b) i) You could be right.
   ii) You might be right.
c) i) He may come.
   ii) He might come.
d) i) Scotland can be warm in September.
   ii) Scotland might be warm in September.
e) i) She can be quite a nuisance.
   ii) She may be quite a nuisance.
f) i) People might swim across the river.
   ii) People can swim across the river.

2 Some of the sentences in Exercise 1 refer to events that are possible in the sense that they could happen in theory, but do not necessarily in fact. For example:
We can go for a picnic on Saturday. (A suggestion of something that would be possible.) Other sentences refer to events that will have some chance of happening. For example:
We may go for a picnic on Saturday. (There is a real chance that the picnic will take place.)

Write *T* (*Theoretically possible*) or *RC* (*Real chance*) against each of the sentences in Exercise 1. Use the guidelines in the Key to help you if necessary. The first one has been done for you. Check your answers with your partner.

a) i) We can go for a picnic on Saturday. *T*
   ii) We may go for a picnic on Saturday. *RC*

Development

Could have, may have, might have: attitudes

Could and *might* are often used in contexts in which talking about a possible past event is more to do with an emotional attitude than the real possibility of it happening. Study the following examples.

1 Reproach, criticism, accusation, etc.: *might, could*

a) *It was stupid to throw the flower pot out of the window. It could/might have hurt someone.*
b) *You shouldn't have gone through those red lights. You could/might have had an accident.*
c) *You could/might have told me.*

2 Irritation: *might*

a) *It might have been all right if you'd asked first.*
b) *I might have come if you'd asked.*

3 Disbelief: *could not*

a) *She couldn't have got a part in a film. She can't act at all!*
b) *He couldn't have been at the party. He never goes to parties.*

4 Strong emotion such as happiness, anger, etc.: *could*

a) *I could have screamed with frustration.*
b) *I was so angry, I could have murdered her.*
c) *I was so happy, I could have danced all night.*

5 Regret: *could*

a) *It hasn't rained. I could have put the washing out after all.*
b) *Just think, we could have been sitting on the beach in the sun by now.*

Practice

1 Work with a partner to decide what is strange about the following sentences. Correct them so they sound more natural.

a) You should have told me you were sick. I might have come and visited you earlier.
b) He mightn't have got the job. He's such a loser.
c) I might have jumped for joy when he asked me to marry him.

2 Work with a partner to complete the following statements with a suitable remark using *could have*. The first one has been done for you.

a) (Reproach or criticism) Why were you playing so roughly with the little boy? You . . . *You could/might have hurt him.*
b) (Strong emotion) I was so pleased with the results, I . . .
c) (Disbelief) Bob is so mean. He . . .
d) (Regret) I was so sad to have to move. I loved living in Madrid so much I . . .
e) (Reproach or criticism) You shouldn't have come home alone down that dark alley. You . . .
f) (Strong emotion) I liked that film so much I went to see it twice. In fact I . . .

Conversational uses of *may, might, can* and *could*

1 [9.1] Read the dialogue below and listen to it. Two people are planning a programme for a film club.

a) Underline all the expressions which contain *may, might, could* and *can*.

MRS GIBBS: We have had far too many big budget adventure films lately, if I may say so. What we need now, if I may make a suggestion, is something a little different, a little experimental. Perhaps from South America, or France, or Italy . . .

MR ORCHARD: You may well think we've had too many adventure films. But they are the ones that draw the crowds, and if we don't attract audiences we won't have a film club much longer.

MRS G: Mr Orchard, may I remind you that the cinema was almost empty last Saturday, when we had one of your adventure films that's supposed to draw the crowds. And might I point out that unless we show people experimental films, they will never know what they are or want to come and see them.

MR O: That may well be the case, but I can't honestly say that I agree with you about your experimental films. I might say, in an ideal world that they would be fine, but here we need an eye-catching programme.

MRS G: Well, you could be right, but I can't say that I'll be that pleased to see that kind of programme and I can't accept that people really want that sort of rubbish.

b) With a partner, look at the list below and the expressions you have underlined and decide what the function (or functions) of *may, might, could* and *can* are each time they are used. For example:
if I may say so – more tentative and more polite
  i) Give extra information
  ii) Lessen any disagreement
  iii) Sound more polite
  iv) Sound more tentative
  v) Sound less direct
  vi) Sound more direct

2 Make the following remarks less direct and more polite using the expressions you have underlined in Exercise 1. The first one has been done for you.

a) That's rubbish.
   That's rubbish, if I may say so.
b) Perhaps that's a good idea.
c) That's not a good idea.
d) I disagree with you.
e) You are wrong.
f) Remember last week's disaster.

3 With a partner, choose one of the following topics and practise disagreeing as politely as possible.

a) A film you have both seen or a book you have both read.
b) A recent event that is being discussed in the news.
c) Your favourite music.
d) Anything else.

Section 3

TALKING EFFECTIVELY

1 Read the short scene below. With a partner, decide briefly what the context is.

> 'Have you had lunch?'
> 'What?'
> 'We could take our repast in a restaurant, or there's some soup -'
> 'Leslie.'
> They looked at each other, and then she went to him and put her arms around him.
> 'I'm sorry, Ron. But did you really tender your resignation? I mean for ever?'
> 'Yes, I'm going to be crowned with success as an artist. A real artist.'
> 'Here?'
> 'I though I'd pursue my activity in my studio, yeah, unless - I mean, is it of any inconvenience to you? You've always said that any time I wanted to - that you earn enough money for both of us …'
> 'Of course. It isn't that.'
> 'Then what?'
> 'It is of no consequence to me. But you always said you didn't want me supporting you.'
> 'It would only be for a little while. I'm sure I can attain my purpose.'
> 'I know you will.'

2 Read the scene again.

a) Some of the original words and expressions have been replaced by expressions which are more likely to be found in written English and do not match the conversational style of the rest of the dialogue. Work with a partner to try and spot them. Try and suggest any alternatives in spoken register.

b) [▣ 9.2] Listen to the tape and note down the expressions which are different on the dialogue above. Were they the ones you noted down in a)? How similar are your own suggestions to the ones on the tape?

3 [▣ 9.3] Listen to the tape and mark in the main stresses and intonation patterns on the corrected tapescript as in the example below. Practise reading the dialogue with a partner, using the same stress and intonation.

'Have you had lunch?'

'What?'

'We could go out, or there's some soup . . .'

'Leslie.'

They looked at each other, and then she went to him and put her arms around him.

'I'm sorry, Ron. But did you really quit? I mean for good?'

'Yes, I'm going to make it as an artist. A real artist.'

SPEAKING

1 You are a group of film producers who are planning a meeting to choose your next film. You are going to consider three projects, all adaptations from novels. This is not a low-budget film, so money is no object. Prepare your meeting in the following way.

a) Divide into three groups of equal size. Decide with your teacher which group prepares book A, which book B and which book C. In your groups, prepare your book in twos or threes after you have read the instructions below.

b) Read the blurb (= the description of a book on the back cover) for your group's book. A film adaptation of this book is the project you want to defend in the meeting. You will have to convince your colleagues that it would make a good film.

c) Write down all the merits you think it will have. You can begin to imagine and develop some of the details of the film script. Make notes under the following headings:

- Title (not necessarily the same as the book)
- Plot and action
- Characters and relationships
- Actors (Who is most suitable to play the parts?)
- Settings, mood and atmosphere
- Moral element (Is there one?)

Book A

Emmanuel is a famous playwright. Lillian is his sickly and embittered wife. They have never fully buried the memory of their dead daughter, Sarah.

Rich but discontented, they flit from capital to capital in the company of their hero-worshipping young manager - nomads on the international air-lines. Then Alberta, straight from an English vicarage and the pages of Jane Austen, is appointed as Emmanuel's secretary. This prim and utterly delightful figure works on the 'family' like milk on a disordered stomach. One by one the leopards change their spots.

Book B

T. H. WHITE
The Goshawk

Stories of close relationships between men and beasts – *Born Free* or *Ring of Bright Water* – possess peculiar fascination. To this T. H. White has added an individuality of style and an independence of philosophy which make *The Goshawk* a classic of its kind. As David Garnett has written:

'*The Goshawk* is the story of a concentrated duel between Mr White and a great beautiful hawk during the training of the latter – the record of an intense clash of wills, in which the pride and endurance of the wild raptor are worn down and broken by the almost insane willpower of the school-master falconer.'

'It is comic; it is tragic; it is all absorbing. It is strangely like some of the classic eighteenth-century stories of seduction.'

Book C

Robert Carey was a spy who had defected to Russia. When the news leaked out that he had changed sides again a ruthless manhunt was on from the glamour of Paris to the violent and scorched wastelands of West Africa.

There is Fat Rossland who doesn't recognise trouble when it sits on his lap; Girland, a dissatisfied agent who is greedy for money - and women; Janine Daulnay who fatally plays the ends against the middle; Radnitz, the sinister tycoon and Malik, the blonde Russian with whom Girland tangles in a lethal battle of wits.

Striking a new note with the background to this action-packed novel of espionage, James Hadley Chase upholds his reputation for compulsive readability.

2 [⬛ 9.4] Prepare your arguments in a convincing manner.

a) Listen to the tape and match the statements to the speakers on the tape. The first one has been done for you.
  i) There is a moral element in it that people will like. *Speaker 1*
  ii) The characters are interesting.
  iii) There is a lot of action and suspense in the story.
  iv) This book has a good plot.
  v) There's plenty of possibility for atmosphere.

b) The remarks on the tape would be more effective in a discussion than the sentences written above. In the list below, tick the characteristics which make them more orally effective.
  i) Telling the truth ☐
  ii) Repetition ☐
  iii) Brevity ☐
  iv) Exaggeration ☐
  v) Colourful vocabulary ☐
  vi) Humour ☐

3 The meeting.

Form groups with one A student, one B student and one C student. You are meeting to decide which of the three projects you are going to adopt. You must all reach a decision within the time limit that your teacher fixes for you. Remember to present your project in a convincing manner and to be polite and indirect when criticising other people's projects (see Conversational uses of *may, might, can* and *could* in *Learning grammar*).

4 Tell the rest of the class which film you have chosen and how your decision was reached.

WRITING

1 Work with a partner to write a mini-scene for one of the films that you talked about in the role play or from another book that you would like to see made into a film. Make sure your scene sounds like spoken English by checking you have included items in the box below.

Characteristics of spoken English
a) Words belonging to spoken register.
b) Colloquial expressions such as *of course* or *just a minute*.
c) Incomplete sentences and interruptions.
d) Hesitation markers (*Well, I mean . . .*, etc.).
e) Redundancy (repeating the same idea in a different way).
f) Simple sentences. Adverbs such as *but* rather than conjunctions such as *although* with complex sentences.

---

2 Swap your scene with another group. Can you make any suggestions for improvement to the other group's work?

3 Mark in appropriate stress and intonation patterns. Give a dramatic reading of your scene to another group.

4 Write an essay on one of the following topics:

a) You have just seen a film you thoroughly enjoyed/absolutely detested. Write a letter to a friend about it.
b) Imagine you were able to observe a film of your choice being made. Describe the scene.
c) The cinema has no future in the twenty-first century. Discuss.

UNIT 10

Star food

Section 1

SPEAKING

1 Read the statements below about family life. How much do you agree or disagree with them? 1 agree strongly; 2 agree mildly; 3 neither agree or disagree; 4 disagree mildly; 5 disagree strongly.

FAMILY BACKGROUND
how much does it count?

1. Children take after their parents. If the parents are materially successful the children will be.
2. In an ideal family, there will always be someone to turn to in times of trouble.
3. Children who are brought up in families with two working parents are more likely to be independent and enterprising.
4. Working mothers cannot provide the emotional security that is essential for children while they are growing up.
5. Everybody in the family must get on well if children are to succeed in life.
6. Children who are never told off for doing wrong and who are allowed to do whatever they like often have problems or become delinquents in their adult life.
7. Children who grow up in a home environment with little discipline take to new situations and ventures more easily than others.

2 Compare your reactions in small groups. Discuss three or four of the comments on which you have different opinions and write one statement about family life that you can all agree with. Report back to the class on your group's discussion.

READING

You are going to read an extract from a story, called *Star Food*, about a young boy growing up in America.

1 Skim the passage very quickly. With a partner, decide whether the family life in the passage is happy, unhappy, neither happy nor unhappy. Refer back to the text to justify your opinion.

THE SUMMER I turned eighteen I disappointed both my parents for the first time. This hadn't happened before, since what disappointed one usually pleased the other. As a child, if I played broom hockey instead of going to school, my mother wept and my father took me outside later to find out how many goals I had scored. On the other hand, if I spent Saturday afternoon on the roof of my parents' grocery store staring up at the clouds instead of counting cracker cartons in the stockroom, my father took me to the back to talk about work and discipline, and my mother told me later to keep looking for things that no one else saw.

This was her theory. My mother felt that men like Leonardo da Vinci and Thomas Edison had simply stared long enough at regular objects until they saw new things, and thus my looking into the sky might someday make me a great man. She believed I had a worldly curiosity. My father believed I wanted to avoid stock work.

Stock work was an issue in our family, as were all the jobs that had to be done in a grocery store. Our store was called Star Food and above it an incandescent star revolved. Its circuits buzzed, and its yellow points, as thick as my knees, drooped with the slow melting of the bulb. On summer nights flying insects flocked in clouds around it, droves of them burning on the glass. One of my jobs was to go out on the roof, the sloping, eaved side that looked over the western half of Arcade, California, and clean them off the star. At night, when their black bodies stood out against the glass, when the wind carried in the marsh smell of the New Jerusalem River, I went into the attic, crawled out the dormer window onto the peaked roof, and slid across the shingles to where the pole rose like a lightning rod into the night. I reached with a wet rag and rubbed away the June bugs and pickerel moths until the star was yellow-white and steaming from the moisture.

Then I turned and looked over Arcade, across the bright avenue and my dimly lighted high school in the distance, into the low hills where oak trees grew in rows on the curbs and where girls drove to school in their own convertibles. When my father came up on the roof sometimes to talk about the store, we fixed our eyes on the red tile roofs or the small clouds of blue barbecue smoke that floated above the hills on warm evenings. While the clean bulb buzzed and flickered behind us, we talked about loss leaders or keeping the elephant-ear plums stacked in neat triangles.

The summer I disappointed my parents, though, my father talked to me about a lot of other things. He also made me look in the other direction whenever we were on the roof together, not west to the hills and their clouds of barbecue smoke, but east toward the other part of town. We crawled up one slope of the roof, then down the other so that I could see beyond the back alley where wash hung on lines in the moonlight, down to the neighborhoods across Route 5. These were the neighborhoods where men sat on the curbs on weekday afternoons, where rusted, wheel-less cars lay on blocks in the yards.

"*You're* going to end up on one of those curbs," my father told me.

Usually I stared farther into the clouds when he said something like that. He and my mother argued about what I did on the roof for so many hours at a time, and I hoped that by looking closely at the amazing borders of clouds I could confuse him. My mother believed I was on the verge of discovering something atmospheric, and I was sure she told my father this, so when he came upstairs, made me look across Route 5, and talked to me about how I was going to end up there, I squinted harder at the sky.

"You don't fool me for a second," he said.

(from *Emperor of the Air* by Ethan Canin)

broom hockey: a ball game played with broom handles
loss leaders: things sold cheaply in stores to attract customers
elephant-ear plums: a type of plum

2 The young boy's father and mother do not agree about what is good for him. Read the list of remarks below and, when you have reread the text, decide which parent made the remark.

a) How many goals did you score today? *Father*
b) Why didn't you go to school today?
c) You mustn't sit around all day doing nothing. You must do as you're told.
d) If you carry on thinking and looking, you'll be a great success one day.
e) Why aren't you more interested in what's going on in the shop?
f) You're so lazy, you're always trying to get out of helping us.
g) You'll end up as a layabout and a tramp, if you go on gazing into space like that.
h) I'm sure you'll find out something really important one day.
i) I can see through you. You're just pretending.
j) You really are a disappointment.

3 Work in groups of three and choose the ending below which you think most likely.

a) The boy refuses to prevent a woman shoplifting. Instead, he explores feelings of human solitude through the strange contact he has with her.
b) The boy grows up, becomes an astronomer and discovers a new constellation. When he becomes famous, he never comes to see his parents and only realises the error of his ways when they are both dead.
c) The boy ends up living in the poor part of town his father used to warn him about, but is in fact very happy and living a very pure and full spiritual life.

4 Discuss these questions with a partner.

a) What symbolic value do you usually attach to a star? Are your ideas relevant to the story?
b) The young boy has many jobs to do in the shop. Is cleaning the star a job he likes or a chore? Give reasons for your answer.
c) What can the boy see from the roof?
d) How is the view of the *curbs* (line 39) to the west different from the view of the *curbs* (line 56) to the east?
e) Why were the men sitting on *those curbs*? (line 58)
f) Why is the father worried about his son?
g) Is the attitude similar to attitudes of parents you know?

TALKING EFFECTIVELY

British English and American English

1 [10.1] Listen to the recording of the first paragraph of *Star Food* read first by an American voice, and second by a British voice. Underline any significant differences in pronunciation. Compare notes with a partner.

2 Work in pairs.

a) Read aloud the dialogue below, first imitating the British accent and then imitating the American accent you have just heard in Exercise 1.
A: Let's go to the beach in my new car.
B: No, let's walk.
A: I'd rather drive, it's quicker and I'm very tired.
B: OK, if you prefer, I don't mind.

b) [10.2] Listen to the tape and compare it with your performance. How good was your performance?

3 In small groups, discuss the following questions.

a) How easy is it to recognise different accents?
b) Do people speak your language with different accents?
c) Which accents do you recognise in English? Why?
d) Does it matter what accent you have when you speak English? Does it matter in your own language?

Section 2

LANGUAGE PATTERNS

Verbs with two objects

The verbs in the box can take two objects.

| cost | give | lend | make | offer | owe |
| send | show | write | | | |

Usually, the indirect object refers to a person and comes first. For example:
She lent her sister £500.
She showed her friend her holiday photographs.
It is possible to put the indirect object after the direct object, but in this case a preposition is needed (usually *to* or *for*). Examples:
She lent £500 to her sister.
She showed her holiday photographs to her friend.
This happens particularly when the direct object is a very short word, for example a pronoun:
She showed them to me.

Note

Explain and *suggest* cannot be used with both patterns, but only with the pattern with a preposition. For example:

~~I suggested her a new plan.~~
I suggested a new plan to her.

~~I explained her the lesson.~~
I explained the lesson to her.

Practice

Put the following parts of sentences into the right order, adding the preposition *to* or *for* if it is necessary. Two solutions may be possible in some cases. The first one has been done for you. Check your answers with a partner.

a) bought/grandmother/Sophie/an ice cream
   Grandmother bought Sophie an ice cream. or
   Grandmother bought an ice cream for Sophie.
b) lend/you/me/it/can?
c) the problem/explain/he/the client
d) I/you/it/owe
e) the car/grandfather/a lot of money/cost
f) another idea/suggested/she/him
g) the person who helped me/sent/I/some flowers
h) made/her daughter/a doll's house/she

LEARNING GRAMMAR

Diagnosis

Expressing contrast

1 Read the paragraph below and work with a partner to underline the contrast words. Two examples have been done for you. Check your answers in the Key.

<u>Although</u> Bill and Bob were not identical twins, they looked almost exactly alike. When you studied them closely, <u>however</u>, it was possible to tell them apart, for there were quite a few tiny differences. Bill had a minute scar over his left eye whereas Bob did not. Bob had neat flat ears but Bill's stuck out a little. Despite these distinctive marks, people often mistook one for the other. Though Bill and Bob were very serious-minded young men, they did enjoy confusing people. So Bob would sometimes go on a date with Bill's girlfriend, while Bill would sometimes go into Bob's office. Friends knew that the terrible twins were likely to get up to tricks, yet they were often taken in all the same. One day, Bob fell desperately in love with Anna. In spite of the fact that he was sure it was 'the real thing' and he wanted to marry her, he couldn't resist having a bet with Bill. Bill was to win the bet if he went on a date with Anna without her realising that he wasn't Bob. Bob was fairly certain he would win. Nevertheless, he waited apprehensively. But Anna was taken in like everybody else, and had a wonderful evening with Bill, thinking that he was Bob. When she found out what happened, she was not amused. However, she soon got her sense of humour back - and sent her own identical twin on the next date with Bob.

2 Look back at the words you have underlined and write them on the chart below. Two examples have been done for you. Check your answers with your partner and use the Key to help you if necessary.

Conjunctions linking two parts of a sentence both with a main verb	Preposition and a noun	Adverb contrasting the ideas in one sentence with the ideas of another
although		*however*

Unit 10

3 With your partner, decide which of the contrast words you are more likely to use in spoken English and which in written English. Check your answers in the Key.

4 Link each of the following pairs of sentences in a different way using a preposition, an adverb or *although/though*. There is more than one answer and the first one has been done for you. Compare your sentences with a partner's. If you have not written the same thing, is one version more concise or elegant than the other, or are they simply two different ways of saying the same thing?

a) It was raining. We had a picnic.
   Although it was raining, we had a picnic.
   We had a picnic in spite of the rain.
b) I know her well. There are many things about her that I don't understand.
c) Your offer is very generous. I can't accept it.
d) She didn't have much money. She decorated her home beautifully.
e) He left school at sixteen. He was extremely well read.
f) There was a risk of another explosion. The rescue workers continued to look for survivors.

▶ Development ◀◀◀

Contrast: difference or surprise?

1 Expressions of contrast can simply express a difference between two sets of facts or ideas. In this case we use *but*, *whereas*, *while*, or *however*. Examples:

a) She would like a beach holiday in the West Indies, whereas/but he would like to go to the mountains.
b) i) Employment figures are up, whereas/while inflation figures are down.
   ii) Employment figures are up. However, inflation figures are down.

2 Sometimes one set of facts is surprising when contrasted with another. In this case, we generally use *although*, *though*, *even though*, *in spite of*, etc. Examples:

a) Though/although it generally rains a lot in Scotland, at the moment there is a drought.
b) Even though she is only twelve, she is already taller than her mother.
c) We bought a new television in spite of the fact that we couldn't really afford it.

3 Sometimes it is difficult to tell whether the contrast is to do with difference or surprise, or it doesn't matter. In this case, you can use either type of contrast word. Examples:

| The main crop in the United States is corn, | although whereas | in Brazil, it is coffee. |

| Sarah has brown eyes, | although whereas but | the rest of the family has blue eyes. |

Practice

Correct the following sentences where necessary. Check your answers with a partner.

a) Whereas I knew Paris well, I got lost.
   Although I knew Paris well, I got lost.
b) The weather will be fine in most places, although coastal areas may have a little drizzle.
c) I like coffee, in spite of the fact that Sally likes tea.
d) Travelling by plane is fast, although travelling by train is pleasant too.
e) The coastal road is more scenic, while the motorway is quicker.
f) A lot of apples are grown in England, although a lot of citrus fruits are grown in Spain.
g) In Europe it often snows on Christmas day whereas in Australia, people go to the beach on 25th December.

Different uses of *though*

1 Study the following pairs of sentences with a partner and decide whether in each case there is a difference of meaning, register (formal/informal, spoken/written) or grammatical structure.

a) i) Even though he hadn't eaten for days, he still looked strong and healthy.
   ii) Though he hadn't eaten for days, he still looked strong and healthy.
b) i) Difficult though it was, it wasn't impossible.
   ii) Though it was difficult, it wasn't impossible.
c) i) Pleased though I was with the results, I did not intend to raise the employees' salaries.
   ii) Pleased as I was with the results, I did not intend to raise the employees' salaries.
d) i) It rained every day. We had a good time, though.
   ii) Though it rained every day, we had a good time.
e) i) There are several ways of treating the problem. The best way, though, is simply to ignore it.
   ii) Though there are several ways of treating the problem, the best way is simply to ignore it.
f) i) She said she won't come. She might change her mind, though.
   ii) She said she won't come. She might change her mind, all the same.

2 With a partner, look back at the examples in Exercise 1 and decide whether the following statements are true or false.

a) *Although* can always replace *though*.
b) *Though* can always replace *although*.
c) *Although* can only replace *though* when it is a conjunction.

3 With a partner, study the following pairs of sentences and decide which ones are alternative ways of saying the same thing and which ones mean something completely different.

a) i) Even though we could afford it, we wouldn't go.
   ii) Even if we could afford it, we wouldn't go.
b) i) Even though she had a lot of money, she wasn't happy.
   ii) For all her money she wasn't happy.
c) i) Even though I admire her, I wouldn't like to be her.
   ii) Much as I admire her, I wouldn't like to be her.
d) i) She behaved as if she wasn't listening.
   ii) She behaved as though she wasn't listening.
e) i) He is very old. He's very active, though.
   ii) He is very old. Still, he's very active.

Practice

1 Rewrite the sentences below with the prompts provided, changing the meaning as little as possible. The first one has been done for you. Check your answers with a partner.

a) Even though we took a lot of trouble, we didn't succeed. (*For all . . .*)
   For all our trouble, we didn't succeed.
b) Even though I love ice cream, I refused the dish I was offered. (*Much . . .*)
c) In spite of many hours of training, the team didn't win the championship. (*Though . . .*)
d) I could change my job, but I don't want to move. (*Even . . .*)
e) We haven't got the time, but if we had, we wouldn't do it anyway. (*Even . . .*)
f) Even though we spent a lot of time on the research, we didn't get much of a result. (*For all . . .*)
g) It won't make any difference if the sun isn't shining, because we'll still have the picnic. (*We'll still have the picnic . . .*)

2 Complete the following sentences so that they make sense. Check your answers with a partner.

a) Difficult though it was, the exam . . . .
   Difficult though it was, the exam *was very fair.*
b) Freezing though it was, we . . . .
c) High . . . , we climbed to the top of the mountain.
d) For all his intelligence, ...
e) Tired as I was, ...
f) Much . . . to help, I'm afraid I'm too busy.
g) The lecture was very long. . . . , though.

SPEAKING

Contrasting opinions

1 Work with a partner. Express contrasting opinions on the moral judgements below. Student A begins by supporting the statement with reasons or examples while student B expresses reservations. Student B supports the next statement and student A expresses reservations, and so on. Examples:

a) If you see someone shoplifting, you should tell the manager and get the person arrested.
   STUDENT A: *Shoplifting is dishonest. It makes prices more expensive for all.*
   STUDENT B: *Admittedly, it's dishonest. However, the shoplifter might be desperately in need. And there are other cases where the shoplifter isn't criminal but suffering from some kind of illness.*

b) If you find something like an expensive camera in a public place, you are perfectly entitled to keep it.
   STUDENT B: *People who are careless with their possessions deserve to lose them.*
   STUDENT A: *Of course people should be careful with their possessions. But it can happen to anyone. And the camera might have a film of great sentimental value in it. You should give it in to the authorities.*

c) Even if you are very hungry and have no money, stealing food is wrong.

d) If you find a wallet which obviously belongs to somebody wealthy, you are quite justified in keeping it.

e) It is immoral to use your company's phone for private phone calls.

f) You shouldn't give money to beggars.

2 In groups discuss other moral dilemmas.

a) You've accepted a date when someone you really like calls and asks you out for the same night. Do you try and get out of the first date?

b) After looking for work for six months, you get a good offer from a large weapons maker. Do you accept it?

c) You come across the diary of someone near to you. Do you read it?

d) You discover that your brother is selling top secret government information to a foreign power. Do you turn him in?

Report your discussion to the rest of the class.

Section 3

VOCABULARY

Idioms

1 The following idioms all contain allusions to families or can be used to talk about families or friends. Match each idiom in column A to its meaning in column B. If you are not sure, check in your dictionary or with your teacher.

A	B
a) chip off the old block	1 difference in ideas and attitudes between old and young people
b) different as chalk from cheese	2 member of the same family
c) sugar daddy	3 person who is very like one of his or her parents
d) generation gap	4 extremely friendly
e) blood is thicker than water	5 family ties are stronger than friendship
f) flesh and blood	6 a rich, older man who gives a young woman money and presents in return for companionship, etc.
g) thick as thieves	7 very dissimilar

2 Complete the gaps in the sentences below with one of the idioms above. The first one has been done for you. Check your answers with a partner.

a) Children often listen to the same music as their parents today, which never used to be the case and means there is much less of a *generation gap* than there was 25 years ago.

b) It's very hard to believe they are twins as they're . . . .

c) If you invited Julia, you had to invite Jenny too, as they were . . . and did absolutely everything together.

d) When her best friend died, she looked after her daughter as if she were . . . .

e) Isn't he like his dad! A real . . . .

3 With a partner decide on a mime to illustrate one of the idioms.

a) Do your mime for another group. Can they guess which expression you are miming?
b) Do you know any other family idioms or sayings? Are there any in your own language? Explain them to other people in your class.

British and American vocabulary

1 Check you know the English equivalent of the following American words or expressions from the passage in Section 1. Work them out from the context, ask other people in your class or look them up in a dictionary.

a) I turned eighteen
b) cracker cartons
c) regular
d) grocery store
e) stock work
f) June bugs

2 In column A there are some very common American words. Can you match them with their British equivalent in column B? Use a dictionary to help you.

A	B
a) sidewalk	1 torch
b) hood (of a car)	2 autumn
c) fall	3 tap
d) flashlight	4 bonnet
e) gas (for cars)	5 public toilet
f) closet	6 pavement
g) faucet	7 cupboard
h) restroom	8 petrol

3 In the following mini-dialogues, which speaker is British and which is American? Explain the misunderstandings.

a) A: Is there a restroom here?
   B: No, I don't think so. Why? Are you feeling tired?
b) A: On my way home, I was knocked down on the pavement!
   B: Serves you right! You should have been on the sidewalk.
c) A: I hurt my back in the fall.
   B: Oh, I didn't know you'd had a fall. Where did you fall from?
d) A: We need a torch to see what we are doing in the cellar.
   B: But we might set the house on fire!

4 With a partner, write a similar dialogue on a misunderstanding with one of the other words from Exercise 2. Read other students' dialogues.

WRITING

Mini sagas

A mini saga is a complete story in not more than fifty words. Read this example from the *Sunday Telegraph* mini saga competition.

> *Grandmama's story of how her father married her mother in 1861*
>
> Exams passed, Leonard set out to request Theresa's hand. At the Inn, he met his best friend, who confided: 'I intend to propose to Theresa!' Leonard said nothing, but arrived first and was accepted. Told years later, she said: 'I had always loved only you!' But did he do right?

to do right: to do what is morally acceptable

1 What do you think of Leonard's behaviour? Would you have done the same thing? Discuss your ideas briefly with other people in your class.

2 It is quite difficult to write a story so concisely! The author of the story above probably wrote his first draft something like this:

> When Leonard had passed his exams, he set out to request the hand of Theresa, the woman he loved. On the way he stopped at an Inn where he often used to go and met his best friend. As they were drinking together, his friend confided that he was intending to propose to Theresa. Leonard said nothing but soon hurried on his way. By the time his friend reached Theresa's house, Leonard had already proposed and she had accepted. When she was told of what had happened many years later, she said 'I had always loved only you!' But Leonard often wondered if he had done the right thing, and never had quite the same relationship with his best friend again.

Study both versions of the story. What has been changed or left out to make the story shorter? Which version of the story do you prefer? Why?

3 Write a draft of a mini saga about a family (or about your own family) in about 150 words.

4 Exchange stories with another student. Reduce your partner's story to a real mini saga of 50 words. After your first draft, consult your partner. Is he or she satisfied with the result? If not, improve it together.

5 Have a mini saga competition. Read other people's stories and vote for the one you prefer.

UNIT 11

Living in colour

Section 1

SPEAKING AND READING

1 What moods and emotions do you usually associate with colours?

a) Fill in the grid opposite.
b) Compare your associations with a partner's. Add as many different associations as you can.

Colour	Moods or emotions
red	anger
green	
blue	
yellow	

c) What moods and emotions do you associate with other colours?

2 The following quiz is taken from the book *The Colours of Your Mind*. In it, the authors show that using colours to label our thought processes can help us understand the workings of our minds, our behaviour, emotions and intellect. For example, we can use red for facts and realities, blue for judgement and opinions, green for ingenuity and imagination. Read the six blocks of questions in the quiz. How much do you agree or disagree with each statement? Discuss your answers with a partner.

a watertight rationale: a very strong, logical argument, which it is impossible to question
hunch: an idea that is found intuitively rather than rationally

THE COLOUR CHART

Quiz questions

BLOCK ONE
If I could choose the problems I had to tackle, my preference would be to:
1 investigate something that has gone wrong.
2 think up all sorts of possible ways to achieve an outcome.
3 evaluate the best way forward from a number of possibilities.

BLOCK TWO
If I am going to buy something:
4 I keep my mind open for opportunities and delightful surprises.
5 I systematically find out what products are available before deciding what I want.
6 I won't even start looking until I really know why I want the product.

BLOCK THREE
The best way for me to deal with an argument or some other conflict is to:
7 seek a way out that is so ingenious it takes the others by surprise and reveals an entirely new dimension.
8 try to prove a water-tight rationale, and show how well my case makes sense.
9 find out what information we have in common and what is different between us, perhaps looking for a more suitable form of expression.

BLOCK FOUR
In times of pressure or crisis, I am in my element when:
10 coming down to things that matter.
11 getting at what needs to be known and putting that across.
12 coming up with an unusual angle on the subject.

BLOCK FIVE
When I need to plan, I like to start with:
13 taking stock and looking at all the data I can easily lay my hands on.
14 feeling my way into the scene, listening to any hunches and intuitions.
15 identifying and naming the main headings.

BLOCK SIX
When anyone asks me to do something for them, I like it best when:
16 they tell me the scale of it — roughly right but fast, or in detailed perfection.
17 I have to find my own ways around awkward aspects of the task.
18 they tell me what matters to them, and ensure I can work with the same kind of aim.

3 Now fill in your answers for each block of questions on the questionnaire. If you agree with only one statement, give it 10 points and the other two 0.

If all three statements reflect your ways of thinking equally, distribute the points as equally as possible: 3, 3, 4.

If you like one statement a lot and didn't feel strongly about the other two, score 6, 2, 2.

If you dislike one statement but agreed equally with the other two, score 0, 5, 5.

Discuss your answers with a partner.

4 Transfer your scores onto the colour score chart below. Put your scores next to the appropriate question number from each block. (Every number should have a score, even if it is 0.) Add up each column and calculate your total.

COLOUR SCORE CHART

Block	Questions		
BLOCK ONE	3	1	2
BLOCK TWO	6	5	4
BLOCK THREE	8	9	7
BLOCK FOUR	10	11	12
BLOCK FIVE	15	13	14
BLOCK SIX	18	16	17
Totals	Blue	Red	Green

5 Now read the analysis of each of your thinking colours according to your totals.

ANALYSIS

40 and over You overuse this Colour, relying on it to the detriment of the other Colours.
30 – 39 This Colour often dominates your thinking.
20 – 29 You should be able to use this Colour as and when needed.
10 – 19 You tend to underuse this Colour in your vocabulary of thinking skills.
under 10 You probably avoid this Colour, maybe to the point of neglect.

▶ Green is the code for the unknown, the as-yet-unrealised future, the possibilities that may or may not materialise. When you are green you are uncommitted to action, just using your mind to throw ideas around which you may or may not pick up and use. All new ideas spring from green thinking. It is divergent, lateral, imaginative, out-of-the-ordinary; Green thinking disturbs the status quo, and so unfortunately can go off at half-cock and be misunderstood and suppressed. But Green is also fun and the fountain of creativity.

▶ Red is the colour for 'what is true', what is already known and what has already happened. This is the thinking that finds out, seeks out information about the world, about people, about things. It collects facts and figures, and organises them in an orderly way. Poetry, dance and novels have the colour Red at their roots, which finds expression in descriptive images to convey the truth of experience and emotion. Red thinking is the Colour of communication. It embodies our desires to be in touch with one another and to co-operate by the exchange of information of all kinds.

▶ Blue is the code of 'coming to judgement', for making up your mind, for deciding. Blue thinking makes choices, gives opinions, has views on things. Blue requires personal values and beliefs to be brought to bear in choices, yet uses a framework of logic and straightforward reasoning to do so. We get things done through Blue thinking. It draws Red and Green together, determining what kinds of idea and information will be relevant. The Blue must weigh it all up.

lateral thinking: creative thinking which makes unexpected associations, as opposed to linear thinking which solves problems in a step-by-step approach
the status quo: the present and well established situation
go off at half-cock: misfire or go wrong, through lack of adequate preparation and prethought

Unit 11

VOCABULARY

Word formation

1 You can increase your ability to recognise new words by becoming more aware of how words go together with other words and with prefixes and suffixes to make up other words.

a) Find the 'parts' in the following:
  i) the noun in *embody*
  ii) the verb in *statement, judgment, measurement*
  iii) the two nouns in *framework*
  iv) the adjectives in *aloofness, reality, creativity*

b) *-ness* and *-ity (-ty)* are suffixes that can be used to turn an adjective into a noun. Fill in the chart below with the adjectives in the box, according to whether they can be made into a noun by adding *-ness* or *-ity /-ty*, or neither. Use your dictionary to check your answers. Note that the spelling of the root word may change when a suffix is added.

| stupid cruel funny sad exciting |
| open opposite safe light fresh |
| futile brief |

-ness	-ity/-ty	neither

2 In the quiz analysis there are two examples of compound adjectives: *out-of-the-ordinary* and *as-yet-unrealised*.

a) Work with a partner to make some more common ones from the box below using each word once. Use your dictionary to help you.

| matter of down fact earth date |
| out of up to to bounds out |
| date of |

b) Write sentences using your new adjectives correctly.

3 In small groups, discuss the following questions.

a) What other difficulties have you had with word formation?
b) What solutions have you found when you come across such words when you are reading or when you try to learn such words?

TALKING EFFECTIVELY

Sounds and spelling

1 The spelling *ough* can be pronounced in a variety of ways.

a) With a partner read aloud the words in the box and then match them to the words with which they rhyme in the list below. The first one has been done for you.

| thought enough cough through |
| plough thorough dough |

  i) stuff *enough*   iv) duller
  ii) oft   v) how
  iii) port   vi) blue
                        vii) toe

b) [11.1] Listen and check your answers.
c) Use your dictionary and write down the phonetic symbols for each sound above.
d) Now decide which sound the following words match. Check your answers in a dictionary. Example: *'nought' rhymes with 'port'*

| nought bough tough borough |
| sought rough wrought |

2 The spelling *ow* can be pronounced either /aʊ/ as in *how* or /əʊ/ as in *know*.

a) Work with a partner to list the words in the box under the phonetic symbol /aʊ/ or /əʊ/.

| show brow tow mow bow |
| vow row |

b) [11.2] Listen and check your answers. Which are the two words that can be pronounced either way according to their meaning?
c) Now list these words according to the sound /aʊ/ or /əʊ/. Check your answers. Be careful: one word has two pronunciations.

| glow glower pow-wow dowdy |
| rowan tree sow frown flow |
| rowdy |

3 Work with a partner to write sentences with some of the words in Exercises 1 and 2 which have at least two words with the same vowel sound. For example:
The conversation flowed and the faces glowed.

Section 2

LEARNING GRAMMAR

▶ Diagnosis ◀◀◀

It and *there*

1 Work with a partner. In each set of three sentences below only one is correct. Write *C* against the correct sentence. Correct the other sentences. The first one has been done for you. Check your answers in the Key.

a) i) She enjoyed the film although was a bit long.
   She enjoyed the film although it was a bit long.
   ii) She unpacked the vase and put it on the sideboard. *C*
   iii) Have some chocolate. No thanks, I don't like.
   Have some chocolate. No thanks, I don't like it.

b) i) 'Joe Cocker is giving a concert at the end of the month.' 'I know it.'
   ii) 'Even Julie's coming to the concert.' 'I don't believe it.'
   iii) 'It'll be a good concert.' 'I know it.'

c) i) The book is on the shelf.
   ii) My aunt she is coming to visit next week.
   iii) It is very funny the film.

d) i) There rained for three days.
   ii) There's a long way to the nearest garage.
   iii) It's late.

e) i) It remains nothing more to be said.
   ii) In a far off country, there lived a beautiful princess in a magnificent castle.
   iii) It is someone at the door.

2 With your partner, write a rule for the use of *it* or *there* for each set of sentences. Use the guidelines in the Key to help you if necessary. The first one has been done for you.
a) *When the pronoun 'it' is the subject or object of a sentence, it should not normally be omitted.*

Common idiomatic uses of *it* and *there*

3 Work with a partner.

a) Complete the gaps in the following sentences with *it* or *there*. There is one example in which you can use either *it* or *there*. The first one has been done for you. Check your answers in the Key.
   i) *There's* no sense in hurrying.
   ii) . . . doesn't make sense to buy a new car.
   iii) . . .'s no use phoning her. She won't be in.
   iv) . . .'s someone sitting here. They've just gone to get a coffee.
   v) . . .'s a shame Joan's not here.
   vi) . . . takes a long time to get there.
   vii) . . .'s no point in talking to her about it.
   viii) . . . doesn't matter what you wear to the party.
   ix) . . .'s a pity you can't come.
   x) . . .'s no need to shout.

b) With your partner, look back at the sentences in a) and complete the two lists below.

A	B
Expressions with *it*	Expressions with *there*
It doesn't make sense	There's no sense . . .

Unit 11

▶ Development ◀◀◀

It, *this* and *that*: referring backwards and forwards

1 With a partner, study the pairs of sentences below and underline what the pronouns *it*, *this* or *that* refer to in each one. If what you have underlined comes after the pronoun, write *F* (*Forwards*) and if it comes before, write *B* (*Backwards*). The first one has been done for you.

a) i) Is it not irrational <u>for pupils studying History or French to lose all touch with the sciences in the VIth form?</u>
   ii) Most boys and girls studying History or English lose all touch with the sciences in the VIth form. This/That is not rational.
b) i) Speaker A: 'I was there at the time.'
      Speaker B: 'That was lucky.'
   ii) Speaker A: 'It was lucky being there at the time.'
c) i) Most people are fated to spend most of their lives in jobs that do not excite them. This/That is intolerable, as is the fact that their schooldays are a mere preliminary to this.
   ii) If most people are fated to spend most of their lives in jobs that do not excite them, it is not tolerable that their schooldays be a mere preliminary to this.
d) i) 'Are they really worth the money?' This/That was always the commonest Republican complaint about the British monarchy.
   ii) It seems that the commonest complaint about the British monarchy is the question 'Are they really worth the money?'

2 Cross out the false information in the statements below about the use of *it*, *this* and *that* when they refer to noun clauses and sentences. Check your answers with a partner.

a) It usually refers/does not usually refer forward to a whole sentence or clause.
b) *This* or *that* is generally used/is not generally used to refer back to a whole sentence.

Practice

Complete the gaps in the following paragraph with *it*, *this* or *that*. The first one has been done for you. Check your answers with a partner.

> Today people's behaviour is analysed constantly by psychologists. I do not think (a)*this* is a good idea. Although (b)..... is essential for us to use the knowledge that modern science has revealed in order to further progress, we should not be overzealous in the study of human beings. (c)..... is important to keep our spontaneity and freedom of action and we cannot do (d)..... if we feel we are continually being observed under a microscope. (e)..... is in any case doubtful whether psychologists' experiments can be called scientific. They are not carried out in laboratory conditions and the results are not reliable. For some people (f)..... is regrettable. They would like to see human behaviour explained with the same scientific accuracy as nuclear fission. However, as far as I am concerned, (g)..... is extraordinary and wonderful that there are still a few unexplained mysteries in the universe.

Using *it* with delayed subjects

1 The reasons for using *it* with delayed subjects (information which comes later in the sentence) are:

a) In comments on a fact, event or situation, the focus of the sentence is on the adjective which expresses an attitude. For example:
   i) *It is essential to understand the basic points.* (The attitude 'it is essential' is more important to the speaker than the understanding.)
   ii) *Understanding the basic points is essential.* (The understanding is more important to the speaker than the attitude.)
b) To avoid *that* clauses, *wh-* clauses, base forms and *-ing* clauses as the subject of a sentence, as this can be inelegant or awkward. For example:
   i) *That she left home eventually was amazing.* (slightly awkward though possible if the focus of information is on leaving home.)
   ii) *It was amazing that she eventually left home.* (more spontaneous, particularly if the focus of information is on 'amazing'.)
c) As an alternative structure which can be used to add variety in spoken or written English.

2 *It* can be used with delayed subjects in sentences with different patterns. With a partner, study the patterns below and match them to the examples in Exercise 1 in the section: *It, this* and *that*: referring backwards and forwards. The first one has been done for you.
Sentence a) i) matches pattern d) (in the interrogative form).

a) It + to be + ADJECTIVE + that + CLAUSE
   It   was   amazing   that she eventually left home.
b) It + to be + ADJECTIVE + *wh- + CLAUSE
   It   was   amazing   when she left home.
c) It + to be + ADJECTIVE + BASE FORM
   It   was   amazing   to see her leave home.
d) It + to be + ADJECTIVE + -ing FORM
   It   was   amazing   seeing her leave home.
e) It + VERB + that + CLAUSE
   It   appears (that)   she eventually left home.

*This pattern can also be used with *Why, What, How,* and *Who*.

Practice

1 With a partner study the differences between the following pairs of sentences and decide which sentence would be most likely in spoken English by answering the following questions:

a) Which sentence is more elegant?
b) In which sentence is the action more important than the attitude?
c) In which sentence is the attitude more important than the action?

You may not agree with your partner, and you may decide that the event and the action are equally important. The first one has been done for you.

a) i) That the mistake has not been noticed before is strange.
   ii) It is strange that the mistake hasn't been noticed before.
   ii) is more likely as i) is clumsy, unless the speaker attaches special importance to 'the mistake'.
b) i) To see you again was really nice.
   ii) It was really nice to see you again.
c) i) To drop out of the competition would be awful at this late stage.
   ii) It would be awful to drop out of the competition at this late stage.
d) i) Climbing Everest completely alone would be exciting.
   ii) It would be exciting climbing Everest completely alone.

2 Rewrite the following sentences beginning with *it*. The first one has been done for you. Check your answers with a partner.

a) Teaching children in hospital must be difficult.
   It must be difficult teaching children in hospital.
b) Living on a nurse's salary is really hard.
c) That nobody was prepared to help the refugees was shocking.
d) Seeing the actual Hollywood film set was extraordinary.
e) Whether we could have won is doubtful.
f) That she should ultimately change her mind seems obvious.

3 Work in small groups to ask and answer questions about attitudes to events, situations and facts from the world around you using *it* and one of the adjectives from the box. Use each adjective only once. For example:

a) *Is it essential that governments pass laws to protect the environment?*
   Yes, and it is surprising that so few laws have been passed so far.
b) *Isn't it wonderful to see the changing seasons?*
   Yes, it's lovely when spring comes.

amazing	awful	bad	doubtful
essential	extraordinary	funny	good
important	inevitable	interesting	likely
lucky	obvious	possible	probable	sad
strange	surprising	true	unlikely
wonderful			

Report back some of your group's comments to the rest of the class.

LANGUAGE PATTERNS

Verbs followed by *it*

It is used in the following cases:

a) with the verbs *find*, *make* and *think* with an adjective:
   i) SUBJECT + VERB + *it* + ADJECTIVE + *that/when* + CLAUSE
      I   find   it   strange   that she didn't come.
   ii) SUBJECT + VERB + *it* + ADJECTIVE + *to* + BASE FORM
       I   find   it   difficult   to make up my mind.

b) with *like, hate, loathe, enjoy, can't stand, can't bear*, etc.:
   SUBJECT + VERB + *it* + *when* + CLAUSE
   She   hates   it   when I drive too fast.

c) With the verbs *owe, leave, take* and *put*, used in the following idiomatic way:
   i) SUBJECT + VERB + *it* + *to* + PERSONAL PRONOUN + *to* + BASE FORM
      I   owe   it   to   her   to   tell her the truth.
      I   'll leave it   to   you   to   lock up.
   ii) SUBJECT + VERB + *it* + *that* + CLAUSE
       I   take   it   that   you are all coming on Saturday.
   iii) SUBJECT + VERB + *it* + *to* + PERSONAL PRONOUN + *that* + CLAUSE
        I   put   it   to   you   that   it's the best idea we've ever had.

Practice

1 With a partner, put *it* in the following sentences where necessary.

a) Sarah hates when the music is too loud.
   Sarah hates it when the music is too loud.
b) I don't know when the elections will be.
c) I found embarrassing to be asked to give a speech.
d) The plaster on my broken leg made impossible to walk.
e) I cannot bear to go out in the dark.
f) I love when it snows.
g) You'll make easier if you do it this way.

2 Complete the following sentences about yourself.

I think it important that . . .   I hate it when . .
I find it essential to . . .   I like it when . . .
I find it difficult to . . .   I wouldn't like it if . . .
I find it embarrassing to . . .   I take it that . . .
I owe it to myself to . . .

Now swap your sentences with a partner. Is anything that he or she has written particularly interesting or surprising? Ask and answer questions about your sentences.

Section 3

READING

Read the poem. Make any comment you like about it to the rest of your class.

> WHAT COLOR IS LONELY?
>
> Since you wrote a poem
> explaining
> the color of Black –
> and I know that I am Black
>   Blacker
>   and Blackless sometimes,
>
> Tell me sister,
> What color is lonely
>
> Is it/am I blue
> when I been hearin the
> Epics sing "Uh Very sad Story"
> ova & ova &
> can't stand tuh hear it anymo-
>
> Is it/am I red
> when uh brotha half hits because
> he's uh 150% player -
>
> Is it/am I green
> when I see two nappy heads
> growin into each otha -
> Is it/am I Black on Black
>
> when I sit for hours that
> trickle befo me like unfreezin water
> & I write poems about Black Unity –
>
> Since you wrote a poem explaining
> the sweet changes we are as Blacks
> and I know how various yet
> unchanging
> Blackness is,
>
> Tell me sister,
> What color is lonely?
>
> (by Carolyn M. Rodgers)
>
> *nappy*: with very curly hair

MINI-PROJECT

The Colour Museum

1 Study the leaflet about the Colour Museum in Bradford. With a partner discuss the following questions.

a) Look at the plate of food. How does colour change our perception of it?
b) What would a world without colour be like?
c) How do colour-blind people see the world?
d) Are some countries more 'colourful' than others? How colourful is your country?
e) Have some periods in history been more colourful than others?
f) There are exhibits in the museum which show how colour looks to a dog, a fish or a bee. Can you imagine how they might perceive colour?
g) In small groups, look at the colours in your present surroundings for a moment or so. Describe them to each other. Be as precise as possible about shades and intensity. Do you agree, or are there significant differences?

Discuss your impressions and decide whether we all perceive colour in the same way.

2 Imagine you are employees of the Colour Museum. It is your job to design a new series of exhibits for the coming year. Work in a small group to design an exhibit.

a) Decide whether you would like to display colour through:
   i) clothes and materials
   ii) food
   iii) interior design
   iv) the colours in the natural world
   v) your own choice of topic
b) Plan your exhibit in detail. Write descriptions of your proposed exhibits, or prepare a sound commentary if you have a cassette recorder.
c) One of your group presents the project to the rest of the class. If possible, make a poster display of your ideas.

COLOUR MUSEUM

An Educational Activity of the Society of Dyers and Colourists

Telephone (0274) 390955
Perkin House, 82 Grattan Road
Bradford, BD1 2JB

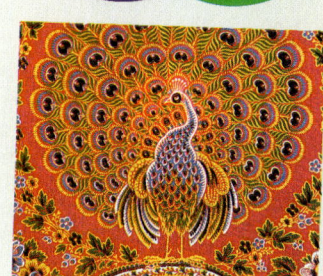

**What is colour? Why is it so important?
How do we use colour?
Would you eat a plateful of blue food? Why not?
What is Turkey Red fabric?**

The SDC's award winning Colour Museum in Britain's only museum of colour. It answers these and many more questions about our colourful world.

The museum consists of two galleries, both of which are packed with visitor operated exhibits.

The World of Colour
This gallery looks at the concept of colour, how it is perceived and how it is used. You can see how the world looks to a dog, a fish or a bee, mix coloured lights and experience strange colour illusions.

Colour and Textiles
In this gallery the fascinating story of dyeing and textile printing, from ancient Egypt to the present day, is examined. You can also use some of the latest computerised technology to take charge of a dye making factory, or to test the colour of any material.

UNIT 12

The quality of animal life

Section 1

SPEAKING AND LISTENING

Caviar

Oysters

Foie gras

Champagne

1 Work in small groups. Discuss the following questions.

a) What do these food items have in common?
b) How many of them have you tasted? What did you think of them?
c) How much would they cost in your country?
d) If you were allowed to choose a menu with anything you liked on it, would you put any of these on it? If not, what would you put on it?
e) What do you know about the way any of the items are made?

2 [12.1] Listen to two people talking about the making of foie gras.

a) Which speaker, *Speaker 1* or *Speaker 2*, expresses which of the following opinions? If neither speaker expresses the opinion, write *N* (*Neither*). The first one has been done for you.
  i) Force-feeding geese is not cruel. *Speaker 2*
  ii) Force-feeding geese is extremely cruel and should be stopped.
  iii) Force-feeding geese is unnatural.
  iv) Geese which are force-fed live normally.
  v) Force-feeding geese is no worse and no better than many things that human beings do to each other.
  vi) Force-feeding makes geese suffer enormously.

b) Listen to the tape again. Note down words and expressions which justify your answers. Compare your notes with a partner.

3 Listen to the first speaker again. Which picture represents the way he says geese are raised?

A   B

C   D

4 Listen to the second interview again and answer the following questions.

a) When the speaker says 'people don't know the backside of a badger from that of an Aylesbury duck', he means that:
  i) people don't realise what they're eating.
  ii) people are generally ignorant about country matters.
  iii) people can only recognise animals from the front.
b) The speaker talks about people working in department stores in order to show that:
  i) the concept 'natural' or 'unnatural' is not appropriate in the modern world.
  ii) human beings are cruel to each other.
  iii) people don't notice their surroundings.
c) The speaker says that 'unhappy' animals:
  i) do not reproduce.
  ii) catch diseases.
  iii) have neurotic behaviour.
d) The expressions 'in inverted commas "happy"' and 'the no doubt very keen MP for Durham' are examples of:
  i) strong feeling.
  ii) sincerity.
  iii) irony.

Check your answers with a partner.

5 Discuss the following questions.

a) Which speaker do you agree with? Why?
b) Do people in your country care about the way we treat animals?
c) Are there any special measures to protect animals? If not, should there be? Can you suggest some?

Report your discussion to the rest of the class.

TALKING EFFECTIVELY

1 Listen to the beginning of the second speaker's interview again. Note the way he uses exaggerated stress on certain words and a wider range of pitch than normal. What adjectives in the box below could you use to describe the effect this has?

| unconcerned | irritated | angry | dogmatic |
| enthusiastic | calm | | |

What other adjectives would you choose to describe the way he talks?

2 [12.2] Listen to this short extract from the tape again and mark on the script below the strongly stressed words or significant changes of pitch. Two examples have been done for you.

Well there again, what on earth is natural these days? People working in department stores, in air-conditioned department stores. That isn't natural, and the French and the E.E.C. people are in many instances ahead of us in implementing regulations which ensure that animals that are kept for human food consumption do not suffer any deleterious or bad effects whatsoever.

ABOUT LANGUAGE

1 In the interview the second speaker uses the expression 'comfortable environmental surroundings' to refer to a farmyard. People often invent expressions such as these to describe things that are thought of as unpleasant. Such expressions are called euphemisms. Can you match the euphemism to its equivalent in plain English? One of them has been done for you.

A	B
a) children with special needs	1 a bloody fight
b) an environmental hiccup	2 cancer
c) improving productivity	3 a large oil spill
d) a cruel illness	4 children with severe learning difficulties
e) a slight disagreement	5 making people work harder for the same salary

2 Invent a euphemism for one of the following. Compare your ideas with a partner.

| a slum   a nuclear war   begging |
| hooliganism   traffic jam |

3 Write your own euphemism for something that you find unpleasant. Read it out to a partner. Can he or she guess what it is?

4 Read an English language newspaper. How many euphemisms can you spot? Report your findings to your class.

Section 2

LEARNING GRAMMAR

▶ Diagnosis ◀◀◀

Nouns in groups: the link with 's or s'

1 Work with a partner to decide which of the following links with 's are normal usage. Check your answers in the Key.

a) The President's assassination shocked the nation. *normal usage*
b) The lion's cage is open.
c) Have you seen today's paper?
d) The door's knob is broken.
e) They never reached the mountain's top.
f) The government's decision was unexpected.
g) England's decline began long before the war.
h) The idea's origin is unknown to me.
i) The boys' football gear is in the cupboard.

2 With your partner, look back at the examples in Exercise 1 to help you circle the categories of nouns in the box below which can normally be used with 's. Refer to the guidelines in the Key if necessary.

| people   animals   organisations |
| abstract ideas   names of countries and towns |
| expressions of time   objects |
| geographical terms (river, mountain, hill, etc.) |

3 With your partner, decide which of the following statements are true. Refer to the guidelines in the Key if necessary.

i) 's is usually preferable to an *of* structure or a noun group when talking about people and living creatures in general.
ii) 's should always be used in preference to an *of* structure or a noun group.
iii) When talking about objects it is usually preferable to use a noun group in preference to 's.
iv) 's always indicates a relationship of possession between one noun and another.
v) 's indicates several different types of relationship between one noun and another.

4 Work with your partner to correct the mistakes in the following sentences where necessary. Check your answers in the Key.

a) The car's factory workers are on strike.
b) The prisoner escape was dramatic.
c) I hate war's films.
d) Where is last month's electricity bill?
e) The Hitchcock's films are full of suspense.
f) The ceiling is covered in spider webs.
g) The soldiers were given a heroes welcome.
h) The river's banks were flooded.
i) The violinist's concert was cancelled.

Nouns in groups: understanding relationships

1 Work with a partner to decide which of the explanations matches each of the noun groups below. Use the Key to help you.

a) Shipwreck salvage operation
   i) A ship wrecked in order to salvage some kind of operation.
   ii) Some kind of operation in order to salvage a shipwreck.
b) Family leisure area
   i) An area specifically for the leisure of families.
   ii) A family who enjoys leisure in a particular area.
c) School perks tax ruling
   i) A school where you get perks in the form of taxes to do with rulings.
   ii) A ruling about taxes on perks gained by people who work in schools.
d) Peace conference vote
   i) Peace which is obtained by a conference at which people voted.
   ii) A vote for or at a conference on the subject of peace.

2 Cross out the false information in the sentence below. Check your answer in the Key.

The best way to work out the meaning of a noun group is to start with the first/last noun.

3 With your partner, write explanations for the following noun groups. Check your answers in the Key.

a) Traffic management system
b) World basketball championship event
c) Heart surgery research breakthrough
d) Toll road development plan
e) Computer software information network

Development

Other ways of grouping nouns

Apart from the 's genitive there are two other common ways of putting nouns into groups.

1 A noun is used as an adjective, for example:
an iron bridge
2 Prepositional structures, for example:
the cost of living, a house in the country

Noun as adjective

a) Noun groups of this type often express two things which make up a single idea. For example: *pet shop, police spokesperson, plant food*. The first noun usually has an 'object' relationship to the noun that follows. That is to say that if we made the relationship explicit, the first noun would be the object of a preposition or a verb. The noun groups above could be expressed as: *a shop where you buy pets, a spokesperson from/for the police, food for plants*.

b) The relationship between the two nouns can be of many kinds. Look at the following examples and work with a partner to add other noun groups in each category. Look at the examples of other pairs in your class.

Relationship	Examples	Your examples
Time	afternoon tea, nightlight	
Place	London airport, kitchen cupboard	
Material	copper wire, marble table	
Function	cookery book, work schedule	
A part of the whole	car door, table leg	
Measurement	litre bottle, mile walk	

Prepositional structures

a) These are often preferred when talking about the following:
  i) A specific case rather than a general concept. Compare the following:
  I couldn't find a taxi in London. (any kind of taxi)
  I couldn't find a London taxi. (the well-known black taxi cab only found in London)
  ii) With words like *a piece of, a bit of, a slice of*, etc. which mean 'a certain quantity'. For example: *a bit of string, a slice of bread*.
  iii) With expressions with *back, front, outside, edge, top, end*, etc. For example: *the edge of the table, the front of the bus*, etc.
  There are a few common, idiomatic exceptions, for example: *a hillside, a knife edge*.

b) An *of* prepositional structure is always used to talk about containers with their contents. For example: *a box of matches* (has matches in it), *a carton of milk* (is full of milk). Compare these to the noun group structure which simply indicates the container: *a matchbox, a milk carton*.

Which noun group to choose?

It is sometimes difficult to know which of the structures above to use, as this is a very idiomatic area of English. For example, we say *leg of lamb*, but *lamb chop*. We can say *goat cheese* or *goat's cheese* but only *cow's milk* and not *cow milk*. When you want to make a noun group, you will be faced with one of the following situations.

1 The case may fit clearly into one of the categories in the guidelines above. For example: *a bookshelf, a cup of tea, Kevin's discovery*.

2 It may not matter which form you use. For example, whether people say *student accommodation, accommodation for students* or *students' accommodation* will depend on personal preferences, on whether you need to be concise or not and possibly even on the rhythm of the sentence.

3 The case may belong to the category of conventional uses which are highly idiomatic and have to be learnt as vocabulary items. For example: we can say *baby clothes* but not ~~*men wear*~~ (*men's wear*), *a dog kennel* but not ~~*a children hospital*~~ (*a children's hospital*). We usually talk about *a birdcage* but *a bird's nest, a frog's leg* but *a fox fur*.

Note

When inventing noun as adjective structures, caution is needed as sometimes they just don't 'sound English'.

Practice

1 Work with a partner to decide what the nature of the relationship is in the following noun groups.

a) a mile walk *measurement*   b) a table top
c) a coal mine   d) a bedtime story
e) a plastic wallet   f) a river bed
g) a 5p stamp   h) a bookshelf   i) office work

2 Complete the gaps in the sentences below by linking the two nouns in a noun as adjective structure or a prepositional structure as appropriate.

a) food/cat
   i) I forgot to buy some *cat food*.
   ii) Look! Somebody has walked in *the cat's food* and made a mess all over the place.
b) guide/tour
   i) I love my job as . . . .
   ii) I need . . . leaving at 9 a.m. on Friday.
c) accident/lorry
   i) John was the victim . . . last Saturday but he wasn't seriously hurt.
   ii) . . . victim claims damages.
d) fruit/bowl
   i) Is that . . . made of ceramic?
   ii) The . . . looked delicious.
e) airport/New York
   i) We're landing at . . . , but I don't know which one.
   ii) . . . is one of the busiest in the world.

3 The noun groups in the following sentences are incorrect or not appropriate in the context.

a) Work with a partner to correct them. Refer to the points above if necessary.
   i) Give me another cake piece, please. *piece of cake, Prepositional structures a) ii)*
   ii) Have you seen the today paper anywhere?
   iii) Have you seen the Sunday's paper anywhere?
   iv) I'm thirsty, I'd like a beer glass, please.
   v) I can't find the quotation I am looking for. I know it's somewhere near the page top.
   vi) Look! The leg of Susan is bleeding.
   vii) He won the race but he sprained a right-leg muscle.
   viii) The tap of the bath is leaking.
   ix) What's my job? I'm a tuner of pianos.
   x) You've given me an empty glass of milk!
b) With your partner, decide which of the noun groups would be correct in a different context.

4 With a partner, make noun groups, using the appropriate way of grouping. There may be more than one solution.

a) Today/living/standard *Today's living standard/ Today's standard of living*
b) holiday/school/scandal
c) filmgoer/companion/Halliwell
d) robbery/train/attack
e) law/Sunday/trading
f) liberation/pressure/animal/group

VOCABULARY

Multi-part verbs

1 The adverbial particle *up* can refer to direction or to the completion of an action. Work with a partner. Write *D* (*Direction*) or *C* (*Completion*) against any of the sentences which, in your opinion, contain one of those meanings. If neither of the meanings are present, or if you are not sure, write *N* (*Neither*). The first one has been done for you.

a) We've used up all our money. *C*
b) I've set up a new business.
c) The goose stretched up its neck.
d) After unsuccessfully trying to find Peta's house for a couple of hours, we ended up going straight home.
e) I picked up my pen.
f) In a fit of rage, the child tore up her painting into tiny shreds.
g) She picked up Spanish very quickly.
h) The price of petrol has gone up again.
i) Eat up quickly, please, Jimmy!
j) We must think up a good explanation for coming home so late!

Check your answers in your dictionary.

2 To what extent can knowing the meaning(s) of an adverbial particle help you work out the meaning of a multi-part verb?

3 List five multi-part verbs whose meaning is clear from the sum of the two parts and five verbs whose meaning is not clear. Compare your lists with another group. Do you agree with their lists? Examples:

Clear	Not clear
to come back	*to take to*

Unit 12

Section 3

SPEAKING

A TV debate: points of view

1 Preparation.

a) What is happening in these photos? What do they have in common?

b) [▣ 12.3] Putting a point of view forcefully. Listen to the speakers on the tape giving their opinions about the photos. What are the words and expressions which make the speakers' messages forceful? The first one has been done for you.
1 *Surely . . .*

2 Role play this situation. You are going to take part in a TV debate. Its aim is to inform the public about animal rights and the views of some active animal rights groups. Prepare your roles in small groups. Decide with your teacher which role card to prepare.

GROUP A

You are television journalists and will be presenting the debate on animal rights, with two animal rights campaigners, one extremist and one non-extremist, and a member of the police force. To help you prepare your role, read article A, *Campaign Catalogue*.

Make a list of questions you would like to ask. Questions with *What . . . ?*, *Why . . . ?* and *How . . . ?* will create a lively debate. Prepare a brief introduction to your programme and make sure you know how to introduce your guests. Plan how to stop the discussion when your teacher tells you that you only have thirty seconds left to finish the programme.

You may use your own ideas and any other information that you know. Use the expressions in Exercise 1 b) to put your opinion forcefully.

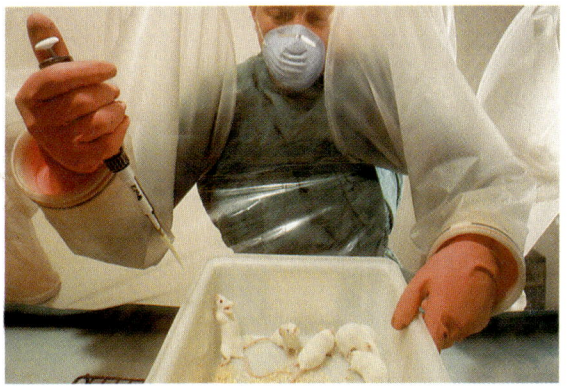

A

Campaign Catalogue

A guide to the main animal organisations and their policies.

British Union for the Abolition of Vivisection: Founded in 1898. 12,000 members. Income £800,000 last year, £500,000 of it from legacies.
Objectives: Ending animal testing and experiments altogether.
Methods: Using consumer pressure and market forces to encourage "cruelty-free" products. No longer involved in direct action or demonstrations, but places sympathisers in animal laboratory jobs to gain information.

Compassion in World Farming: Started 1967 by a former dairy farmer and his wife, Peter and Anna Roberts. 10,000 members, "growing rapidly." Last year's turnover: £100,000.
Objectives: Ending factory farming and genetic engineering of farm animals; reducing society's dependence on animal products.
Methods: Political lobbying in Westminster and Brussels, producing exhibitions, a magazine and educational material. No direct action, opposed to any law-breaking.

Lynx: Started 1985. "We don't give our membership because we don't want the fur trade to know," says the director, Ms Lynne Kentish. "We don't reveal our budget set for the same reason, but it's minimal."
Objectives: Ending the fur trade.
Methods: Advertising, campaigning, merchandising and political lobbying to make wearing fur socially unacceptable.

Animal Liberation Front: Began 1979. Activities mostly illegal. Founding a mystery. Information on membership unavailable/scarce.

Unit 12

GROUP B

You are members of the Animal Liberation Front. To help you prepare your role, read article B, *Militant decries legal protest*, and make notes on:
a) the type of activity you believe is effective.
b) practical suggestions for the protection of animals that you would like to see made legal.
c) how you see the future.

You may use your own ideas and any other information that you know. Use the expressions in Exercise 1 b) to put your opinion forcefully.

GROUP C

You are members of the British Union for the Abolition of Vivisection, Compassion in World Farming and Lynx. To help you prepare your role, read article C, *Animal rights legal protest*, and make notes on:
a) the type of activity you believe is effective.
b) practical suggestions for the protection of animals that you would like to see made legal.

You may use your own ideas and any other information that you know. Use the expressions in Exercise 1 b) to put your opinion forcefully.

GROUP D

You are members of the police force and you are responsible for law and order in an area where there has been a lot of animal rights campaigning. Read article D, *Police list 50 as terrorists*, and make notes on:
a) the type of activity you have come across.
b) the problems that you have come across when dealing with animal activists.
c) the means you have available for coping with activists and the means you would like to have.

You may use your own ideas and any other information that you know. Use the expressions in Exercise 1 b) to put your opinion forcefully.

B Militant decries legal protest

Militancy in the Animal Liberation Front earned Ms. Vivien Smith a four-year prison sentence for conspiracy in 1987. The 18 months she served were 'an interesting time to sit back and review things'. Now she helps imprisoned friends and runs an ALF newsletter. She is convinced that militant activities have reduced animal experiments. 'In the ten years since the ALF started, the number has gone down.'

A conventional-looking 27-year-old, she likens the campaign to women demanding votes or black people equal rights. 'But people are able to defend themselves; animals can't. Our aim is economic sabotage, inflicting the maximum damage to property, rescuing as many animals as we can and gaining evidence of conditions in which animals are kept. Most ALF activities are illegal, whether they are breaking and entering or criminal damage or theft. We want to put people who exploit animals out of business. Even if someone could prove that a life-saving drug came from such experiments, we should do without that drug.'

C Animal rights legal protest

SOME BRANCHES of the animal rights movement are gaining in respectability. The British Union for the Abolition of Vivisection has abandoned illegal activities in favour of promoting the sale of 'cruelty-free' products. Lynx, the group which opposes the fur trade, claims to have used advertising – principally the famous David Bailey poster of the coat trailing blood – to make fur so unfashionable and unacceptable that hardly anyone still buys it. It insists that retailers have stopped selling fur because people no longer want it rather than because of the spate of firebombs set off by the extremist movement, Animal Liberation Front.

Law-abiding campaigners say that illegal activities are counter-productive and discredit the whole movement. However, it is open to argument whether the law-abiding groups would do so well without the activities of the militants over the last ten years, shocking public opinion with photographs and documents obtained by breaking into laboratories.

D Police list 50 as terrorists

Police believe there are about 50 people prepared to use explosives, incendiaries or guns in the cause of animal rights, many of them young and well-educated with anarchist, anti-capitalist sympathies.

They are listed as terrorists because of their willingness to damage not only property, such as research laboratories and fur shops, but also to put lives at risk.

They are regarded as the extremist fringe of a general environmental movement, concerned not only about animals but also about the rainforests, pollution and the Third World.

Police say they are unpredictable, travelling long distances to carry out attacks, drifting in and out of the movement, and likely to move into respectable organisations. Officers find it hard to keep track of them and decide when to act.

A complication for police is that some of their illegal activities command public sympathy, for example when they break into a chicken farm and produce photographs of hens living in cramped conditions with their feathers pulled out.

3 When you have prepared your role, make new groups of four, one A student, one B student, one C student and one D student. Role play the situation in your groups.

4 Discuss the following questions in your groups. One member of the group makes notes and reports back the discussion to the class.

a) Which point of view seemed the most convincing?
b) How did each member of the group's participation contribute to the debate?
c) Was any member of the group particularly good at getting across his or her ideas? If so, how did he or she do it?
d) Did any good ideas emerge?
e) Other good points in your debate, or other difficulties.

WRITING

A balanced view

1 You are going to write an article about protecting animal rights. You have been given the following notes on the subject by someone who watched a recent TV debate on the subject. Before you begin to write, work with a partner to decide whether the points argue for the protection of animals or whether they argue against them or against the way they are being protected at the moment. The first two have been done for you.

a) Treating animals badly is degrading for mankind. *For*
b) Animal experimentation does not actually make animals suffer. *Against*
c) People do not need fur coats.
d) People should never use violence to achieve their ends.
e) Most of the products that are tested on animals are not really necessary.
f) The animals used for testing are treated with terrible cruelty.
g) Meat and other animal products are not necessary for a balanced diet.
h) We would not be able to cure a great many diseases if we had never experimented on animals.
i) Making sure that people have enough to eat is more important than being kind to animals.
j) Looking after animals properly contributes to the preservation and respect of our environment.
k) If people knew the conditions in which industrial farming is carried out they would stop eating meat.
l) Animals used in medical research are treated humanely.
m) Violence must be used to protect animals if governments take no notice of peaceful means of pressure.
n) Most people do not mind animals being killed for food, so why should they mind them being killed in experiments which will save lives?
o) Animal experimentation is a necessary evil.

2 Work with your partner.

a) Group together the points for and against according to topic. For example, both d) and m) relate to violent action.
b) Put your points into a logical order to make the outline of an article.
c) Work on your own to write up the notes into two or three short paragraphs, presenting a balanced view of the issues. Look back at Unit 10 to remind yourself of the contrast words you will need. Add examples or other information if you wish. Example:
Although most of the speakers agreed that any kind of violent action was unacceptable, one member of the panel argued that violent actions, for example sabotaging animal experimentation laboratories, might be the only way of drawing the matter to the public's attention.
d) Compare your paragraphs with a partner's. Can you make any suggestions for improvement?

3 Work in small groups.

a) Make a list of issues about which people campaign in your countries or in other countries you know about.
b) With a partner, select one topic and prepare to write a balanced report of it. First brainstorm a list of all the arguments for the campaign and all the arguments against it. Then group together points in your lists which relate to the same topic. Order the points into a coherent sequence, and eliminate any points which are not directly relevant. Write your report of the campaign.
c) Read other people's reports.

UNIT 13

How zany are you?

Section 1

SPEAKING AND READING

1 Work in small groups.

a) Read the following list and compare your experiences. Have you ever:
  i) got on a train going the wrong way?
  ii) started driving to the wrong destination?
  iii) got into bed with your clothes on?
  iv) tried to light an electric fire with a match?
  v) forgotten the name of someone you know well?
  vi) put something away in a particular place and forgotten where?
  vii) started to look for something and forgotten what it was that you were looking for?
  viii) done anything else strange?

b) Make a list of all the 'peculiar' actions that anyone in your group has done while their mind was on other things.

2 In small groups, discuss the following questions.

a) Do you know why we sometimes do the strange things you have listed in Exercise 1?
b) Is this kind of behaviour completely random and without any rational explanation?
c) Is one sex more likely to behave in this way than the other?
d) Are people in certain kinds of jobs more likely to behave in this kind of way?
e) Do we make more 'mistakes' of this kind when we are doing something we don't know how to do? Or do we make more when we are doing something we know how to do well?
f) Can you avoid making errors or slips of this kind by concentrating more?

3 Read the article opposite by Professor Reason. Are your ideas in Exercise 2 the same as his?

4 Study the following words and expressions in their contexts in the passage and write out what you think they mean in your own words.
a) programme assembly failures (lines 25–26)
b) test failures (line 45)
c) overshooting (lines 53–54)
d) undershoot (lines 60–61)
e) storage failures (line 66)

5 In small groups, look back at your list of 'bizarre' actions in Exercise 1. Which of the categories in Exercise 4 do they fit into?

6 Over the next week or so, note down your lapses. Mention the time of day and the circumstances, for example if you were pre-occupied. With a partner, discuss how they fit in with Professor Reason's findings.

The Zany World of Professor Reason

Professor Reason recently persuaded 35 people, 23 of them women, to keep a diary of all their absent-minded actions for a fortnight. When he came to analyse their embarrassing lapses in a scientific report, he was surprised to find that nearly all of them fell into a few groupings. Nor did the lapses appear to be entirely random.

One of the women, for instance, on leaving her house for work one morning threw her pet corgi her ear-rings and tried to fix a dog biscuit on her ear. 'The explanation for this is that the brain is like a computer,' explains the professor. 'People programme themselves to do certain activities regularly. It was the woman's custom every morning to throw her dog two biscuits and then put on her ear-rings. But somehow the action got reversed in the programme.' About one in twenty of the incidents the volunteers reported were these 'programme assembly failures.'

Altogether the volunteers logged 433 unintentional actions that they found themselves doing – an average of twelve each. There appear to be peak periods in the day when we are at our zaniest. These are two hours some time between eight a.m. and noon, between four and six p.m. with a smaller peak between eight and ten p.m. 'Among men the peak seems to be when a changeover in brain 'programmes' occurs, as for instance between going to and from work.' Women on average reported slightly more lapses – 12.5 compared with 10.9 for men – probably because they were more reliable reporters.

Twenty per cent of all errors were 'test failures' – primarily due to not verifying the progress of what the body was doing. A man about to get his car out of the garage passed through the back porch where his garden jacket and wellingtons were kept, put them on – much to his surprise. Sometimes these 'test failure' abbreviations result in the brain 'overshooting' its programme. Getting home from work tired one evening, another man went to the bedroom to take off his jacket and tie and ended up in his pyjamas.

The automatic 'stop' mechanism of the programme sequence can 'undershoot' as well, according to Reason. A woman victim reported: 'I got into the bath with my socks on.' Not surprisingly, the commonest problem, accounting for 40% of all errors, was information 'storage failures.' People forgot the name of people whose faces they knew, went into a room and forgot why they were there, mislaid something, or smoked a cigarette without realising it.

The research so far suggests that while the 'central processor' of the brain is liberated from second-to-second control of a well-rehearsed routine, it must repeatedly switch back its attention at critical decision points to check that the action has proceeded as intended. Otherwise the activity may be 'captured' by another frequently and recently used programme.

A startling finding is that the absent-minded activity is a hazard of doing things in which we are skilled. Normally, you would expect that skill reduces the number of errors we make. But trying to avoid silly slips by concentrating more could make things a lot worse — even dangerous. 'If we had to think about every single activity the brain just could not cope. For instance, you could fall if you concentrated on what your feet were doing as you were running down stairs,' says Professor Reason.

Having studied a number of aircraft accidents and near-miss inquiries, including the Trident air disaster at Heathrow in 1972, Professor Reason is struck by the number of actions of crews which were similar to absent-minded behaviour. Inquiry reports often refer to a pilot 'inadvertently' or 'inexplicably' moving a switch or a control.

(from *The Sunday Times*)

aberrations: a change away from one's usual way of thinking, usually sudden and undesirable

VOCABULARY

Multi-part verbs

1 Work with a partner to explain the following children's jokes and riddles. They are based on two different meanings of the multi-part verb. Use a dictionary to help you.

TEACHER: Anyone here quick at picking up music?
TWO PUPILS: I am, sir!
TEACHER: Right, you two, move that piano.

A: Who is always being let down by his mates?
B: A deep sea diver.

2 Put one of the multi-part verbs in the box into the jokes below.

| get over | keep in | pull together | slip on |
| help out | | | |

a) A chap goes to the doctor and says: 'Doctor, doctor, my hair's falling out. Have you got anything to . . . it . . . ?', and the doctor gives him a cigar box.
b) A: Why is a banana like a pullover?
   B: Because it's easy to . . . .
c) A: Have you heard the joke about the high wall?
   B: Yes and I'll never . . . it.
d) A man goes to the doctor and says: 'Doctor, doctor, I think I'm a pair of curtains.' The doctor says: 'Come on now, . . . yourself . . . !'
e) A: Doctor, doctor, can you . . . me . . . ?
   B: Certainly, which way did you come in?

Section 2

LEARNING GRAMMAR

▶ Diagnosis ◀◀◀

Link words

1 Underline the conjunctions in the sentences below. Work with a partner to decide whether they express reason or cause, purpose or consequence or result. The first one has been done for you.
  i) The bridge collapsed <u>because</u> it had been badly designed. *Reason*
  ii) I missed the last bus, so I had to get a taxi home.
  iii) As she was constantly late, she lost her job.
  iv) He left early so that he could catch an early train home.
  v) Since there's no chance of finding our way home, we might as well set up camp here.
  vi) It had hardly rained for months, with the result that there was a serious water shortage.
  vii) I worked hard (so as) to pass my exams.

2 Underline the prepositional phrases in the sentences below. With a partner decide whether they express reason or cause, purpose or consequence or result. The first one has been done for you.
  i) We have introduced new measures <u>for</u> improving safety in factories. *Purpose*
  ii) Owing to the rain, the match has been cancelled.
  iii) She was sick as a result of eating too many chocolates.
  iv) We have developed a new product for making plants grow faster.
  v) As a consequence of the fog, the plane was late and we missed our connection.
  vi) We won't be going on holiday this year on account of the expense.
  vii) We never go out in the day because of the heat.

3 Look back at Exercises 1 and 2 and write the conjunctions and the prepositions on the table below. Check your answers with a partner. The first one has been done for you.

	Conjunction	Prepositional phrase
Reason, cause	because as, since	
Purpose		
Result, consequence		

4 Join the pairs of sentences below, using either a conjunction or a prepositional phrase. Make any other changes that are necessary and make your sentences as concise and elegant as possible. There is more than one answer. Compare your answers with a partner.

i) I bought a giant TV screen. I wanted to watch documentaries.
ii) I didn't visit my aunt. I didn't have time.
iii) We didn't go out. The weather was too bad.
iv) I lost my money. I had to walk home.
v) We're going past your house anyway. It's no trouble to give you a lift.
vi) More people than expected came to the party. There was nothing left to eat for latecomers.

▶ Development ◀◀◀

Linking ideas: relative clauses

It is important to distinguish defining clauses from non-defining ones, as there are several important grammatical differences between them which may affect the meaning of the sentence. Study the following pair of sentences.

The Browns, who sold us their house, moved to America.
The people who sold us their house moved to America.

If you cross out the relative clause in the first example, the sentence still makes sense. The function of the clause is to add extra information. It is non-defining.

In the second sentence, if you remove the relative clause the sentence no longer makes complete sense. There is not enough information, 'Which people?', you might ask. The function of the clause is to define the people.

Defining clauses

1 Defining clauses are not usually separated from the rest of the sentence by commas or in any other way. Example:
The person who told me the way knew where you lived.
2 The relative pronoun *that* very often replaces *which* or *who* in defining clauses, particularly in conversational style. It is also often used after superlatives and the following words: *all, everything, anything, nothing.* Examples:
That was the best meal that I have ever had.
Have you got anything that will relieve my headache?
3 The relative pronoun is often left out if it is the object of the verb in the relative clause. Example:
That was the best meal I have ever had.
The relative pronoun cannot be left out if it is the subject of the clause. Example:
The friend who helped me lives down the road.
4 Defining clauses are not used when the noun is already fully defined in another way, for example by a proper name, a superlative, or a possessive. Example:
~~My best friend that lives next door has gone on holiday.~~
Correct formulation of this idea would be either a non-defining clause:
My best friend, who lives next door, has gone on holiday.
Or a subject which is not already defined:
The good friend who lives next door has gone on holiday.

Non-defining clauses

1 They are separated from the noun they refer to by a comma and if the sentence continues there is another comma. For example:
The new book by Frederick Forsyth, which I am thoroughly enjoying, is 800 pages long.
2 They are found more often in written English than in spoken, conversational English, in which shorter, simple sentences are often preferred. For example:
The new book by Frederick Forsyth is 800 pages long. I am thoroughly enjoying it.
3 Non-defining clauses do not contain *that*.
4 The relative pronoun is never left out.

Relative pronouns in defining and non-defining clauses

1 *Whom* is an object relative pronoun. Example:
The Managing Director, whom the board had trusted for many years, turned out to be dishonest.
However, *whom* is rarely used today in spoken or informal English.

2 Relative pronouns can also be used with prepositions. Examples:
The box in which I keep my spare glasses has disappeared.
The person on whom I was counting for help has let me down.
The prepositions can be put after the verb, particularly in informal or in spoken English. Examples:
The box I keep my spare glasses in has disappeared.
The person who I was counting on has let me down.

3 *When, where, whose* can also be used as relative pronouns. Examples:
I remember the time when I lost my passport.
The place where Stephany goes dancing is quite near.
Jo often reads aloud to her grandmother, whose eyesight is failing.

Practice

1 Write *D* against the following sentences which contain a defining clause and *ND* against those which contain a non-defining clause. If you are not sure, use the rules above to help you.

a) Could you pass me the hammer which is on the table over there.
b) I sold the Rolls Royce, which I always thought was uncomfortable anyway.
c) I didn't like the way in which she looked at me.
d) The people who I work with are very nice.
e) This is Sharon Smith, who plays the guitar.

2 Delete the relative pronouns in the sentences in Exercise 1 whenever it is possible.

3 Correct the mistakes in the following sentences.

a) The music is by Vivaldi who I love.
b) I am selling my house that I bought last year.

c) The small man in the black raincoat, who nobody recognised, was in fact a famous pianist.
d) A singer, which I have always loved but who I have never heard live, is performing in town tonight.
e) The planet on that we live is becoming very overcrowded.

4 Work with a partner. Put one of the following relative pronouns into the gaps in the text below: *when, where, whose*.

> Students (a) whose parents cannot afford to pay for higher education must find ways of earning their living. Stephanie, (b) family is unable to help her and (c) student grant is inadequate, tells us what it is like to study and work at the same time: 'The restaurant (d) I work as a waitress pays quite well as the clients are well-off and the tips are good. But I finish at 1 a.m. every morning (e) there is no public transport, so I have to walk home. North street (f) I live, is fairly deserted and its pretty scary sometimes. The alarm goes off at 7 every morning, (g) I have to get up to go to lectures or get on with my studying. Yes, even Saturdays and Sundays – I can't remember the time (h) I was able to lie in bed in the morning.'

5 Rewrite the following sentences, which include non-defining clauses, into simpler, conversational English. The first one has been done for you.

a) The poet, who had instructed his executors, who were his best friends, to destroy all his unpublished work, died suddenly.
The poet died suddenly. He'd asked his best friends to destroy his unpublished work. They were his executors.
b) We've tried fifty different brands, none of which is really satisfactory and all of which contain dangerous additives.
c) Magnificent prizes, which the headmistress herself had chosen, were given to fourteen children, all of whom had worked extremely hard and the youngest of whom was only eight.

TALKING EFFECTIVELY

1 [📼 13.1] Listen to the tape and read the tapescript below.

a) Mark in commas at the points at which the speaker makes natural pauses.

b) Listen to the tape again and underline the parts of the tapescript that are lower pitch than the rest. Are these the defining or the non-defining clauses?

```
This is the hotel that we stayed in
which was very pleasant. And this is
the little fishing port I told you
about which was extremely lively and
noisy. And here's my niece who's a
little devil. That's the waiter that
served our table the whole time - he
was very nice and he had a friend who
knew all the interesting things to
do. This friend who was born in the
village knew absolutely everyone.
```

2 Work in groups of three. Student A continues to describe the photos, imagining they are his or her own and adding more details from his or her own experience. Student B asks questions, e.g. *Who is this? What is that?* Student C monitors student A's intonation patterns: high pitch for defining clauses, low pitch for non-defining clauses.

READING

1 [▣ 13.2] Read and listen to the poem.

a) How is it related to the theme of this unit?
b) What do the combination of the words *honest idiocy, flying-crooked gift* and *hope and hopelessness* tell you about the observer's attitude to the butterfly?
c) Which is the line that tells you that the observer in the poem has a great deal of sympathy for the butterfly and understands it very well?
d) Write down, for yourself, any thoughts you have about the poem.

FLYING CROOKED

The butterfly, a cabbage white
(His honest idiocy of flight)
Will never now, it is too late,
Master the art of flying straight,
Yet has – who knows so well as I? –
A just sense of how not to fly:
He lurches here and here by guess
And God and hope and hopelessness.
Even the acrobatic swift
Has not his flying-crooked gift.

(by Robert Graves)

2 Work with a partner to decide what conflicting emotions you might feel when considering the following: a tiger, a rose, a jungle, a snake, a giraffe. Write a few sentences about one of them, or about something else from the natural world about which you might have conflicting emotions. Read out your sentences in small groups.

3 In your groups, discuss the following questions.

a) What is your attitude to people and things that are unusual?
b) What unusual people or things are you attracted to? What are you not attracted to? What do you have mixed feelings about?

Section 3

SPEAKING AND LISTENING

1   The following headline appeared in the newspaper. In small groups, imagine briefly what the story behind the headline is.

Dandelion eater is 'caught in mid-bite' in a New York park

2   The dandelion-eater was arrested and brought to court for 'criminal mischief'. You are going to hear extracts from his trial. There are four witnesses in the case:

Henry Stern, the Parks Commissioner whose job is the care and protection of all city parks. He is being questioned by Steve Brill's lawyer.

Steve Brill, the dandelion-eater himself. He is being questioned by the prosecution.

Sarah Stokes, the park ranger who trapped Steve and helped arrest him. She is being questioned by the prosecution.

Alexandra Brown, a person who has been on several tours organised by Steve Brill. She is being questioned by the lawyer defending Brill.

Before you listen, work with a partner and note down the kinds of things that you think each witness might say.

3   [▣ 13.3] Imagine you are one of the magistrates judging the case. Listen to the four witnesses and note down the facts of the case.

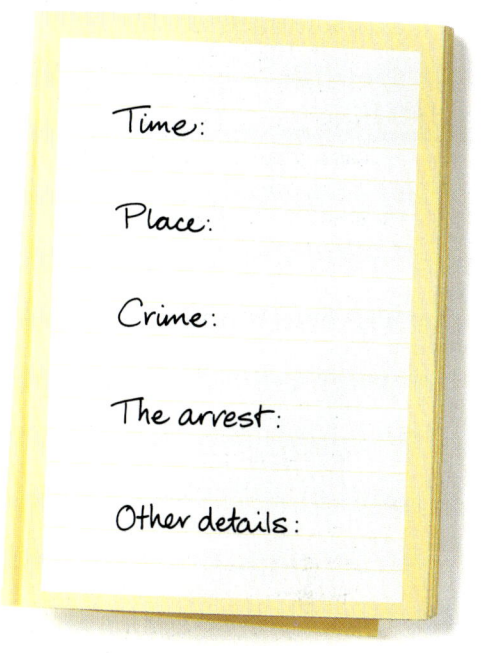

Time:

Place:

Crime:

The arrest:

Other details:

Compare notes with a partner.

4   Listen to the tape again. Make notes in two columns. In column A, write things that make you think Steve Brill should be judged guilty. In column B write things which make you think he should be judged not guilty.

5   What's the verdict – criminal or just eccentric? Work in groups of three magistrates to decide whether Steve Brill is innocent or not. If your group has decided he is guilty, choose an appropriate sentence for him. If your group has decided that he is simply eccentric, brainstorm a list of other types of behaviour which may appear eccentric to some people, for example vegetarians or other health freaks. Choose one type of behaviour and note down a few ideas for a campaign to publicise and fight against the victimisation of such eccentrics.

WRITING

Narrative points of view

1 Read the story of an eccentric below.

● Ed has survived for many years on a weird daily diet of 4lb boiled brown rice, supplemented only by chocolate bars, Vitamin C tablets and endless cups of coffee. Although he lives in an elegant, antique-filled Georgian house, he rejects the comfort of its spacious bedrooms. All four of these are rented out although he does not need the money. He himself sleeps on the painfully hard wooden floor of his gloomy study which is stacked from floor to ceiling with books on just three topics – travel, plants and rice.

Ed, aged 39, has the curious job of inspecting vegetables, but in his free time he is what he likes to call a 'freelance vegetable consultant'. His ideal holiday? Going to India, birthplace of rice, to visit the International Rice Centre.

Underline the words and expressions that indicate that the author thinks that Ed's way of life is eccentric. Compare with a partner.

2 Rewrite the passage about Ed's life from his own point of view.

a) Use the first person, 'I'. You will need to replace the words you have underlined with words that Ed would use to describe the way he lives – he probably likes it and sees nothing bizarre in it! You can change other parts of the passage and add things if you wish.

b) Swap your passage with a partner. Does your partner's passage really express the view of Ed?

3 Work with a partner.

a) Decide which of the words in the box describe things that are strange because they are unusual but not frightening and which ones things that are strange because they are mysterious.

> uncanny   peculiar   eerie   odd

b) Check your answers in the entries from the LLA below.

c) What other words do you know that mean *strange*? With your partner, discuss how you can know the various associations of these words.

uncanny /ʌnˈkæni/ strange and hard to explain and therefore rather surprising and frightening [adj] *Gina had an uncanny ability to tell when I was lying.* | *The two women, who had been friends for over twenty years, bore an uncanny likeness to one another.* | *It was almost uncanny the way the room had suddenly become filled with people without her noticing.*
uncannily [adv] *The house was uncannily quiet.*

peculiar /pɪˈkjuːliər/ strange in a way that is very surprising or rather unpleasant [adj] *Her jacket is a peculiar shade of mauve.* | *The taxi came from the farm and had a peculiar smell of stale straw.* | *During our stay on the island I had a most peculiar feeling of being transported back in time.*

eerie /ˈɪəri/ eerie darkness/sound/feeling/voice/silence etc. (=strange and frightening) [adj] *I woke with the eerie feeling that somebody was watching me.* | *My grandfather's voice sounded distant and eerie in that house in which so few words were spoken.* | *The pumps were shut off now. It was eerie, being in the factory without their sound.* | *The tropical forest through which the boat was gliding remained eerily silent.*
eerily [adv]

odd /ɒd ‖ ɑːd/ strange in a way that is interesting or amusing [adj] *Isn't that odd? She's never done that before.* | *When I got to the party I couldn't see one person I knew, which was very odd.* | *That's funny. That dog doesn't like strangers but he likes you.* | *The funny thing was, I sort of missed him after we moved to Illinois.*
oddly [adv] *Oddly, I felt little conscious fear of prison itself.*

(from the *Longman Language Activator*)

4 Work in small groups.

a) Discuss any eccentrics you know personally or that you know of.

b) In pairs, choose one of the characters you have been talking about. Write about the person from different points of view. One of you describes the person's behaviour as admirable and the other describes it as strange. Before you start, look back at the list of words you underlined in Exercise 1 and the words you discussed in Exercise 3c). Make two lists of opposite attitude words that you would like to use about the person you have chosen.

5 Write an essay on one of the following topics:

a) There is no place for eccentrics in the world today. Discuss.
b) Describe the strangest person you have ever met.
c) You are a sociologist and have been interviewing people about their attitudes towards eccentrics. Write a report of those interviews.

UNIT 14

Girls + boys = mixed blessings

Section 1

SPEAKING

1 Work in small groups. Look at the pictures and discuss the following questions.

a) How similar or dissimilar are the schools in the photos to schools in your countries?
b) What aspects of the life shown in the photos would you particularly like or dislike?
c) Are primary or secondary schools in your country coeducational or single sex?
d) Describe the secondary school you went to. Was it single sex or coeducational?
e) Which system is better? What do you like and dislike about the system you went through or are going through at the moment?

2 Do you all agree? Report your discussion back to the class.

VOCABULARY

Studying culture-related vocabulary

1 Do this quiz to see how much culture-related vocabulary you know on the topic of education. Work with a partner, and check your answers with the dictionary entries in the Key.

a) An independent school is:
   i) a non-religious school.   ii) a non-political school.   iii) a fee paying school.
b) Pupils in the sixth form are:
   i) 16–18.   ii) 14–16.   iii) 12–14.
c) In British English, a high school is:
   i) a certain kind of private school.   i) any secondary school.   iii) a school for very bright pupils.
d) Extra-curricular activities are:
   i) academic activities done outside the classroom.   ii) non-academic activities.
   iii) activities which cost parents extra money.
e) 'A' level and 'GCSE' are:
   i) public exams.   ii) school entrance exams.
   iii) school leaving exams.
f) Oxbridge is:
   i) a prestigious British university.   ii) a word made up from Oxford and Cambridge.
   iii) a non-university institute of higher education.
g) A 'first' is:
   i) the first degree or diploma taken at university.   ii) the result of the best student on a university course.   iii) very good results in final exams at university.

2 Think of other ways to find out the meanings of culture-related vocabulary. Compare your ideas in small groups. Then think of other categories of words for which you might need a dictionary with cultural content as in the Key.

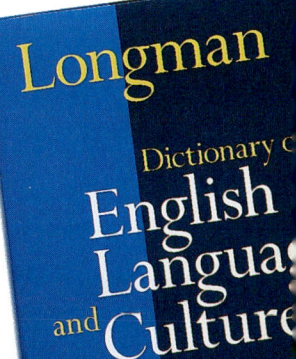

Unit 14

LISTENING AND READING

Group A (half the class)

[▶ 14.1] You are going to listen to Mrs Townsend, a headmistress, talking about single sex education. Note down her remarks about how this type of school affects girls under as many of the following headings as you can. An example has been done for you.

a) academic record *Girls do better academically.*
b) self-confidence
c) behaviour in the classroom
d) attitude of teachers
e) job prospects

Group B (half the class)

Read the article on the right about coeducational education and make notes about how this type of education affects girls and boys under as many of the following headings as you can. An example has been done for you.

a) academic record *under-achievement in science and maths*
b) self-confidence
c) behaviour inside and outside the classroom
d) attitude of teachers
e) job prospects

SPEAKING

1 Work in small groups, two students from group A and two students from group B. Compare the information from the tape and the article and discuss the questions below. You may refer to the article or the tapescript to check.

a) What are the main advantages and disadvantages of single sex schools for girls? For boys?
b) What are the advantages and disadvantages of coeducational schools for girls? For boys?
c) What type of coeducational schools are criticised most?
d) Is the situation similar in your country?
e) Are the reasons for having single sex education the same all over the world? If not, what are they?

2 Report back your discussion to the rest of the class.

Co-education: a high price to pay

Research carried out in the Eighties indicated strongly that co-education was generally better for boys than for girls. The dangers of single-sex education for boys have often been stated, and there has long been an assumption that girls benefit from co-education in the same way. Recent research tells us that this assumption is wrong. Girls studying in co-educational schools can, it seems, pay a high price in diminished career ambitions, poor self-confidence and under-achievement in academically rigorous subjects such as science and mathematics.

Girls' schools are working hard to compete with the independent boys' schools that are currently increasing their intake. Marlborough, the pioneer, has increased its number of girls and begun admitting them at 13. The battle for girl pupils is growing fiercer all the time. Averil Burgess, headteacher of South Hampstead High School, believes parents needs to consider the effect of mixed classroom learning on reinforcing gender 'stereotypes'. She believes that in the halfway house type of co-education favoured by independent boys' schools, men become 'macho' and girls are forced to be inarticulate and passive. This is inevitable, she says, when the school is still run by the male-dominated senior teachers with little insight into gender education issues. She points to a study by Professor Hoyle of London University showing how boys were allowed to jump the queue to gain access to limited computer facilities. As a result girls' choice of career of computing suffers.

The recent introduction of co-education by Oxbridge colleges seems to have had the same harmful effect on girls' academic performance as identified in schools. In 1958, 8.1 per cent of men and 7.9 of women won firsts. In 1973, the corresponding figures were 12 and 12.1 per cent. Since the mid-Eighties, when both men and women's colleges have admitted members of the opposite sex, 16.1 per cent of men have gained firsts, but only 9.8 per cent of women. As Averil Burgess argues: 'Maybe the girls fall too readily into the sock-washing and meal-providing mode for the benefit of male colleagues and to the detriment of their work. At least a single sex institution offers the freedom not to behave as a woman.'

No one is suggesting that boys should be restricted to single-sex education; co-education is here to stay. But boys' schools with a minority of girls should take care to protect the latter from social domination by the boys. Parents should consider a single-sex school as a first option for their daughters, even if they choose co-education for their son. Maybe the implicit contradiction in that statement will only be resolved when girls' schools admit boys on gender-aware terms. ∎

(from *The Observer*)

Section 2

LEARNING GRAMMAR

Diagnosis

Ellipsis and substitution

1 Complete the following sentences so that they make sense. Avoid repetition, and use a substitute word such as *do* or *did, so, to, not, neither,* etc. Check in the Key if necessary.

a) Are you going on holiday this year? No, we can't afford *to*.
b) Make up your mind. Are you coming on Monday or . . . ?
c) A: Why are you painting that cupboard?
   B: My father told me . . . .
d) A: I'm tired. B: . . . am I.
e) A: I'm not hungry. B: . . . am I.
f) He said he'd phone but he . . . .
g) A: Is Barbara a doctor? B: I think . . . .
h) A: Did you want to go to a single sex school?
   B: No, I . . . . It was my parents who wanted me . . . .
i) A: Where is Ben? Do you think he's got lost?
   B: I expect . . . . He often . . . .

Omissions in spoken English

2 [▣ 14.2] People leave out the subject quite a lot in informal spoken English.

a) Listen to the dialogue and fill in the gaps with a pronoun if you hear one or Ø if you do not.
   TRACEY: (1) Ø went to the cinema last night.
   KATE: Did (2) . . . . . ? What (3) . . . . . see?
   TRACEY: Well, (4) . . . . . wanted to go to a French one at the cinematheque but my boyfriend wanted to see that awful horror film, *Green Gnomes Come To Town*. Of course, (5) . . . . . went where (6) . . . . . wanted to go, didn't (7) . . . . . ?
   KATE: (8) . . . . . see. (9) . . . . . make such terrible films these days. Still, (10) . . . . . lucky (11) . . . . . any cinemas left, I suppose. (12) . . . . . come to that French film with you next week, if (13) . . . . . like.
   TRACEY: Oh, thanks, (14) . . . . . be great.
b) With a partner, decide which pronoun has been left out every time you have written Ø.
c) What else would you have to add to the dialogue writing it out in correct, written English? (e.g. auxiliaries/verbs)

Development

***One* as a substitute word**

1 Work with a partner and correct the mistakes in the following sentences where necessary. Refer to the guidelines below if you are not sure. The first one has been done for you.

a) Leave your car in the garage. We'll go in my one. *in mine*
b) I caught ten fish yesterday, but I only caught five ones today.
c) I'll have five red apples and five green ones, please.
d) Are you going to buy a new car or a second-hand one?
e) Your work is interesting. The one I do isn't.
f) I don't like my watch. I prefer the one of Sarah.
g) I'm quite fond of little dogs but I'm scared of the big.
h) I don't just want a house in the country. I want a one with old wooden beams and a thatched roof.

Guidelines for using *one* as a substitute word

2 The pronoun *one* is used as a substitute word to avoid repeating a noun.

a) *One* is used to replace count nouns in the singular and the plural. Examples:
   I don't want a wooden table. I want a plastic one.
   I don't want blue balloons. I want red ones.
   Pass me a knife please. 'Which one?' The sharp one.

b) It is usually necessary with an adjective, which in most cases cannot stand alone as a replacement word. For example, you cannot say:
   ~~I don't need a new television. My old is perfectly all right.~~
   You must say:
   I don't need a new television. My old one is perfectly all right.

c) If it is used without an adjective, no indefinite article is used. Examples:
   ~~I'm looking for a new raincoat but I don't want a one with a belt.~~
   I'm looking for a new raincoat but I don't want one with a belt.

3 *One* is not usually used in the following cases:

a) With uncountable nouns. Examples:
   ~~'I'd like some dark chocolate please.' 'I'm sorry, I've only got some milk one.'~~
   ~~I haven't time today, but I've got one tomorrow.~~

b) To express possession. Examples:
   i) Possessive pronouns (*mine, hers, yours,* etc.) are used instead of possessive adjectives (~~*my one, her one, your one,* etc.~~) in cases where no adjective is used. For example, we do not say:
   ~~That's not your bag. It's my one.~~
   We say:
   That's not your bag. It's mine.
   ii) *'s* acts as a replacement word by itself and it is not necessary to add *one*. Examples:
   Whose bag is that? It's Joan's.
   not ~~It is the one of Joan.~~ or ~~Joan's one.~~

Ellipsis

1 To avoid repetition it is preferable to leave out nouns, main verbs, modal verbs, relative pronouns, etc. as long as the meaning of the sentence is clear. For example, in the following sentence, the meaning is quite clear although the main verb is not repeated:
Susan paid for the food and her friend the drinks.

2 Although leaving out some words leads to concision and brevity, complex sentences can be difficult to understand if too much is left out. With a partner, read the sentences below and write them out in full so that they are easier to understand.

a) The police stated that the victim should be heard and eyewitnesses looked for.
b) Emma and Mark began an exotic dance which was applauded wildly and after plenty of encouragement from the audience danced a brilliant tango.

3 Sometimes a sentence can be ambiguous if too much is left out. What must be added to the following sentence to make it clear that the policewoman would say no more or the suspect would say no more?

The policewoman informed us that the suspect had revealed his whereabouts at the time of the crime but would say no more.

Practice

1 Rewrite the following paragraph, which is longer than necessary and a little repetitive. Leave out as much as possible, but make sure the meaning is still clear.

> RESEARCH which was carried out in the eighties indicated strongly that co-education was generally better for boys than it was for girls. The dangers of single-sex education for boys have often been stated, and there has long been an assumption that girls benefit from co-education in the same way as boys benefit from it.

2 Look back at the first paragraph of the reading text in Section 1. Have you left out absolutely everything that you can?

3 Rewrite the following sentences leaving out as much as possible.

a) Many women today will move into a wider range of professions than their mother's generation could have hoped to move into.
b) Women have long found it easy to pick up work when economies boom. Now they are picking it up fast even in hard times.
c) In some countries almost as many women go out to work as men go out to work, which is causing problems for childcare.
d) British evidence suggests that staying at school improves girls' employment prospects more than staying at school improves boys' employment prospects.
e) The reporter said that many women should have top jobs in the future and that many women should be earning more than their husbands.

Section 3

READING AND LISTENING

Just an ordinary school

1 [▶ 14.3] Read and listen to the extract from the sketch on the right, in which three girls at a very expensive independent school are being interviewed.

a) With a partner, tick any of the adjectives in the box below which describe its style. You may add other adjectives of your own.

| realistic | humorous | satirical | ironic |
| serious | caricatural | | |

b) Compare your answers with other people in your class.

2 Some slang words are used in the sketch. Work with a partner to circle the right meaning for each one below. Look back at the context and see if there are any clues to help you.

a) *booze:* i) luxuries ii) gambling iii) drink
b) *awfully poor:* i) impoverished ii) destitute iii) bankrupt
c) *hideous:* i) repugnant ii) unappealing iii) inaesthetic
d) *loot:* i) credit ii) money iii) gold

What clues did you find to help you? Why do you think the girls use slang like this?

3 Explain the following words and phrases from the sketch.

a) New taps for his yacht (line 6)
b) extras (line 15)
c) There's only . . . their own balloons now (lines 18–19)

4 Imagine the girls ten years later. Work in small groups to improvise a short sketch in which an interviewer asks them questions. To prepare your sketch, think about their lives:

a) Who will they be with? Will they be married?
b) What will they be doing? Will they have a job?
c) What will they be thinking?

Male Interviewer (*Voice over*):   And do you ever feel guilty about your fathers spending five thousand pounds a term on you?
Anthea: Not really, do you? I don't really.
5 **Babs:** My father would only spend it on booze or something.
Ceal: New taps for his yacht or something.
Interviewer (*Voice Over*): But I mean some parents can't spend that amount of money on their daughter's education.
Anthea: Oh, can't they? No, I suppose no …
10 **Babs:** But you make an effort, don't you?
Ceal: Yes, you find the money, because my cousin's father's a duke, and he's awfully poor actually, and they sold a Gainsborough, quite a hideous one actually, and that sort of brought in enough loot to cover quite a few terms.
15 **Babs:** Anyway, you don't have to have all the extras.
Anthea: Scuba diving — quite a lot of the girls don't do that now, do they?
Ceal: Or ballooning, hot-air ballooning. There's only about ten girls here with their own balloons now.
20 **Interviewer** (*Voice Over*): What I mean is: does it make you work harder, knowing the amount that's been invested in you?
Anthea: No.
Ceal: I mean, a lot of things one learns here, they're not
25 really going to be very much use when one leaves.
Babs: I mean, we're not going to talk Latin, are we?
Laughter
Anthea: Or French!
Laughter

ABOUT LANGUAGE

Gender issues in language

1 Work with a partner.

a) Read the entry from the *Longman Dictionary of Language and Culture* and discuss whether people react in a similar way in your country.

> **per·son** /ˈpɜːsən ‖ ˈpɜːr-/
> ▷ USAGE 2 Many people, especially women, do not like the use of words such as **chairman** or **spokesman** to refer to both sexes. They also dislike the use of these words to refer to women. They prefer to use words which can refer to both men and women: *She/he is our new **chairperson**. | She/he agreed to act as **spokesperson**.* ◁
> **per·so·na** /pəˈsəʊnə ‖ pər-/ *n* (in psychology) the outward person takes on in order to persuade

b) Do you know, or can you invent, a non-sexist term for the following words using the words in the box.
  i) policeman
  ii) salesman
  iii) congressman
  iv) air hostess
  v) headmaster
  vi) nurse

| person | teacher | officer | member | attendant |

2 Study the two versions of the extract from a company brochure below and underline the differences. Which is the sexist version and which is the non-sexist version?

A

WECARE CORPORATION has positions available for the man who wants to be in management, finance, statistics, communication, marketing or accounting. Whether running a one-man show or working on multiple-man teams, the employee at Wecare has a great deal of freedom to engage in the kind of creativity that has brought mankind to the level of productivity it now enjoys.

B

WECARE CORPORATION has positions available for the graduate who wants to be in management, finance, statistics, communication, marketing or accounting. Whether working alone or with others, the employee at Wecare has a great deal of freedom to engage in the kind of creativity that has brought humanity to the level of productivity it now enjoys.

3 Rewrite the following paragraph in a non-sexist way.

> Although our craftsmen, under the direction of our fine foremen, produce an outstanding manmade material, we always need bright, young men for the position of salesmen so that the product can be sold. Certainly the wife and children of the salesman must be willing to have a weekend husband and father and to move frequently as he advances from one territory to another.

WRITING

Planning a sequence of paragraphs
You are going to write a sequence of paragraphs with the information in the chart below. Work in groups of three. Begin by deciding which topics go together well to make a coherent paragraph. For example, the topic of children probably goes best with the topic of families, but you may use your own criteria for organising the information.

Writing a paragraph
Each person in the group chooses one paragraph and writes it up. Link the information together using cohesive devices where appropriate. For example you can contrast two pieces of information using *whereas, but, in spite of*, etc. or you can use *as well as, besides, furthermore*, etc. when you are adding some information.

Linking paragraphs
In your groups, look at the three paragraphs and link them with cohesive devices. Make any changes necessary so that the three paragraphs are coherent.

Revising
Read through your work a final time. Can you use any of the types of ellipsis you have studied in this unit to make it more concise and elegant? Make sure you do not leave out words that are vital to the sense or the coherence of your writing.

Different ways of organising information
Put your articles on the wall and see how other groups have organised the information. Which passage has the best organisation? Why?

Women in the U.S. - A New Look

NUMBER:
More than half of the population

The nation's 119.1 million females comprise 51.3 percent of the total population. Ten years from now, they will number 130.3 million, but their proportion of the total population will be about the same as today. Now, there are 88.4 million women age 18 and up.

LIFE SPAN:
Women live longer than men

The average female lives to a little more than 78 years, or nearly eight years longer than the average male. The gap in life expectancy is widening - it was little more than seven years two decades ago.

FAMILIES:
Those headed by women rise sharply

More than 1 in 7 families - 9.1 million - are headed by women. The number has risen by 65 percent since 1970, largely because of the climbing divorce rate.

RACE:
6 of 7 are white

Of all females –
101.6 million, or 85 percent, are whites.
14.6 million, or 12 percent, are blacks.
2.9 million are of other races.

EDUCATION:
More likely to attend college

Among persons age 18 to 24, 35 percent of women are enroled in college, compared with 34 percent of men. At last count, 23.4 percent of graduating medical doctors were women, as were 30.2 percent of lawyers.

CHILDREN:
Women want fewer offspring

Of childless married women age 18-34, 23 percent expect to have one child or none, while 72 percent expect to bear two or three children. Only 5 percent expect four or more. If fulfilled, these plans mean little population growth.

AGE:
Older than men on the average

The median age of females is 31.9 years, compared with 29.3 years for males. And females are getting older; in 10 years, their median age will be 34.5 years, and by the year 2000, 36.8 years.

MARRIAGE:
More women are putting It off

Just over half of the women age 20-34 have never been married, compared with 35.8 percent in 1970 and 28.4 percent in 1960. But 83 percent of women ultimately do marry.

POLITICAL POWER:
Edge in numbers at the top

Women of voting age are 52.2 percent of all Americans age 18 and up. With women living longer than men, the proportion is growing.

UNIT 15

Looking ahead

Section 1

SPEAKING AND READING

Predictions

1 In small groups, think about the next two generations and decide which of the following questions are relevant to your own country or countries.

a) Will the consumer market aim at single people or families?
b) Will the wealthiest bracket of the population be old people, young people or middle-aged people?
c) Will more people live in the country or in the town?
d) Will it be easier or harder for young people to find jobs?
e) Will it be easier or harder for women to get jobs?

2 Add two or three more questions about the future which are relevant to the contexts in which you live.

3 Discuss your answers to the questions about your own country, Great Britain or the world in general. One member of the group should make notes on the discussion, particularly on any disagreement.

4 Report your discussion briefly to the whole class. Are most people's predictions for the future generally optimistic or pessimistic?

5 Quickly read the article opposite about Great Britain's population in the future. Look back at your group's notes from Exercise 3. Were your group's opinions the same as the writer's or were they different?

So how many? Who, what, when, where and why?

Whatever else happens in the next twenty years, some things are reasonably certain. Demographic trends tell us that more babies will be born in the last decade, and the number of children at primary
5 school will grow, but the overall numbers of retired people will not change very much. But older people will live longer: a twenty per cent increase in the number of over-eighties is expected between now and the next century.

Bodies to babies in the High Street

10 High streets are likely to change. The 1980s have seen fortunes made from the rock - denims - Body Shop generation. At the end of the century we will see that power transferred to home-building and family-expanding. Fewer Body Shops, more baby
15 shops?

The middle-aged and the new wealth

The biggest upheaval of all is likely to revolve around the generation of people who will have reached their fiftieth birthday by the year 2001. Numbers tell part of the story: there will be a
20 million and a quarter more of us at the turn of the century than there are now. There is a further factor which arises out of a social revolution that has already taken place. At the end of the Second World War barely one quarter of the population of
25 Great Britain lived in their own homes. Today the proportion is two-thirds. The decade of most rapid expansion was the 1950s when home ownership rose from 28 to 42 per cent of households. In the

116

future we will not see anything like that. What we will see, however, is a vast growth in the number of people of about fifty, already home-owners, who will receive a windfall dollop in the form of their parents' homes (or, rather, the value of their parents' homes).

A back-of-the-envelope estimate means that £50bn spare cash will become available to spend or save. This is a lot of dosh, and will affect everything from high street shops and financial institutions to the leisure industry and political parties.

People will choose where they live

During the middle decades of this century - the Second World War apart - around half the working population held jobs in production industries - agriculture, mining, manufacturing, construction and so on. Since the 1960s that proportion has fallen rapidly to 30%. Those jobs have been replaced by the services, both public (education, health, etc.) and private (such as banking, insurance, shops, hotels).

Since people go where jobs go, this has meant a drift of the population from the industrial north to the service-dominated south. Many of today's services are more footloose. Already banks, civil service departments and other large employers are relocating where rents and staff are cheaper. What is more, modern information technology allows a growing number of their employees to work away from base. Why bring up a family in a noisy, dirty run-down city when the country beckons and the job could be done just as well in either place? The year 2001, I predict, will see the beginning of a boom decade for villages.

6 Read the following paragraphs A and B.

a) With a partner, decide which one you would choose to conclude the survey you have just read about the UK.

Paragraph A

Green Power

The next twenty years will see a resolution of the problems that entered the centre stage of politics in the late 1980s. Products and processes that harm the environment will be outlawed or taxed to oblivion. Virtue will be rewarded with large subsidies. By the end of the decade we shall consume less energy than today, and it will be cleaner energy more efficiently used. Farmers will discover that they can grow more - and tastier - food, using fewer chemicals. As a result, our water supplies will contain less in the way of fertilisers and other unwelcome additives. It will taste sweeter. Consumers will be happy, although shareholders in water companies will be less pleased by the costs that dent their dividends. Perhaps the biggest single sign that the Government takes the environment seriously will be the announcement of an integrated transport policy. Motorists will be required to pay the full congestion and pollution costs. Petrol prices will rise; drivers will have to pay to enter city centres. The extra revenue will finance investment in buses, trams and trains, and subsidise their running costs.

Paragraph B

Green Power

Environmental policy will be summed up in one word: prevarication. Ministers will find that the time is never right for long-term reform: short-term electoral interests will always intervene. Farmers, water and electricity shareholders and, above all, motorists will always provide too powerful a political lobby. As a result, congestion will increase, pollution will become more severe, and forests will be felled to provide the paper that goes into the impotent reports that fill up the shelves of the department of the Environment. Sometime in the late 1990s a major international conference will be held to debate the mounting crisis. Everyone will say how dreadful things are and how everyone else should follow their own impeccable example.

b) Would you choose the same paragraph if the article was about your own country?

c) Which paragraph have the other groups in your class chosen? Find a group which has decided on the other ending. Try to make them change their minds and agree with you. To support your point of view, think of all the things that are either already being done, or are not being done.

Unit 15

VOCABULARY

Vocabulary and style

The writer achieves a certain ironic style in the article by mixing precise almost technical language and humorous, almost slangy expressions. With a partner, look back at the context in the article and in paragraphs A and B for each of the words or expressions below. Write *T* (*Technical*) or *H* (*Humorous*) against each of them.

home ownership (line 27)
windfall dollop (line 32)
back-of-the-envelope estimate (line 35)
dosh (line 37)
production industries (lines 43–44)
footloose (line 53)
a boom decade (line 62)

Cultural allusions

Find out the meanings of the following words by looking back at the context, checking in your dictionary, guessing or asking your teacher if all else fails.

a) The rock-denims-Body Shop generation (lines 11–12) means:
   i) people who like rock music.
   ii) young people with spending power.
   iii) very rich people.
b) The Body Shop (line 14) sells:
   i) synthetic spare parts for the body.
   ii) modern, trendy bathroom accessories.
   iii) fashionable, natural cosmetic products.
c) High street shops (line 38) means:
   i) small businesses in the retail trade.
   ii) shops in the main street of any town.
   iii) shops in the centre of a particular town.
d) The service-dominated south (line 52) is:
   i) the part of England where there is very good service.
   ii) the part of England in which people complain about bad service the most.
   iii) the part of England in which most people work in the service industries.

What helped you to guess most: the context, your dictionary, or pure guesswork? Ask other people in your class what helped them most.

LISTENING

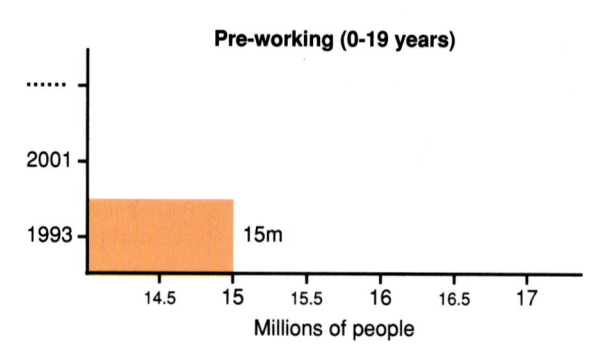

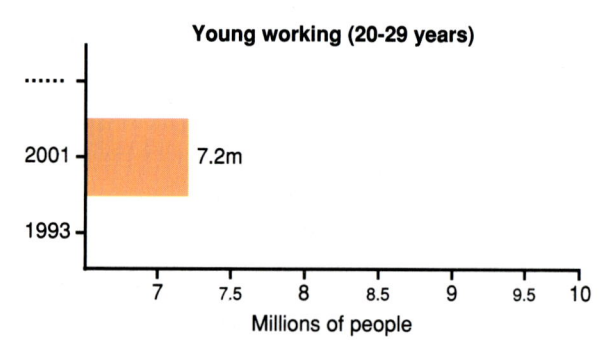

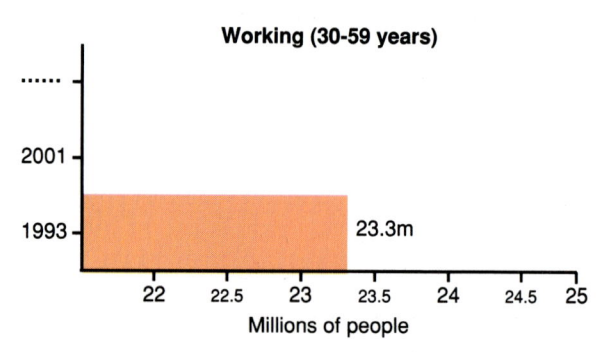

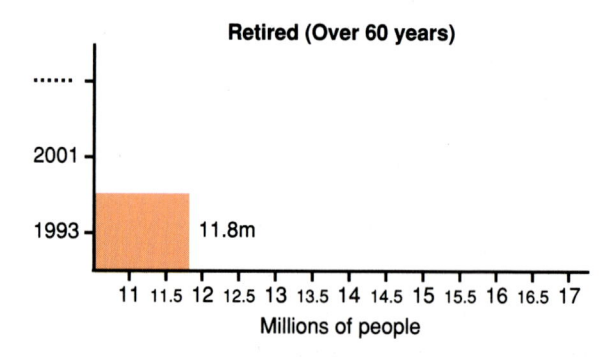

1 [▶ 15.1] Look at the charts below. Listen to the tape and shade in the missing numbers. Compare your answers with a partner. Listen again and check.

Pre-working (0-19 years)
1993: 15m
Millions of people (14.5–17)

Young working (20-29 years)
2001: 7.2m
Millions of people (7–10)

Working (30-59 years)
1993: 23.3m
Millions of people (22–25)

Retired (Over 60 years)
1993: 11.8m
Millions of people (11–17)

2 Ask people in your class about statistics for population changes in their country or countries. Are they very similar to Britain or very different?

Section 2

LEARNING GRAMMAR

▶ Diagnosis ◀ ◀ ◀

Conditional sentences

1 Work with a partner to correct the following sentences where necessary. Refer to the Key if you are not sure.

a) If you had loved me, you had not left me.
If you had loved me, you would not have left me.
b) If I have time, I would have helped you.
c) If it will be fine tomorrow, we can play tennis.
d) If you came to the party, you'll meet Susanna.
e) If you would have asked me for some money, I would have lent you some.
f) We went to the seaside if the weather was fine.
g) I would have gone if I hadn't been so busy.
h) I enjoyed the dinner more if those people over there were not making so much noise.

2 With your partner look back at Exercise 1 and answer the following questions.

a) In which sentence does *if* have almost the same meaning as *when*?
b) Write Type 1, 2 or 3 against each of the other sentences you have corrected. Refer to the Key if necessary.

3 Use the prompts below to make conditional sentences. There may be more than one answer. Check your answers in the Key.

a) I can't buy you a diamond ring because I have no money. (*If I . . .*)
If I had any money, I'd buy you a diamond ring.
b) We may go on holiday. It depends if we have enough money. (*If we . . .*)
c) He's overweight because he eats far too much. (*If he . . .*)
d) We cancelled the picnic. It looked like rain. (*We wouldn't . . .*)
e) We must buy some petrol soon. We may run out. (*If we don't . . .*)
f) The house was burgled while we were on holiday. We really should have installed a burglar alarm. (*The house . . .*)

▶ Development ◀ ◀ ◀

Mixed conditionals

1 With a partner, study the following pairs of sentences. Use the questions to help you imagine a context for each one. The first one has been done for you.

a) i) If you knew me better, you wouldn't have said that.
   ii) If you had known me better, you wouldn't have said that.
Which conditional clause is talking about the present and which about the past?
In the first sentence, the speaker is talking to someone who doesn't know him or her well and is referring to something that has just been said. In the second sentence, the speaker knows the person he is talking to well enough to discuss something hurtful or insensitive that was said some time before in the past.

b) i) If Alan missed the train, he won't be here on time and we'll have to go without him.
   ii) If Alan misses the train he won't be here on time, so we should make alternative arrangements just in case.
In which sentence has Alan already tried to catch the train? In which sentence is the fact that Alan may miss the train a future possibility?

c) i) If Ben has already bought a car, he wouldn't have wanted to buy mine, so there's no point in talking about it.
   ii) If Ben had already bought a car he wouldn't have wanted to buy mine. He was prepared to pay whatever I wanted.
In which sentence is it clear that Ben has already bought a car? In which sentence is it clear that Ben wanted the speaker's car at some time in the past?

d) i) If Sophie works as hard as you say she does, she would have passed her exams by now.
   ii) If Sophie worked as hard as you say she did, she would have passed her exams by now.
In which sentence is the speaker questioning Sophie's general capacity for hard work? Which sentence questions whether Sophie worked hard at a specific moment in the past?

2 Read the sentences again and write *M* after the ones which mix two different types of conditionals. Which types does each one mix? The first one has been done for you.

a) i) If you knew me better, you wouldn't have said that. *M (type 2 + type 3)*

3 Which of the following statements about conditional sentences is correct?

a) You can use any sequence of tenses in conditional sentences.
b) Any sequence of tenses is possible, provided the sentence makes sense in its context.
c) There are very strict rules about tense sequences.

Modal auxiliaries in conditional sentences

1 With a partner, decide whether the modal in the *if* clause in the following sentences is a politeness marker in a request, an offer or a suggestion, or an expression of strong volition. The first one has been done for you.

a) If you would drive me to the station, I can catch the 7 o'clock train.
   A politeness marker in a request
b) If you will fill this registration form in, I'll have your luggage sent up to your room.
c) I would be grateful if you would help me.
d) If you will play with fire you must expect to get burnt.
e) If you should need any help, I'll be right next door.
f) If I may make a suggestion, we could postpone the meeting till next week.
g) If Bob will keep coming to work late, he must accept the consequences.

2 [15.2] The modal auxiliary can be left out in all the sentences in Exercise 1 except f). Listen to the recording of the sentences with and without the modal auxiliary and with a partner discuss how the modal auxiliary and the intonation pattern change the meaning. The first one has been done for you.

a) i) *'If you would drive me to the station, I can catch the 7 o'clock train.' A tentative and polite request.*
   ii) *'If you drive me to the station, I can catch the 7 o'clock train.' A matter-of-fact statement of possibility, not necessarily a request.*

Practice

Make the following remarks more polite by adding a modal auxiliary and making any minor changes that are necessary.

a) If you lent me a hand, I could do the job much more quickly.
   If you would lend me a hand, I could do the job much more quickly.
b) Phone me if you want anything else.
c) If you deliver the goods tomorrow morning, that will be fine.
d) If Bob called round tomorrow, we could discuss the matter then.
e) If you hold this piece of wood for a moment, I can bang in the nail.
f) If you want a lift tomorrow morning, give me a call.

Hypothetical situations

1 The following pairs of sentences all contain verbs in the simple past, but they do not all refer to past time. Write *H* (*Hypothetical* or *Imaginary*) if it does not refer to past time.

a) i) I would stay, as long as you stayed too.
   ii) She stayed as long as I did.
b) i) It's time we got used to living here.
   ii) In time we got used to living here.
c) i) In fact, they got lost when the mist came down.
   ii) Suppose we got lost and the mist came down!

2 The following pairs of sentences all contain the past perfect but they do not all refer to the past-in-the-past. Write *PP* (*Past perfect*) if the sentence refers to the past-in-the-past and *H* (*Hypothetical* or *Imaginary*) if it does not.

a) i) What if we had broken down in the middle of the desert?
   ii) It took ages for the rescue team to arrive after we had broken down.
b) i) You look as if you'd seen a ghost.
   ii) He hadn't really seen a ghost but he had had a fright.
c) i) I knew you had been there before.
   ii) I wish you had come earlier.

3 In small groups, look at the sentences marked *H* in the last 2 exercises. Is the imaginary time past, present or future? How do you talk about similar hypothetical situations in your language?

Practice

1 · In the following sentences, put the verb in brackets into the simple past form when the situation is hypothetical or imaginary. Put it into an appropriate present or future tense when it is not. There may be more than one answer.

a) It's about time Sam (*go*) *went* to bed.
b) Sam (*go*) to bed at nine o'clock.
c) I wouldn't go ahead with the deal unless you (*agree*).
d) You (*agree*) that I was right?
e) I lent Sarah the car as she (*be*) a very sensible driver.
f) It's time we (*have*) a housewarming party.
g) In time we (*have*) a housewarming party.

2 In the following sentences put the verb in brackets in the past perfect when the situation is hypothetical or imaginary. Put it into the simple past tense when it is not. The first one has been done for you.

a) If I (*know*) *had known* at the time that he had a criminal record, I would never have employed him.
b) Although I (*know*) at the time that he had a criminal record, I still employed him.
c) Suppose the epidemic (*spread*)! We'd all be dead by now!
d) It (*be*) a rather unpleasant experience as it rained the whole time.
e) What if they (*lose*) the match! There wouldn't have been a party.
f) They unexpectedly (*lose*) the match so the party was cancelled.

3 Write sentences about small changes you would like in your life now or about things that might have been different in the past. Use the prompts below. Examples:
If only I had more time to spend on learning English!
Suppose I'd gone to an English school as a child! I'd speak English perfectly now.

If only . . . / Suppose I . . . / It's time I . . . / I'd rather . . .

Discuss your sentences in small groups. How can you make those small changes happen? Do you often think about things that might have been different? Is there any point in doing so?

LANGUAGE PATTERNS

Verbs with *-ing*, base forms and *should*

1 Study the following patterns for making suggestions and recommendations.

a) *Suggest* or *recommend* + *-ing* or base form
   Examples:
   i) *The advertising company suggests launching a new campaign in the autumn.*
   ii) *The Managing Director recommends taking an immediate decision.*
   iii) *He said it is essential for the whole board to agree.*
b) *Suggest* or *recommend* + *should* + base form
   Examples:
   i) *The advertising agency suggests the company should launch a new campaign in the autumn.*
   ii) *The Managing Director recommends that a decision should be taken immediately.*
   iii) *He said it is essential that the whole board should agree.*
c) *Suggest* or *recommend* + base form (even in 3rd person singular). Examples:
   i) *The advertising agency suggests the company launch a new campaign in the autumn.*
   ii) *The Managing Director recommends that a decision be taken immediately.*
   iii) *He said it is essential that the whole board agree.*

2 Look back at the examples and with a partner decide which pattern(s) you would use in an informal spoken context and which pattern(s) you would use in a more formal written context.

3 Other verbs and adjectival expressions following the patterns are:
propose, demand, recommend, order, command, insist, request, it is essential/important/necessary/ vital that . . .

4 Write a sentence of your own for each of the patterns a), b), c) above.

Practice

Rewrite the sentences below using the prompts. Change the meaning as little as possible. The first one has been done for you.

a) My host insisted that I should stay another couple of days.
My host insisted on *my staying another couple of days*.

b) It is normal for dissatisfied customers to complain.
It is normal that . . .

c) It is vital that every single instruction be followed to the last letter.
It is vital to . . .

d) The instructions recommend regular cleaning of the device.
The instructions recommend that . . .

e) Gina has proposed leaving first thing tomorrow morning.
Gina has proposed that we . . .

f) The ambassador suggested starting the meeting at 11 a.m.
The ambassador suggested that we . . .

Section 3

SPEAKING

You are about to enter the competition described in the advertisement below.

a) Work in groups of four or five. Each person thinks of three objects which would reveal interesting information about our lives to future generations, who may be living in a completely different way.

b) The group selects the six most representative objects and prepares short notes on the reasons for their choice.

c) The class chooses a judging panel – probably one member from each group and your teacher. A spokesperson from each group presents the group's list, explaining the reasons for the choices. The panel awards each team points out of ten. The points are added up and the winners declared.

TIME CAPSULE COMPETITION

THE INSTITUTE OF FUTUROLOGY is organising a competition in order to leave a heritage of the 1990s to future generations.

★ The competition is open to groups or individuals who should select a list of objects which they consider would reveal the most interesting information about life in our times to future generations. After a preliminary selection, entrants will be invited to present their lists and the reasons for their choices to a panel.

★ The objects on the winning list will be ceremoniously buried for future generations to find.

★ *The winners will be invited to visit current archaeological excavations in Greece.*

WRITING

1 Read the accounts opposite of the *Time Capsule Competition*. Match each one to one of the following sources. Justify your answer with reference to stylistic features in each paragraph.
  i) *The Institute of Futurology Newsletter*: the chatty, in-house newsletter of the company which organised the competition
  ii) *The Stockport Weekly Echo*: a local newspaper which reports mostly human interest stories, such as weddings and personal success stories, in a concise and factual way
  iii) *Public Relations Today*: a professional journal dealing with public relations and circulating ideas among its readers

2 You are living in 2030. The group of objects which won the Time Capsule Competition has just been found. You are going to write a short article about the find. Before you start, answer the following questions in groups of three.

a) Which articles will still be used and which will not?
b) What kind of guesses will people make about articles and objects that are no longer used?
c) How will life be different in 2030?

3 Work in your groups of three.

a) Choose three different newspapers or magazines for which you will write three different articles. For example, you could choose a serious history magazine, a sensational newspaper, a young person's magazine or think of an idea of your own.
b) Look back at the articles in Exercise 1 and decide what makes each one different. Discuss how each of your articles will be different. Use the following check list.
  i) Vocabulary: simple, accurate, idiomatic
  ii) Sentence structure: simple or complex
  iii) Register: informal, chatty, ordinary, formal
  iv) Tone: factual, educational, descriptive, serious, light-hearted, etc.
  v) Reader: child, young adult, adult, professional, general interest, etc.

4 Now write your article.

a) Show it to the other people in your group. Are each of the articles in an appropriate style? Suggest improvements.
b) Read other groups' articles.

A

A GOOD WAY to bring your company to the public's notice is to organise a competition of some kind. The Institute of Futurology recently gained a lot of press coverage with just such an event called the **Time Capsule Competition**... This kind of initiative is not cheap, as if the initial outlay is not so great as it is in a normal advertising campaign, the costing of staff time must be taken into account...

B

Here at the Institute of Futurology, we have hit the headlines again with our highly successful Time Capsule Competition. The number of entries for this exciting event far exceeded our wildest dreams and although the competition was not directly open to our employees, I know many of you have taken a lively interest, encouraging your families to enter and visiting the exhibition we have set up with the entries. But finally, an outstanding entry from Janet Stowe won by a narrow margin. 'I am over the moon,' said the happy winner, clutching her prize, an envelope containing a ticket for a wonderful trip to Greece. **Well done, Janet! And well done, The Institute of Futurology!**

C

The internationally famous Institute of Futurology which has its headquarters just outside Stockport recently organised a Time Capsule Competition... Our very busy Mayor, Mr Adam Smith, found time to take part in the competition judging and he was helped by the President of the Institute of Futurology, Sharon Lee and the eminent scientist Cyril Smith who was born here in Stockport. There were 352 entries in the adult category and 471 in the young person's. The overall winner, Janet Stowe, is 29 and a well-known local figure who has an arts and crafts shop in the High Street. The judges were very impressed by the high standard of the entrants' ingenuity and imagination.

UNIT 16

Creators and creativity

Section 1

LISTENING

1 You are going to listen to an interview with P.D. James, a famous crime story writer. Before you listen, work with a partner and list the questions you would ask a crime writer for a radio interview.

2 [16.1] Listen to the interview. Were your questions the same as the interviewer's? Does anything P.D. James says answer your questions? Make notes as you listen. Compare your notes with your partner.

3 P.D. James talks of 'revelation' rather than 'creation'. Listen to the tape again and note down words and expressions which tell you exactly what she means by this. What other points does she make about the creative process?

TALKING EFFECTIVELY

Pace

1 [16.2] Listen to part of the interview again while you read the script below.

a) Notice the way the speaker varies her pace. Sometimes she speaks very quickly, with the words almost running together. Sometimes she makes long pauses. Mark in the pauses // and underline the fluent passages as in the example.

b) What do the pauses contribute to the speaker's effectiveness? What effect does this variety of pace have on your impression of the speaker? Discuss your ideas with a partner.

> PDJ: I think it's a strength,// but I think it has its dangers. As C. P. Snow, a writer not perhaps much regarded now, said in one of his books that there's great dignity in being an observer, that if you do it for too long you lose your soul. And I think there is a danger. I think one needs the involvement. It's possible I think for certain people to feel, writers particularly, that life is a messy business and that it's better to stand on the sidelines, observing the mess and recording the mess. But I think occasionally, we have to join in and get as messy and dirty as all other human beings. And indeed we don't often have the choice, I mean, this is what happens to us, so we have to.

2 Tell your partner about a writer you like. Spend a few minutes preparing what you are going to say and thinking about where you can vary the pace as you talk, and about the strategic points where you can pause.

SPEAKING

1 Work in small groups to compile a list of people who are, in your view, creative. Think of other people in the arts (painters, sculptors, etc.), but also think of other professions (architects, furniture makers, etc.) and of ordinary people that you know. Compare your list with other people in your class. Have you listed the same or different kinds of people?

2 Think about how creative people go about their work. In your groups discuss the following questions in relation to the people on your list.

a) What materials does the creator need?
b) Does he or she need solitude?
c) Does he or she need detachment from reality or involvement in it?
d) Does the artist have a complete idea of the work before he or she begins or does the work of art 'take over' and have a life of its own?
e) How do creators go about the practical business of creating?
f) How different from other people are they?

Compare your notes with another group.

Section 2

VOCABULARY

Collocation

With a partner, use your dictionary to find out which of the words in column A go with the words in column B. Which is the word in column A with the most general meaning? Which words have the connotation 'with intent to deceive'?

A	B
a) invent	1 a plan
b) hatch	2 a story
c) concoct	3 a lie
d) fabricate	4 an alibi
	5 a device
	6 a meal
	7 a plot

Multi-part verbs

In pairs use your dictionary to help you decide which of the multi-part verbs in the box below go with the words in column B above.

make up	dream up	think up
hit upon	conjure up	

Which of the verbs has connotations of suddenness, magic, or a derogatory nature?

Practice

Complete the sentences with an appropriate verb from the sections above. There may be more than one answer. Compare your answers with a partner. Where there is more than one possible answer, how does each affect the meaning of the sentence?

a) She was always *dreaming up/inventing* weird new gadgets.
   'Dreaming up' reinforces the derogatory connotation already present in the sentence.
b) It looked as if a conspiracy was going on – I'm sure they were . . . a plot of some kind.
c) She used the leftovers in the fridge to . . . something wonderful.
d) He is always . . . wild schemes for making money, but they never work.
e) We had been trying to work out what to do for ages when suddenly Brian . . . an idea.

LEARNING GRAMMAR

▶ Diagnosis ◀◀◀

Preferences

1 With a partner, correct the mistakes where necessary. Check in the Key if necessary

a) I prefer tea than coffee.
   I prefer tea to coffee.
b) I prefer playing the guitar to playing the piano.
c) Rob prefers go out to eat rather than cook at home.
d) A: Can I give you a lift?
   B: No thanks, I'd prefer walking.
e) 'What about going to Guatemala for our holiday?' 'I'd prefer Mexico.'
f) I would prefer not to go out this evening.
g) On Sunday I'd prefer to stay at home to drive all that way to the seaside.
h) I'd rather stay at home tonight.
i) I'd rather we stay at home tonight.

2 Look back at the sentences in Exercise 1 and complete the following statements with your partner. Refer to the guidelines in the Key if necessary.

a) To express preferences in general, *prefer* can be followed by . . . , by . . . or by . . . .
b) To say what you prefer in a particular situation you use the structure: . . . + *prefer*.
c) The full structure with *prefer* in a particular situation is: . . . *prefer to* + base form . . . *than* + (to) + base form.
d) When *would rather* is used to state a preference about what someone else should do in the present or in the future it is followed by the . . . tense.

Note

1 *Would rather* is sometimes confused with *had rather,* probably because both forms can be contracted to *'d rather*. However, *had rather* is no longer used in standard British English.
2 *Would rather* is sometimes confused with *had better*. However, *had better* is used for advice or to express something one ought to do. Examples:
*You'd better put a coat on as it's very cold out.
I had better stay at home (or my cold will get worse).*

Practice

1 With a partner, ask and answer questions using the following prompts. The first one has been done for you.

a) this evening/ disco – cinema
   What shall we do this evening? Go to a disco or to the cinema?
   I'd rather not go to the cinema. I'd prefer the disco.
b) weekend / go to the country – stay at home
c) for our holiday / travel abroad – visit family
d) this afternoon / skating rink – play dungeons and dragons
e) on Friday / do a computer program – play tennis
f) have for dinner / spaghetti – ravioli
g) have for pudding / ice cream – fresh fruit
h) this evening / take the car – bus
i) buy Jenny for her birthday / a book – a record

2 In small groups, plan an outing together. Decide where you will go, what you will do, who you will invite to come with you, what you will take with you, etc. Make sure you ask everybody in the group about their preferences.

Development

Hopes and wishes

Wish + would and could

With a partner, look at the following sentences and imagine a context for each of them, for example who the speaker is talking to. In which of them does the modal auxiliary express willingness, habit or ability?

a) You're late again, Jim. I wish you would catch an earlier train.
b) I wish you wouldn't fiddle with that pen while I'm talking.
c) I wish you would come on holiday with me.
d) I wish you could come on holiday with us.

I wish you would take up tennis instead!

Sequence of tenses with *wish* and *hope*

2 With a partner, look at the following sentences and answer the questions. To help you, you can imagine a context and think of who the speaker is talking to.

a) i) I wish she would come with us.
   ii) I hope she comes with us.
   Which of these sentences can only refer to one event in the future? Which can refer to one event in the future or in the present?
b) i) I wish I was invited to the party.
   ii) I hope I am invited to the party.
   In which sentence is there no chance of the person going to the party?
c) I hope Greg would help us.
   I wish Greg would help us.
   In which sentence is it certain that we need help right now?
d) I hope I haven't offended Jill.
   I wish I hadn't offended Jill.
   In which sentence is it not certain that Jill is offended?

3 Look back at the sentences with *wish* in them. Read the statements below and tick the ones that are correct. Correct the ones that are not. Compare your answers with a partner.

a) The past tense is used after *wish* to express a wish in the present.
b) The verbs *hope* and *wish* are used with the same tense sequence.
c) *Will* is used after *wish* to express future meaning.
d) The past perfect is used after *wish* to express a wish about the past.
e) Any modal auxiliary can be used after *wish*.

Practice

1 With a partner, write *C* against the sentences which are correct. Correct the ones which contain a mistake. The first one has been done for you.

a) I wish you live nearer. *I wish you lived nearer.*
b) I wish you would live nearer.
c) I wish it will snow.
d) I wish I hadn't been so rude.
e) I wish she can stop smoking.
f) I wish she came with us – it was a wonderful evening.
g) I wish I do not worry so much.

2 What would each person say in the following situations? Work in small groups and think of as many remarks as you can for each situation. Begin each remark with *I wish . . .* or *If only . . .* (see Unit 15). The first one has been done for you.

a) Jim wants to go on a diet but finds it difficult not to eat large quantities.
   I wish I could eat less!
   If only I didn't like eating so much!
   I wish I wasn't so fond of food!
b) Joanna finds it difficult to pass her history exam because she forgets important dates.
c) Diana wants to learn to pilot a plane but does not have enough money.
d) Ben needs to speak foreign languages for his job, but thinks he is hopeless at them.
e) Jill wants to be a ballet dancer, but can't because she is too tall.

3 Complete the following prompts with your hopes and wishes. Read them out to a partner.

a) I hope I . . .
b) I wish I could . . .
c) I wish it was . . .
d) I hope they will . . .
e) I wish they would . . .
f) I wish it had been . . .

Unit 16

Section 3

READING

1 Look at the Celebrity Questionnaire below from a British Sunday newspaper. Choose ten of the questions. Work with a partner to ask and answer the questions about yourselves. Make notes of your answers.

CELEBRITY Questionnaire

1. What is your idea of perfect happiness?
2. What is your greatest regret?
3. What is your favourite word?
4. What is the trait you most deplore in yourself?
5. What is the trait you most deplore in others?
6. What is your greatest extravagance?
7. What objects do you always carry with you?
8. What do you most dislike about your appearance?
9. What is your favourite journey?
10. What is your greatest fear?
11. On what occasions do you lie?
12. Which living person do you most despise?
13. What do you consider the most overrated virtue?
14. Which words or phrases do you most overuse?
15. What single thing would improve the quality of your life?
16. Which talent would you most like to have?
17. What would your motto be?
18. How would you like to be remembered?
19. What keeps you awake at night?
20. What is your present state of mind?

(from *The Sunday Correspondent*)

2 Now read David Bowie's answers to the questionnaire below and work with a partner to answer these questions.

a) What do you think David Bowie means when he says:
   i) that he regrets taking his ambitions too seriously.
   ii) that his favourite word is 'today'.
   iii) that his greatest extravagance is believing he has anything worth saying.

b) Which of his answers do you find the most surprising? Which do you find the most predictable? Give reasons for your answers.

c) What kind of person does David Bowie appear to be? Tick any of the adjectives in the box that you think apply to him. You may add more adjectives of your own.

humorous	down-to-earth	original	serious
clever	kind	sarcastic	imaginative	creative
sensible	conceited	romantic

d) Which of the following statements about David Bowie's answers do you agree with most? If you agree with neither, write a sentence about your impression. Compare your answers with other people in your class.
   i) His answers are gimmicky and irritating.
   ii) His answers show a truly creative mind.
   iii) His answers . . .

DAVID BOWIE was born David Jones on 8 January 1947 in Brixton, south London. The son of a public relations officer for Dr Barnardo's, he left school at 16 and worked in advertising before becoming a musician. He had his first hit in 1969 with 'Space Oddity', but it was his creation of Ziggy Stardust in 1972 that secured him an international reputation. He went on to star in seven films and took the title role on Broadway in *The Elephant Man*. He has just completed an album and a tour with his band, Tin Machine. He is divorced with one son and based in Switzerland.

1. Being lost in the streets of a very foreign city with someone greatly loved
2. Taking my ambitions too seriously
3. Today
4. Indifference
5. Indifference
6. Believing I have anything worth saying
7. Guitar pick, a photograph or two, cigarettes
8. Its deceptiveness
9. There is only one
10. Not feeling amazed or curious anymore
11. I have no idea
12. Anyone who has the ability but won't read; anyone who has the means but won't travel
13. Originality
14. Tomorrow; is it not …? I have no idea
15. Imagination physically manifest
16. To be able to ask personal questions of perfect strangers
17. Generally the last clever thing I heard. Aren't mottoes rather prison-like?
18. By whom?
19. Seventies revival parties next door
20. Delightfully irrational

3 Read the interview again.

a) Compare your and your partner's answers in the *Reading* exercise on page 128 with David Bowie's answers. Were yours as unusual and surprising as his or were they more natural and factual? Would you now like to change any of your answers and make them more original, or are you happy with them as they are?

b) Report back your impressions to another group.

4 Roleplay this situation. In groups of three, choose an artist, writer or other creative person that you would like to meet. Imagine two of you are journalists who have been commissioned by your newspaper to interview the person in question and the third student is the creator. Decide whether your interview will be serious, like P.D. James's, or more frivolous, like David Bowie's, and prepare your questions accordingly.

WRITING

Creative writing

1 In small groups, look at the photograph and imagine what the little girl is thinking and what she has been doing.

2 Discuss the following writing tasks – which is the easiest? Which is the most difficult?

a) Write a paragraph about what the little girl is thinking. Write in the first person or the third person.

b) Write a very short story or a poem about the little girl.

c) Look at the poem in the shape of a tree. Write a poem in a shape which evokes the sea for you.

Tree Poem

d) Write a poem using the following letters for the first line.

S . . .
E . . .
A . . .
S . . .
C . . .
A . . .
P . . .
E . . .

3 Choose one of the tasks above to do, or do a piece of creative writing on a topic of your choice. Then read other students' writing.

UNIT 17

A world of difference

Section 1

SPEAKING AND READING

1 In small groups discuss the following questions.

a) If you had a problem and wanted to talk to someone about it, would you go to your parents or someone their age, your grandparents or someone their age, or a brother or sister or a friend your own age? Explain the reasons for your answer.
b) Do you find it easy or difficult to communicate with old people? Why? What topics of conversation can you talk about with old people? What topics are difficult to discuss with them?
c) Which of the people in the photos above would you like to interview about their lives? Why?
d) In your country, who has more social status – old people, young people, or middle-aged people?
e) In your country, who appears most in adverts on TV and in magazines – old people, young people, or middle-aged people?
f) How do you ask people's age in your language? *How old,* as in English, or the number of years or in another way?

2 Report back your discussion to the rest of the class.

3 Look at the two photos below. Imagine you are lost in a big city and want to ask the way. Which of these two people would you ask? Discuss your reaction briefly with a partner.

4 Read the article on page 131. Each sentence below summarises one of the paragraphs. With your partner, match the sentences to the paragraphs.

a) People's differing attitudes to the old and the young.
b) An experiment in what it is like to be old.
c) Old people's feelings.
d) The practical problems of disguising oneself as an old person.

The Incredible Ageing Woman

In an amazing three-year experiment, Pat Moore, a young product designer, lived as an elderly woman on the streets of New York. As 'Old Pat' she roamed around trying to find out what it was like to be old. During the controversial experiment, Pat, now 36, was short-changed by shopkeepers, verbally abused when she got in the way and assaulted and left for dead by a gang of youths out for drugs money. By going into disguise, she had intended to find out hard architectural, design and engineering data. But soon her strict design aims were lost in the welter of new and shocking experience.

One of the most alarming discoveries was the difference in attitude the same people had to the old and the young Pat. Typically, a shop assistant in a Manhattan stationery store ignored the old Pat. He barked at her when she asked if he sold typewriter ribbons and when she genuinely misheard his question about what kind of typewriter she owned, he yelled out her mistake to humiliate her. To ensure she wasn't encountering people's off-days, Pat would return to the same store the next day as her young self, with shoulder length blond hair, young tanned skin and often the same cheap print dress as the Old Pat - not that anyone ever noticed. In the stationery shop the next day the exchange followed the exact same format, right down to her making the same mistake. This time, however, it elicited laughter and jovial response. The young Pat left distraught and dazed. Irascible behaviour became almost a Pavlovian response to her 'aged' appearance.

As far as the disguise was concerned the clothes were the easy part. With the help of friend Barbara Kelly, a make-up artist, they built up a latex mask. To simulate as many of the sensory conditions of the ageing as possible was as important to her as the facial ageing. She put high density 'steel worker's' wax in her ears to impair her hearing and dabs of baby oil in her eyes to cloud her vision. For her body, she developed a wrap that stopped her standing upright and even gave her a slight dowager's hump. Small splints of balsa wood placed at the back of each knee restricted her flexion and a tight tube of material around both thighs stopped her walking too fast. She taped her fingers to simulate arthritic hands and the gloves concealed the tape. She could bend her fingers only with difficulty. The two features which risked giving her away were her voice and her bright white teeth. A paste of crayon and oil stained her teeth and an actor friend advised her that a paste of salt and water held at the back of the throat for several minutes ensured a rasping voice for the next six hours.

Despite the success of the disguise, Pat Moore continually felt guilty that she could change back to being Young Pat. 'I was always painfully aware the disguise was just a shell for me.' To her surprise, however, when she voiced this guilt to her elderly friends, they confirmed the feeling. They too felt they were in a shell - young minds trapped behind old faces. This discovery was a turning point for her. It confirmed her in the growing knowledge that the elderly weren't handicapped by their own physical disabilities so much as by the attitudes and psychological barriers set up by others. A fear of ageing is even built into the English language. We ask 'How old are you?' Whereas other languages ask 'How many years?' or, 'What age?'

(from *The Guardian*)

5 Look at the sentences below in context in the article. With a partner, study the three suggested alternatives for each sentence and decide which one could replace the original sentence in context. The meaning does not have to be exactly the same, but the alternative must make sense in the article and match its style. Give reasons for your choice. The first one has been done for you.

a) As 'Old Pat' she roamed around trying to find out what it was like to be old. (lines 5–7)
   i) She tested people's attitudes to old age.
   ii) Thus disguised, she was able to make a significant contribution to gerontology.
   iii) She used the disguise in order to discover what old people go through.

   The third sentence is the best. In the first one, there is no link with the previous sentence and the writing would be lacking in cohesion. The second one is in the wrong style for a newspaper article.

b) This time, however, it elicited laughter and jovial response. (lines 41–42)
   i) On the second occasion, people started to laugh.
   ii) But on this occasion, the shop assistant was charming.
   iii) But this time, the shop assistant split his sides.

c) A paste of crayon and oil stained her teeth . . . a rasping voice for the next six hours. (lines 72–77)
   i) However, she borrowed a couple of actor's tricks which enabled her to overcome these difficulties.
   ii) Her very original disguise was complete.
   iii) To overcome these problems a friend advised her to treat her teeth with a substance composed of sodium chloride and H_2O and to use a crayon and oil compound which provokes a grating voice.

d) This discovery was a turning point for her. (lines 88–89)
   i) It was a sad day for all.
   ii) These revelations gave her new insight.
   iii) Findings of this nature could only bear out her initial research.

6 Has the article made either of you change your opinion? Report back to the rest of the class.

VOCABULARY

Dealing with difficult words and expressions

1 With a partner, look at the words below from the article on page 131 and then tick the correct definition. Check your answers in the dictionary. The first one has been done for you.

a) roamed (line 5) means:
   i) walked slowly
   ii) walked in a specific direction
   iii) walked with no particular purpose ✓
b) shortchanged (lines 8–9) means:
   i) shouted at
   ii) ignored
   iii) robbed
c) the welter (lines 16–17) means:
   i) the great variety
   ii) the strength
   iii) the overwhelming amount
d) barked (line 25) means:
   i) spoke roughly
   ii) imitated a dog
   iii) made strange noises
e) off-days (line 31) means:
   i) days when most people are on holiday
   ii) days when people are not feeling good
   iii) odd days of the month, e.g. 1st, 3rd, 5th etc.
f) distraught and dazed (lines 43–44) means:
   i) surprised
   ii) upset
   iii) unperturbed
g) irascible (line 44) means:
   i) thoughtless
   ii) violent
   iii) bad-tempered
h) impair her hearing (line 56) means:
   i) protect her hearing
   ii) make her hearing better
   iii) make her hearing worse
i) a rasping voice (line 76) means:
   i) a rough voice
   ii) a soft voice
   iii) an unnatural voice

What else helped you guess: word formation, metaphor, or anything else?

2 Look at the diagram.

a) Label the diagram with the words below. Refer back to the article, and use your dictionary to help you.

latex mask
'steel workers' wax
dabs of baby oil
a slight dowager's hump
wrap
balsa wood splints
a tight tube of material
oil stained teeth
paste of salt

b) With a partner, decide on an area of vocabulary that you need to know well. Choose a topic that you can visualise well rather than something abstract. Draw a diagram or picture and use your dictionary to help you label it. Show your picture or diagram to other people in your class.

Section 2

LEARNING GRAMMAR

▶ Diagnosis ◀◀◀

Comparisons

1 With a partner, correct the mistakes in the following sentences. Refer to the Key if necessary. The first one has been done for you.

a) Champion tennis player Judith Syone uses the same technique to serve than her great rival Mariella Sanchez.
   Champion tennis player Judith Syone uses the same technique to serve as her great rival Mariella Sanchez.
b) Inflation in Italy is higher that in Germany.
c) It was more hot today than yesterday.
d) Of all the movies I have ever seen that one really is worst.
e) I'll have the same pudding like her.
f) You can have as good meal in New York as in Paris.
g) The situation is bad enough, but it would be worst if it was raining.
h) It's the biggest diamond of the world.
i) My kitchen is not so well-planned than yours.

2 Write your own comparative sentences with the prompts below. Underline the complete comparative in each one. Use the corrected sentences in Exercise 1 to help you. Check your examples in the Key. The first one has been done for you.

a) *the same* + noun + ...
   Cara works at the same speed as Ben.
b) short adjective + *-er*
c) *more/less* + adjective + ...
d) *as* + adjective + ...
e) *so* + adjective + ...
f) *as* + adjective + *a* + noun ...
g) *the* + superlative form ...

3 Look at the survey below of men's participation in housework. With a partner make up sentences comparing men from different countries using the following prompts. The first one has been done for you. Check your answers in the key.

a) Laundry / Italy/Britain
   Italian men do not do as much laundry as British men.
b) Ironing / France/Spain
c) Cooking / Italy/Switzerland
d) Cleaning / Italy/Spain
e) Dishwashing / Italy/Britain
f) Shopping / Germany/Italy

Jobs for the boys	Britain	Switzerland	France	Germany	Italy	Spain
Dishwashing	77%	64%	55%	38%	22%	26%
Shopping	48%	58%	60%	41%	43%	45%
Cleaning	73%	35%	51%	40%	34%	32%
Cooking	47%	51%	40%	21%	25%	15%
Laundry	34%	15%	25%	16%	5%	11%
Ironing	29%	6%	20%	10%	3%	6.5%

4 Refer back to the chart and fill in the gaps in the following sentences with one of the modifiers in the box below. The first one has been done for you. Check your answers in the Key.

| much   many   a lot   far
| a great deal   a bit   a little
| slightly   nearly   quite
| twice   half   three times
| etc.

a) *Many* more Spaniards do the shopping than do the washing up.
b) ... as many Germans help with the cleaning as with the shopping.
c) ... more British men help with the laundry than Italian men.
d) ... fewer Germans help with the shopping than Italians.
e) Men in Britain do ... more washing up than men in Germany.
f) ... as many men in Italy do the ironing as men in Switzerland.
g) German men do ... less cooking than British men.

5 Work with a partner.

a) Make other comparisons between the different countries using modifiers from the box above.
b) In small groups, compare men in your own country to the men in the survey.

Unit 17

▶Development◀◀◀

Other comparisons

Continuing processes
A comparative form can be repeated to suggest a process. Examples:
I liked him more and more.
People are living longer and longer.
Parents are less and less strict and more and more understanding.
Fewer and fewer shops are offering discounts.
She is getting better and better every day and will be out of hospital soon.

***the* + comparative + *the* + comparative**
This construction can be used to show cause and effect: when one thing happens, another follows. Examples:
The harder you work, the better you will succeed.
The higher you climb, the more you can see.
You may sometimes come across the structure used in an incomplete and idiomatic way. Examples:
Do come to the party – the more the merrier. (The more people there are, the merrier we shall be.)
Serve champagne cold. In fact the colder, the better. (The colder it is served the better it is.)

More* and *less
This construction can be used to indicate an extreme degree. Examples:
I was more than pleased with the result. (I was delighted.)
We were less than satisfied. (We were not satisfied at all.)

Least
You can indicate that something has less of a quality than anything else with *least*. Example:
That is very unlikely and the least probable solution to the problem.
The first singer was the least popular and no one clapped.

Practice

1 Each of the following sentences illustrates one of the comparisons above. With a partner fill in the gap with an appropriate word or expression. The first one has been done for you.

a) I was *more than* suspicious, I thought she was definitely guilty.
b) . . . it rained, . . . difficult it became to drive.
c) This book is really boring. It is . . . interesting book I have ever read on the subject.
d) I was . . . concerned, in fact I was completely indifferent.
e) Over a period of six months interest declined, the show was . . . popular and . . . people came.

2 Look at the following sentences about continuing processes.

a) Complete them using the repeated comparative form. There may be more than one answer. Check your answers with a partner. The first one has been done for you.
  i) Global warming means that summers are getting *hotter and hotter*.
  ii) There are roughly the same number of daylight hours the whole year round near the equator whereas if you go towards the north or south days get . . . in winter and . . . in summer.
  iii) The mass rural exodus means that big cities are growing . . . .
  iv) Pollution in the world today is getting . . . .
  v) In future there will be more leisure for everybody and people will work . . . .
  vi) In response to a great variety in consumer demand, our company is developing . . . .

b) With your partner, talk about other processes and developments in contexts you know. Example:
We have been doing more and more homework lately.

3 Work with a partner.

a) Match the topics in column A to one of the expressions in column B. Check your answers with a partner.

A
a) Air travel:
b) Holidays:
c) A TV screen:
d) An exam:
e) Strawberries:
f) Rent for accommodation:

B
1 the cheaper the better
2 the riper they are the tastier they are
3 the bigger the better
4 the safer it is the better
5 the easier it is the more chance I have of succeeding
6 the longer the better

b) In small groups use the same structure to express your views on some of the topics in the box below and on other topics of interest to your group.

Children	Cars	Films	Food	Music
Housework	Medical research
TV	Books	Sport

LANGUAGE PATTERNS

Like and As: conjunctions

1 *As* is normally a conjunction and is followed by a clause. Example:
He stays up working all night and drinking black coffee, as I used to when I was young.
As can also be used for comparisons in prepositional phrases. Example:
The pound dropped suddenly, as in 1973.

2 *Like* is sometimes used instead of *as* as a conjunction. In this case it can means 'in the same way as'. Example:
No one can hit a ball like she used to.
It is also used with the meaning 'as if', although some British people consider this use of *like* to be incorrect. Example:
He ran like a pack of wolves were after him.

Like and As: prepositions

Like is normally a preposition and is followed by a noun. Example:
She ran like the wind.
As is also used as a preposition which indicates a role or a function of the person or thing. Example:
She's got a job as a computer programmer.

Verbs with *as* or *like*

The following verbs are followed by *like*: *be, look, seem, feel, sound, smell, taste*
The following verbs are followed by *as: portray, depict, describe* Examples:
She looked like an ordinary, elderly woman with grey hair.
She was described as an ordinary, elderly woman with grey hair.

Practice

Work with a partner to fill in the gaps in the following sentences with *like* or *as*. When both are possible, explain why, with reference to the points explained above. The first one has been done for you.

a) That box serves *as* a table.
b) She plays tennis . . . a champion.
c) In the travel agent's brochure the hotel was described . . . a palace, but in reality it looked more . . . a slum.
d) He worries when his children come home late, just . . . I do.
e) In this biography, Grace Kelly is portrayed . . . a goddess.
f) He is working . . . a waiter in a local restaurant.

VOCABULARY

Idioms with *like*

These idioms are often used informally. Study column B and find the idiom which is related in context and meaning to the sentences in column A.

A
a) She has a huge appetite.
b) They are very good friends.
c) We were so tired after our walk.
d) She was so frightened.
e) It was the most exciting news we had heard for ages.
f) She is always broke.
g) He's so clumsy.

B
1 spend money like water
2 tremble like a leaf
3 spread like wildfire
4 eat like a horse
5 get on like a house on fire
6 be like a bull in a china shop
7 sleep like a log

With a partner, think of other contexts in which you could use the expressions in column B.
Example:
Have you broken the teapot again? You're just like a bull in a china shop.

Unit 17

Section 3

READING

1 Look back at the pictures at the beginning of this unit and answer the following questions with a partner.

a) Do any of the photos remind you of old people you know?
b) Which of the following statements describe the old people you know?
 i) They have time to enjoy life. ii) They are lonely. iii) They are much loved by their families. iv) They are often sick and in pain. v) They command a lot of respect. vi) They like to talk a lot. vii) Anything else

2 [17.1] Read and listen to the poem.

TWO OLD WOMEN

The two of us sit in the doorway,
chatting about our children and grandchildren.
We sink happily
into our oldwomanhood.
Like two spoons
sinking
into a bowl of hot porridge.

(by Anna Swir)

a) Which of the adjectives in the box below could describe porridge? Which ones do you think the writer of the poem was thinking of particularly?

spicy	nourishing	comforting	soft
thick	healthy	grey	sweet	tasty
sticky	pleasant	bland

b) Think of images to describe the old people you talked about in Section 1 of this unit. For example:
My great aunt is magnificent despite her age. She is like a setting sun.
I have a friend who is as dignified and elegant as a silver birch tree.

3 Write your own poem about two people of your choice. You can work with a partner or alone. Then read out your poem to other people in the class. Begin like this.
Two . . .

TALKING EFFECTIVELY

1 Listen to the poem again and mark in the way the words are linked together. For example:

The two of us sit in the doorway,

chatting about our children and grandchildren.

2 Practise reading out the poem to a partner, making sure you link the words as on the tape.

SPEAKING

Personal and cultural differences

1 In small groups, discuss the following questions.

a) Look at the photos below and decide who you would find it easy to communicate with and who you would not. Give your reasons.

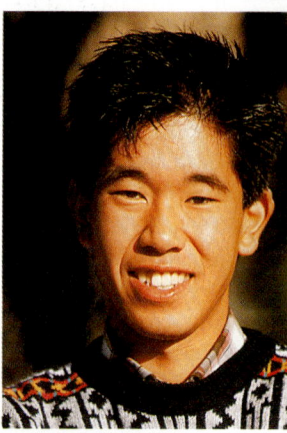

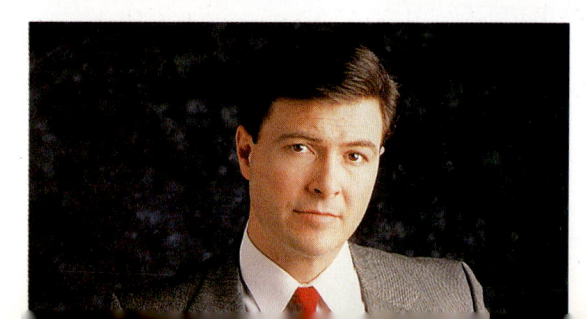

b) Study the diagram below of the way in which certain nationalities reveal their personal thoughts and ideas to a greater or lesser extent. If you come from one of these countries, how much do you agree with the diagram and how much do you disagree? If you come from somewhere else, how does your country compare with the countries in the diagram?

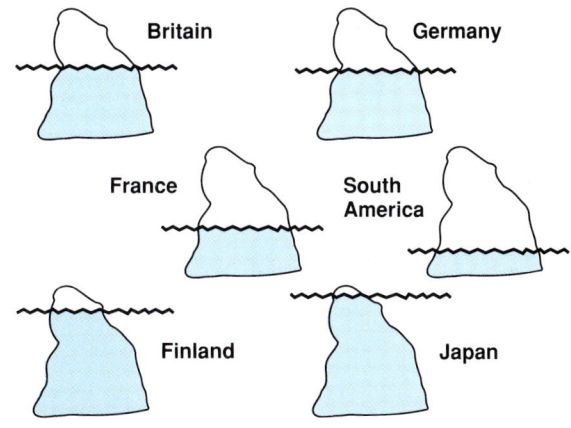

Britain   Germany
France   South America
Finland   Japan

Different nationalities reveal their ideas to a lesser or greater degree. As with Icebergs, most thought is kept below the surface.

c) What else do you know about the cultural characteristics of nationalities you know of? Think of some of the following:
   i) How formal or informal are people in the way they meet and entertain friends or business acquaintances?
   ii) How formal or informal are people in the way they dress?
   iii) Do people make a lot of gestures or only very few?
   iv) How much physical contact do people have, a lot or only a little (handshaking, kissing, hugging, putting a hand on someone's shoulder)?
   v) How close to each other do people from different countries stand when they are chatting together?
   vi) How much emotion do people show, a lot, or only a little?
   vii) What sort of attitude do people have to punctuality and time, strict or not strict?
   viii) Any other differences?
d) What kind of people do you like being with, people who are similar to yourself or people who are different?
e) How can we gain a better understanding of people who are very different from ourselves?

Report back your discussion to the whole class.

2   Be someone different for a day!

a) If you could be someone completely different for a day, who would you be: somebody much older, somebody much younger, somebody of another nationality or from another walk of life? Would you choose out of curiosity like the woman in the article? Or would you choose for pleasure? Make notes on the person of your choice under the following headings:
   i) What is a typical day for this person?
   ii) What are the pleasures/difficulties of the person's life?
   iii) What is special about the person's life?
   iv) How do people treat this person?
   v) What are the person's relationships like at work, with friends and family, etc.
   vi) How would people's attitudes to this person be different from people's attitudes to you in your life?
b) Choose a partner. Interview each other about your 'new' life. Talk in the first person ('I').

WRITING

1   Work in groups of three.

a) Discuss interesting personal experiences. You can choose a dramatic experience, a frightening experience, an enjoyable experience or any other experience which is interesting. Choose one person's experience and discuss it in detail.
b) Each student writes up the experience in the first person ('I') as if it had happened to him or to her. Do not include real names of people and places, but try and write from a personal point of view and give lots of details in order to be convincing.
c) Join up with two other groups. In turn each of the three students in a group reads out his or her story. When all three stories have been read out, the other groups try to guess which of the three stories was written by the person to whom the experience really happened.
d) Discuss the reasons for your guesses and why one account seems more plausible than another.

2   Report back to the whole class and read out some of the accounts which were written very convincingly.

UNIT 18

A current affairs documentary

Section 1

LISTENING

1 You are going to listen to Nigel Chapman, editor of a weekly current affairs TV documentary programme. Before you listen, discuss the following questions with a partner.

a) What kind of current affairs programmes are broadcast on TV in your country?
b) Can you remember any which you found particularly interesting?
c) Make a list of interesting topics for a current affairs documentary in your country today.

2 [18.1] Listen to the tape. Are Nigel Chapman's topics similar to the ones you have thought of or are they different? Compare notes with another pair.

3 Listen to the tape again and answer the following questions.

a) According to Nigel Chapman's definition of his programme, which of the following topics might interest him?
   i) educational reforms
   ii) world trade
   iii) general elections
b) In which of the following ways does Nigel Chapman find his stories?
   i) a member of the public tells him
   ii) a government institution asks him to cover a story
   iii) a story is already in the news

4 Listen to the tape again. What does Nigel Chapman mean by the following?

a) going downhill
b) whistle-blowers
c) spot on
d) crystal ball gazing

5 Work in pairs.

a) Before you listen to the second part of the tape, match the definitions below to the words in the box. Use a dictionary to help you.

rushes	videotape editor
cutting room	rough cut
dubbing	script
early out	transcript

   i) The person responsible for cutting and splicing the final version of a film.
   ii) The soundtrack that is added to the film.
   iii) The commentary written by the reporter.
   iv) The place where the film is edited.
   v) All the material that has been filmed.
   vi) The written record of an interview.
   vii) An interview which is cut in an unnatural place.
   viii) The film when it is more or less the right length for the final version.

b) [18.2] Listen to the tape and check your answers.
c) With a partner, write down from memory the process of making a documentary. Listen again and check your work.

138

6 In small groups, discuss the following questions.

a) Do journalists always respect the truth in news programmes in your country? Can you remember precise examples when they did or they didn't?
b) In what ways can journalists disguise the truth?
c) What news is important in your country? What comes first – the political news or the football results?

TALKING EFFECTIVELY

Sounding interested

1 [18.3] Read the dialogue below and listen to the two recorded versions of it. In which version is Speaker B interested? In which does she sound bored?

A: I'm leaving for Rio on Saturday.
B: How lovely. What for?
A: Well, for my job, mostly, but I'm having a bit of a holiday as well.
B: Are you? Lucky you.
A: Yes, I've never been to South America before.
B: Really. How very exciting.
A: Yes, I'm really looking forward to it.
B: Are you?

2 With a partner, mark in the intonation pattern which shows interest/shows boredom.

Practice

1 Work in pairs. Student A reads out the statements below to student B who responds as in the dialogues above (either bored or interested). Then swap roles.

a) I'm having a party on Saturday.
b) I had an accident on the way.
c) I've got a new job.
d) We're going to that new vegetarian restaurant this evening.

2 Tell your partner what you did yesterday. Is he or she interested or bored? Swap roles.

Section 2

LEARNING GRAMMAR

Diagnosis

Question tags

1 Work with a partner.

a) Correct the following question tags where necessary. There may be more than one answer. Refer to the guidelines in the Key if you are not sure.
  i) Let's go, go we?
  ii) Come and visit us, won't you?
  iii) She isn't coming, isn't she?
  iv) You are taking your exam next week, are you?
  v) Bob arrives at 8 o'clock, isn't he?
  vi) There's not been a mistake, has there?
  vii) Open the door, wouldn't you?
  viii) Sit down and behave, will you?
  ix) She can leave now, doesn't she?

b) With your partner, decide if the sentences in Exercise 1 are:
  i) a request.
  ii) an invitation.
  iii) a suggestion.
  iv) an order.
  v) a request for confirmation or agreement.
  vi) a way of showing interest.

2 [18.4] Listen to the tape.

a) Note whether the intonation pattern on each question tag is rising or falling. Check your answers in the Key.
b) Look at the sentences which are a request for confirmation or agreement. How certain of the answer is the speaker when the intonation is rising, and when it is falling? Refer to the Key if you are not sure.
c) Write *R* (*Rising*) or *F* (*Falling*) or *R* and *F* (*Rising* and *Falling*) against the list of different functions of question tags in Exercise 1b). The first one has been done for you.
  i) a request R

3 With a partner complete the following sentences with a question tag. Decide whether the intonation is rising or falling, or could be either. Practise saying them. The first one has been done for you.

a) She can't be hungry, *can she? Rising or falling intonation*
b) Phone me next week, . . . ?
c) You had spent too much money, . . . ?
d) Let's have a look, . . . ?
e) I'm coming with you, . . . ?
f) She usually has three lumps of sugar, . . . ?
g) Shut up, . . . ?
h) You'd like a cup of coffee, . . . ?
i) We haven't been here before, . . . ?
j) Come to dinner next Friday, . . . ?

4 Role play this situation.

a) You are having a party this evening with a friend. One of you is checking that the other has done everything he or she should have done.

STUDENT A
Check some of the following by asking questions with question tags. Decide which ones you are almost sure of which will have a falling intonation pattern, and which ones you are not sure of which will have a rising intonation pattern. The first one has been done for you.
  i) bought enough drink. *You have bought enough drink, haven't you?*
  ii) ordered the food.
  iii) invited the Smiths.
  iv) arranged sleeping accommodation for the guests who are staying the night.
  v) arranged the furniture.
  vi) asked two students to help serve food and drink.
  vii) arranged for someone to help clean up tomorrow.
  viii) anything else

STUDENT B
The ticks correspond to what you have done and the crosses to what you have not done. Respond with short answers. The first one has been done for you.
  i) bought enough drink. ✓ *Yes, of course I have.*
  ii) ordered the food. ✓
  iii) invited the Smiths. X
  iv) arranged sleeping accommodation for the guests who are staying the night. X
  v) arranged the furniture. ✓
  vi) asked two students to help serve food and drink. ✓
  vii) arranged for someone to help clean up tomorrow. X
  viii) anything else. ✓

b) With a partner, ask and answer questions with tags to check other things. Example: *The course ends next week, doesn't it?*

▶ Development ◀◀◀

Focussing on information: auxiliary verbs

1 Study the two sets of sentences below which illustrate the two types of context in which auxiliaries are stressed to give special emphasis.

a) i) I *have* loved being here.
   ii) I *must* have something to drink.
   iii) You *do* look nice in that dress!
   iv) You *will* come, won't you?
   v) She *does* complain a lot, doesn't she?
   vi) *Do* come in!
   vii) I *was* pleased to see him.
b) i) 'You haven't been listening to a word that I've been saying' 'I *have* been listening.'
   ii) I don't usually go to rock concerts but I *did* go to see the Rolling Stones.
   iii) 'There's another packet of biscuits in the cupboard.' 'There *isn't*, or at least I *can't* see any.'
   iv) 'Why didn't you tell them?' 'I *did* tell them. They must have forgotten.'
   v) Classes usually finish at 4 o'clock but students *do* stay later when we put on social activities.
   vi) I've never been to China, but I *have* been to Hong Kong.

2 Discuss the following questions with a partner.

a) What is the context in each sentence?
b) What do the examples in set 1 a) have in common? What specific meaning is conveyed by stressing the auxiliary?
c) What do the examples in set 1 b) have in common? What specific meaning is conveyed by stressing the auxiliary?

3 With your partner, look back at the sentences in Exercise 1 and decide which of the following statements are true.

a) The auxiliary *do* is added to express emphasis in sentences in which no auxiliary is already present.
b) The auxiliary *do* can be added to any sentence to give special emphasis.
c) The simple auxiliary (*do*, *be* or *have*) or the modal auxiliary has strong stress.
d) A stressed auxiliary is used in contexts of strong emotion and of conflict, contradiction or exception.

Practice

1 In pairs, take it in turns to respond to the following sentences. One of you reads out the prompt and the other replies using a simple or a modal auxiliary or the verb *to be* and stressing it correctly. The first one has been done for you.

a) A: I don't think you're really interested in this project.
   B: *But I am interested in it.*
b) A: I could be right.
   B: No, . . .
c) A: You don't understand.
   B: But . . .
d) A: You've made a mistake again.
   B: No, . . .
e) A: Why didn't you tell her?
   B: But I . . . .
f) A: You thought I would agree.
   B: Yes, . . .
g) A: We're not there yet.
   B: Yes, . . .
h) A: You can't leave like that.
   B: . . . if I want to.

2 Expressing enthusiasm: the overenthusiastic host/hostess. In pairs, you are going to role play a situation in which a host or hostess is trying to do everything to make his or her guest happy for the weekend. Before you begin, imagine the situation. Who are you? What is your relationship to each other? What are you going to do for the weekend? You can choose one of the situations below or imagine your own. Situations:

a) You are staying with a business colleague and will be working some of the weekend.
b) You are staying with your girlfriend's or boyfriend's family for the first time.
c) You are staying with your favourite aunt, who has provided a weekend full of social activities.

STUDENT A
You want your guest to be happy. Express concern about all aspects of the person's well-being and use the ways of giving emphasis you have studied in this section. Here are some examples to help you get started.
You would like some more tea, wouldn't you?
You do like breakfast in bed, don't you? I'll bring it at eight o'clock.
You would like to spend some time visiting the surrounding countryside, wouldn't you? We can't work all the time.

STUDENT B
You have come to stay with a very kind friend for the weekend. He/she cannot be helpful enough and is very concerned about your welfare. Respond politely to his or her concern with expressions like:
That's very kind of you.
Of course.
I'd love to. I'd love some.
Everything's fine.
Please don't bother.

Unit 18

Focussing on information: cleft sentences

1 Look at the following pairs of sentences and note the different ways in which the information is presented. The second example in each case contains a clause beginning with *it, what* or *all*, to focus on a particular element in the sentence.

a) i) Brian arrived on Saturday.
   ii) It was on Saturday that Brian arrived.
b) i) Getting that job was a turning point in my life.
   ii) It was getting that job that was a turning point in my life.
c) i) We need a new manager.
   ii) What we need is a new manager.
d) i) I just need a holiday.
   ii) All (that) I need is a holiday.

2 In the following sentence, focus on the different elements of information with the prompts provided.

a) Sarah Bright gave a lecture in Westminster Hall on 1st April at 6h30.
b) *It was on 1st April that Sarah Bright gave a lecture in Westminster Hall.*
c) It was at . . .
d) It was in . . .
e) What Sarah Bright did . . .

3 You can focus on information in this way after the verb as well as before it if you use *what* or *all*. Examples:
A new manager is what we need.
A holiday is all (that) I need.

You can use other *wh-* words in this structure: Examples:
Where I'm going is none of your business.
The boss is who I'm going to see.

4 This way of focussing is used in various contexts, particularly the following:
a) to clarify information. Example:
   'So you lost your passport, did you?' 'No, what I lost was my wallet.'
   'So you lost everything, did you?' 'No, all I lost was my passport.'
b) to talk about likes, dislikes, wants and needs. Examples:
   What I liked most about the film was the wonderful photography.
   What I really enjoy is a good walk in the country.
   All Bob needs is a bit of encouragement.

Practice

1 Clarify the misunderstandings in the following sentences with the prompts. There may be more than one answer. Check your answers with a partner. The first one has been done for you.

a) So you are writing a biography, are you?
   No, . . . (novel)
   No, what I'm writing is a novel.
b) So you went to Italy next, did you?
   No, where . . . (Spain).
c) So you'd like a book token for Christmas, would you?
   No, . . . (record token)
d) We're leaving on Sunday, aren't we?
   No, . . . (on Monday)
e) Emma brought you home, did she?
   No, . . . (Julie)
f) So I should ask Sarah, should I?
   No, . . . (Fiona)
g) So everybody knows where he's gone, do they?
   No, . . . (a secret)
h) So you won first prize, did you?
   No, . . . (second prize)
i) So Tracey and John have started a small printing business, have they?
   No, . . . (travel business)
j) So Aunt Emma has written an autobiography, has she?
   No, . . . (mostly fiction)
k) So the dates of the conference are settled, are they?
   No, . . . (the venue)

2 In small groups, talk about people, things and activities using a focussing structure and one of the verbs in the box. Examples:
It's his kindness that I appreciate most.
What I can't stand about TV is the ads.
What I enjoy about sailing is the sense of freedom.

appreciate	admire	adore	love	enjoy
want	prefer	dislike	can't stand	
need	hate	loathe		

LANGUAGE PATTERNS

No matter, whatever, however, etc.

In the following pairs of sentences, the speaker's message is similar but one of them expresses it more strongly and suggests that absolutely nothing could change the situation. With a partner, compare each pair and answer the question below it.

a) i) I couldn't say anything to make her change her mind.
   ii) No matter what I said, I couldn't make her change her mind.
   In which sentence did 'I' try the hardest?
b) i) Bob works hard but he fails his exams.
   ii) Bob fails his exams, however hard he works.
   In which sentence does the speaker think that Bob can just never work hard enough to pass his exams?
c) i) I'll follow you wherever you go.
   ii) I'll follow you everywhere.
   In which sentence is 'I' absolutely determined not to lose sight of 'you'?
d) i) I like her paintings.
   ii) I like whatever she paints.
   Which sentence expresses more admiration for the painter?

Practice

Rewrite the following sentences using the prompt given so that they express greater emphasis. The first one has been done for you. Check your answers with a partner.

a) Tell anyone who phones that I am out.
   Whoever phones, tell them I am out.
b) She would eat nothing that I gave her.
   No matter . . .
c) Even if he has a lot of money, he still wants more.
   However . . .
d) Which one do you want? Take either of them.
   Take whichever . . .
e) It will upset her, even if you break the news very carefully.
   However . . .
f) Every time I take an exam, I get butterflies in my tummy.
   Whenever . . .

Section 3

PROJECT WORK

Making a documentary

1 In small groups, think of as many possible topics for a documentary as you can. It could be a radio programme or a video depending on the technical support available in your school. As you think of ideas, you will need to take the following into consideration:

a) Are you able to interview native speakers of English? If you are not in an English-speaking country, speakers of English, native and non-native, may be visiting your town as tourists or on business. Failing this, you will need to plan to interview speakers in other languages and translate them into English, or other people in your school or class who are willing to be interviewed.

b) What is the strong point of the topic you are considering? Has it got good narrative or descriptive possibilities? If you are going to present conflicting views, can you think of sufficiently varied sequences?

c) If you are short of ideas, look through the newspapers of the past few days or look back through this book and develop a topic such as ageing, the future or education, or any other which has interested you. You might also think of something of local interest, such as reactions to a local tourist sight or museum, a local industry or craft or a local artist.

2 Choose one of the topics on your list that you would like to make into a documentary and present your topic to the class. The class will give you feedback, suggestions for improvement and so on.

3 Write a draft script for your documentary. Use the following checklist to help you.

a) How will you introduce the topic?
b) What different points do you want to make?
c) How many interviews do you need? Will they be the same point of view or different points of view?
d) What questions will you ask your interviewees?
e) How will you conclude your documentary?

4 Collecting the interviews. Your teacher will help you organise this stage of your work. Remember to encourage your interviewees by using the intonation pattern for showing interest practised in *Talking effectively*, Section 1.

5 Editing. Decide on the most interesting bits of your interviews. You will have to cut pitilessly – your programme should not last more than ten minutes! Write the narrative to link up the interviews. Record your programme, if you have the technical support to do so. If not, be prepared to present your documentary live.

6 Feedback. Swap your tape with another group, or present your documentary to the class. Look at the feedback sheet below before you listen to other people's documentaries.

WRITING

1 Choose one of the documentaries made by someone else in your class and write a review of it for the television pages of a media magazine.

a) Make a plan, deciding how much of your review will be descriptive and how much opinion. Remember that your job is to interest the reader, but also to leave something for him or her to discover on viewing.
b) Look back at the section *Focussing on information: cleft sentences*. Write some sentences about the documentary you have chosen using this structure. Example:
What this documentary was illustrating was . . .
What I really liked about this documentary was . . .
c) Write your review.

2 Make all the reviews into a class catalogue of your documentaries. Find another class which has done the same activity. Read their catalogue and borrow the documentaries which interest you.

---

1 Before you listen to or look at each documentary, with a partner jot down two or three questions about the topic to which you would like to know the answer.

2 Listen to or look at the documentary.

3 Ask the production team any of your questions which have not been answered.

4 What did you learn from this documentary?

5 Did it make you want to know more about the topic? What, in particular?

6 How did you react to it? Describe your feelings.

Key to grammar diagnosis

UNIT 1

Answers

1 Tenses and verb forms
a) are having / has not rained / continues / will be 4 marks
b) has been / went 2 marks
c) passes / runs / kicks / puts 2 marks ($1/2$ mark each)
d) be doing / have been waiting 2 marks
e) had known / would not have invested 2 marks
f) is rising / is decreasing 1 mark ($1/2$ mark each)
g) have gone 1 mark
h) would be able to / will be (or are) 2 marks
i) to go / would be 2 marks
j) living 1 mark
k) Will you marry 1 mark
TOTAL 20 marks

2 Score 1 mark for each correct answer.
a) fewer (for a countable noun) – though many native speakers of English do not make this distinction any longer, at least when they speak.
b) latest c) as d) people e) said
TOTAL 5 marks

3 The problem is word order. Score 1 mark for each sentence you wrote out correctly. Take off one mark for anything that you changed which was correct.
a) I don't know where the treasure is.
b) She picked up the phone again and called her parents.
c) Are you coming tonight?
d) I would like to explain the problem to you.
e) She's a very good blues singer.
TOTAL 5 marks

4 Score 1 mark for each correct answer.
a) in b) for c) on d) no preposition e) no preposition
TOTAL 5 marks

5 Score as marked for each sentence. Take off one mark for anything that you changed which was correct.
a) The receptionist gave me a lot of information about London. 1 mark
b) Human beings are made that way! 1 mark
c) There will be a new economic crisis if inflation is not stopped. 1 mark
d) Government policies on the immigration question are becoming more and more strict. 1 mark
e) My father gave me a lot of advice before I came to London and said studying English was very hard work.
1 mark ($1/2$ mark for each mistake)
TOTAL 5 marks

6 Score 1 mark for each correct sentence. Take off one mark for anything that you changed which was correct.
a) I was born in Buenos Aires.
b) This Friday I am meeting an American business man. (capital letters)
c) I lived in Tokyo for two months.
d) You can stay longer if you like.
e) My hotel was near the Tower of London.
f) The people who left the meeting all disagreed with the speaker.
g) I want us to begin the meeting at 8 a.m.
h) You mustn't smoke on the Tube in London. You will be fined £50 if you do.
i) I had dinner before coming here.
j) I do not agree with you.
TOTAL 10 marks

Now add up your score out of 50 and read the analysis which follows.

Analysis

40–50 marks. You know a lot of English grammar and are ready to embark on this course. You may not even need to look at the *Diagnosis* sections very much.

35–45 marks. You know the right amount of grammar to start out on this course. When you do the *Diagnosis* sections, you may occasionally need to ask your teacher for more practice exercises.

25–35 marks. Your reading, speaking and listening skills are probably fluent enough for you to be able to use this course book without any problem, but you still have quite a lot of work to do on your basic English grammar and may well need quite a lot of extra practice if this area of your learning is important for you.

Less than 25. You may well find the grammar section of this course book quite difficult and need quite a lot of extra revision work as you go along.

UNIT 2

Guidelines: Continuous tenses

1 The choice of simple or continuous tenses is sometimes directly related to the meaning of a sentence. For example:
a) We usually use the simple present for a habitual event: *Stephany **goes** to school every day.*
b) We usually use the present continuous tense for an action in progress: *Stephany **is doing** her Homework.*

2 However, the choice of tense can also simply represent a different way of presenting information. For example, the difference between the following two sentences would probably be insignificant.
*I **live** in Hampstead.*
*I**'m living** in Hampstead.*

3 Overuse of the past and past perfect continuous tenses could become very heavy stylistically. Ultimately, it is often the rhythm of the sentence which governs a writer's choice. Fortunately most of these decisions are made subconsciously once you have a sufficient command of the language!

Answers

1 a)
i) This sentence expresses a temporary event in progress. However, the presence of 'every day . . .' would make the simple present quite appropriate and the emphasis would then be on the habitual action.
ii) 'have taken' would be possible but the sentence refers

Key

to foods taken at any period in the speaker's life rather than the period up to the moment of speaking.
iii) 'still emanate' would be possible and would present the information as permanent truth or scientific fact, rather than a description of what was actually happening.
iv) 'had developed' would imply that the phobias were now fully developed, whereas 'had been developing' implies that the process is incomplete.
v) The continuous tense describes the action in progress and emphasises the duration. 'Recorded' and 'made' are possible: the action would be seen as an event.

2 a) The continuous tense would not make much difference here, but it would emphasise the duration of the action. If both verbs were in the past continuous, the actions would be parallel.
b) The present continuous here would emphasise the continuity or regularity of the 'leadings' whereas the simple form merely indicates the fact that leadings have occurred. *are being* is not possible.
c) No change possible for either verb. 'Had' here expresses a state rather than an activity. 'Learned' refers to what has just been learned, therefore to a completed action.
d) The continuous form would make very little difference here, simply emphasising the duration of the action.

UNIT 3

Guidelines: *Used to and Would*

a) The modal auxiliary *used to* is followed by the base form of the verb. Example:
Jane **used to have** long curly hair.
Be careful not to confuse it with the multi-part verb *to be used to + -ing*. Example:
Jane **was used to living** in the big city and didn't mind the people and the dirt.

b) There are two negative forms of *used to*:
i) Graham **didn't use to** have a car. (Found mostly in spoken English)
ii) Graham **used not to** have a car. (Found mostly in fairly formal English.)

Used to and *would*
c) *Used to* can be used to talk about actions and states in the past. Examples:
i) We **used to go** to the cinema on Saturdays.
ii) There **used to b**e a cinema in the centre of town.
Note: You cannot use *would* to talk about states in the past.
~~There would be a cinema in the centre of town.~~

d) *Used to* always refers to an event or state in the past which no longer exists and can be understood without any extra context. Example:
I **used to** smoke.
Would is not used with the meaning of habitual action in the past unless the context is clear. Example:
I **would smoke** a cigar after Sunday lunch.

Answers

1 b) Jane used to buy a new car every two years.
c) Correct
d) Sally used to have a dog when she was little.
e) People do not work as hard as they used to.
f) Correct

2 Note that the scene is set with *used to*. It would be unusual to start a story with *would*.

UNIT 4

Guidelines: *The, a, or Ø (zero article)*

1 Uncountable nouns which refer to general things such as qualities, processes, substances or topics are not usually used with the determiners *the*, *a* or *an*. For example: *freedom, music, glass*.

2 No definite article before *most* when it means 'the majority of'. Compare 'the most beautiful' superlative structure.

3 In some common expressions with prepositions, no determiner is used with a count noun. For example: *at school, in church, on foot, by rail*.

4 The determiner *the* is used with the names of musical instruments in British English. For example:
I play the violin. (cf Am. English *I play violin*.)

5 The general determiner *a* or *an* is used with names of professions. For example:
She wants to be a scientist.

6 Proper names are not usually used with determiners. See 7 for exceptions.

7 The determiner *the* is used with names of seas and oceans, rivers (*the Amazon*), mountain ranges (*the Alps*), groups of islands (*the Canaries*), etc.

8 No determiner is used with the possessive *'s* and a proper name. Compare '*I.B.M.'s excellent results.*' and '*The company's excellent results.*'

Answers

1 a) Apples are my favourite fruit.
b) I love travelling by plane.
c) Correct
d) The Himalayas are higher than any other mountains in the world.
e) What a beautiful view!
f) I have never been to South America.
g) Correct

2 The numbers in brackets refer to the guidelines above
a) Ø (1) b) Ø (3) c) the (4) d) a (5) e) Ø (6) f) The (7)
g) Ø / the (8) h) Ø i) Ø (2)

UNIT 5

Guidelines: Uses of the past perfect

1 The past perfect is often used with conjunctions of time (*when, after, as soon as, by the time that*). However, it is not always necessary unless you want to make the sequence in time very clear. Notice the difference in the following examples.
When I **did** the shopping, I **had** a cup of coffee. (I had a coffee while I was shopping.)
When I **had done** the shopping, I **had** a cup of coffee. (I had a cup of coffee after I had finished the shopping.)

2 The past perfect cannot be used to make an event more distant in the past in an isolated context. For example, you cannot say:
~~We had been to Venice a long time ago.~~

3 The past perfect is not always necessary when we talk about two things that happened at different times in the past. It is usually used when we are talking mainly about one moment but want to refer back to another.

4 The past perfect is not usually repeated in a sentence or a paragraph if the time sequence is obvious from the context or because one verb is already in the past perfect.

5 The past perfect is usual when the subject of the two clauses in the sentence are the same. Notice the difference in the following examples.
When I **had done** the shopping, I **drove** home.
When I **gave** the little girl a lollypop, she **said** thank you.

6 The past perfect continuous is used to express duration up to a point in the past.

Answers

1 a)
i) We lived in Hong Kong when I was a child.
ii) Correct
iii) When Noah set sail on the ark, he took every kind of living creature with him.
iv) Correct
v) By the time I got there the room was empty and everyone had left.
vi) I left my shoes to be repaired on Monday. Are they ready yet?
vii) Correct. or When I had finished my speech, I sat down.

2
b) arrived – specific action in the past
c) had left – the action needs to be situated in a sequence before Harry appearing
d) appeared – another action in the past
e) explained – another action
f) had been looking – duration up to the point when he appeared
g) had put/put – past perfect not obligatory as sequence clear from context. Repetition would be inelegant.
h) had got/got – past perfect not obligatory and repetition of past perfect here would be very inelegant
i) thought – past perfect not obligatory
j) was – past perfect not obligatory
k) was eating – temporary duration in the past

UNIT 6

Guidelines: Adverbs

1 a) Adverbs are normally placed after the verb at the end of the clause. However, they can be placed in initial or mid-position and there is often a choice. Factors governing this choice can be:
i) the focus or emphasis that the speaker or writer wishes to give.
ii) the rhythm of the sentence.
iii) the complexity of a sentence with several adjuncts.
b) Adverbs most often found in end-position: place, manner, time.

2 a) Adverbs at the beginning of a clause have special emphasis. Notice this difference in the following examples:
We are leaving **tomorrow.**
Tomorrow we're leaving.
b) The following adverbs are not usually used in this position:
i) Adverbs of degree (*nearly, totally, very,* etc.)
ii) Frequency adverbs
iii) Adverbs of place (for exceptions, see *Development*)
Some other adverbs do not sound right at the beginning of a clause. For example, you cannot normally say:
~~Thoroughly she cleaned the room.~~ or ~~Late she came.~~

3 a) Adverbs in mid-position have less emphasis than adverbs in initial position but more emphasis than adverbs in end-position. Compare the following examples:
Slowly she opened the parcel.
She **slowly** opened the parcel.
She opened the parcel **slowly**.
b) Frequency adverbs (*often, frequently, never*), adverbs of degree (*nearly, almost, thoroughly, hardly*) and some other common adverbs (*certainly, recently, still,* etc.) are usually in this position.
c) When these adverbs are used in sentences with *auxiliary + verb*, they go between the two parts of the verb.
d) When the verb has more than two parts (including a modal auxiliary), the frequency adverb comes after the first auxiliary.

4 In general, adverbs of time ('when') come after adverbs of manner ('how') and place ('where').

5 Some adverbs, e.g. those used to evaluate (*well, badly*) normally go in end position. Note, however, that they can come before a past participle in a passive structure used as an adjective, e.g. *This interior is **well** designed. Hard* is used in the same way.

Answers

1 a) ii) Jane often visits her parents.
    iii) Sharon always works on Sundays.
   b) i) The postman delivers the mail at noon.
    ii) We celebrated Jacky's birthday yesterday.
    iii) The committee meets monthly to discuss general business.
   c) i) The policewoman examined the evidence carefully. (possibly: The policewoman carefully examined the evidence.)
    ii) Rosie walked through the room elegantly. or Rosie walked elegantly through the room. or Rosie elegantly walked through the room.
    iii) Joe failed his exam badly.
   d) i) We nearly missed the bus.
    ii) They almost had an accident.
    iii) She hardly smiled the whole evening.
   e) i) We drove southwards yesterday.
    ii) After the party we went home.
    iii) I have never been there.

2 a) b) time c) manner d) degree e) place
b) b) end-position c) end-position, though they can go in mid-position. (See guidelines) d) mid-position e) end-position

3
a) ii) The plane was late.
    iv) I always make the same mistake.
    ix) Ben plays the piano badly.

Key

b) i) The place of an adverb sometimes depends on fixed rules.
ii) The place of an adverb sometimes depends on the emphasis the speaker wants to give.
iii) Some adverbs of time can go in initial position.
iv) Adverbs of manner rarely go in initial position.
v) Adverbs expressing attitude, comment or viewpoint can always go in initial position.

4 Brackets (. . .) indicate a choice of position.
b) (Sometimes) I may (sometimes) have been a little harsh with my children (sometimes).
c) Karen walked into the room backwards.
d) I know the area well.
e) (Honestly) I don't (honestly) know.
f) She hurt her arm badly.
g) Although I have broken a leg three times, I still like skiing.
h) You have designed this interior well.
i) I hardly knew Kate.

UNIT 7

Guidelines: Present and past participles

1 We can use certain past participles such as *interested, bored, excited, frightened, tiring,* etc. to describe the way people feel about something. For example:
Bob was very **excited** about the holiday.
Megan was **tired** after the journey.

2 We can use the present participle to talk about the person or thing that causes these feelings (*interesting, boring, exciting, frightening, tiring,* etc.) For example:
The holiday was **exciting**.
The journey was **tiring**.

3 We usually use the participle before a noun when we want to talk about a fairly permanent characteristic or a state. For example:
a **barking** dog (barking is a characteristic of the dog), a **sleeping** dog (a dog which is in a temporary state of sleep), a **torn** curtain (a description of the state of the curtain after it has been torn).

4 We usually put the participle after the noun if we are thinking more of the action than of a characteristic or a state. For example:
Who does that dog **barking** out there belong to?
It will be difficult to repair the curtain **torn** last night.
This use of the participle is like a relative clause in which the relative pronoun and the auxiliary verb have been omitted.
Who does that dog **which is barking** out there belong to?
It will be difficult to repair the curtain **(which was) torn**.

5 Present participles are usually only used to talk about actions which happen at about the same time as the main verb in the sentence. For example, you can say:
Passengers travelling to any other destination should go to the transfer desk.
But you cannot say:
~~Passengers will receive compensation for any luggage having been lost.~~
You must use a relative clause instead. For example:
Passengers will receive compensation for any luggage **which has been lost**.

6 A present participle used after a noun usually has a progressive meaning, that is, it describes something that lasts for a certain duration, usually at the time of speaking. For example:
The man **sitting** over there is my uncle.
In other cases you must use a relative clause. For example, you cannot say:
~~The man losing his job is my uncle.~~
You must say:
The man **who lost** his job is my uncle.

Answers

1 a) ii) (I was bored, the party was boring) b) i) (The subject is interesting, I am interested.) c) ii) (I was exhausted) d) i) (The action of climbing is more important than a description of the man) e) i) A characteristic of the plants is that they are 'climbing'. f) i) The machine was bought at a different time. A relative is needed. 'Anyone who has bought a faulty machine . . .' g) ii) A relative needed as the sentence means 'The person who teaches our class on a regular basis', and not 'The person who is teaching it at the moment'.

2 I was very *excited* at the prospect of going on holiday to China. I packed a very small bag with only a very few toiletries and a spare set of clothes. At first, the flight seemed very long and I was very *bored*. I couldn't sleep, for the man *sitting* next to me snored all night and the book I bought at the airport turned out to be one I had already read. Suddenly, the *sleeping* passengers were woken up by the captain's voice. Two hi-jackers *wearing* balaclavas and *carrying* guns were in the cockpit *threatening* him. He explained the situation and told us to keep calm. Everyone was very *frightened*, but the flight personnel were very good and calmed most of the passengers down. However, one person spent the rest of the flight screaming. We landed somewhere in Malaysia. Most of us were allowed off the plane almost immediately and I was very *relieved*. The army soon arrived and encircled the plane. The hi-jackers seemed discouraged and soon gave up their fight. Police took the *captured* hi-jackers off the plane. That was the last I heard of them. I never found out what happened afterwards.

UNIT 8

Guidelines: The future

The choice of which form to use to talk about the future is complicated because it is to do with the way we envisage in our minds events which have not yet happened. In many contexts, there is a choice of several forms because talking about the future involves the concepts of intention, probability and planning which seem to overlap. In other cases, you have to be more careful and respect the following guidelines carefully.

a) The present continuous is used for talking about future, or 'diary', arrangements. For example:
I'm seeing my mother on Sunday. We do not use 'will' in this context.

b) 'Going to' is used in the following contexts:
i) to predict something that is very obviously about to happen. For example:

148

Look! that man is going to step in the puddle. (The man is very distracted and not looking where he is going. The puddle is enormous).
The difference between 'will' and 'going to' is often insignificant.

ii) to express intention, for example:
I'm going to take the car to the garage tomorrow.
In this example, you have already made up your mind to take the car to the garage when you speak. If you say, *I'll take the car to the garage tomorrow.*, it also expresses intention but your mind is only made up as you speak. This is a subtle difference which is often insignificant.

c) 'Will' is used in the following cases:
i) to make predictions about the future. For example, in weather or economic forecasts: *Tomorrow will be sunny and warm.* or *Inflation will fall in the next three months.*
You can often use 'going to' instead of 'will' in this context.
ii) to decide or to offer to do something, for example: *I'll carry your suitcase.* or *I'll drive today.*
iii) Agreeing, refusing or promising to do something. *Jill **will help** us* (promises or agrees) *but Bob **won't**.* (refuses)
iv) Asking someone to be something, for example: ***Will you open** the window, please.*

d) The present tense, never 'will', is used after time conjunctions such as *when, before, until, by the time*. For example:
*When she **arrives**, we'll have dinner.*

e) The future perfect is used to talk about:
i) a period of time up to a moment in the future. For example:
*Sara **will have spent** five whole years here by the time she leaves in March.*
ii) about a predicted action in the future which is viewed from a point even further in the future. For example:
*By the time we get home, they **will have gone**.*

Answers

1 a) 'I'm having lunch with James.'
b) 'Oh look! The train is going to run him over!'
c) 'You'll meet a tall handsome stranger. You'll win a lot of money.' ('going to' would also be possible here)
d) 'You can have it when you say please.'
e) 'In the year 2016, Shakespeare will have been dead for 400 years.'

2 Alternative answers in brackets.
b) are spending (going to spend)
c) we'll be (are going to be)
d) leaves (will leave)
e) will have been married
f) get
g) is going to train (will train/is training, etc.)
h) will have found

Key: About language

1 a) I'll phone when I get there. Unusual mistake for a native speaker.
b) I can't get any satisfaction. Considered grammatically wrong but very common in some contemporary spoken English (particularly American) as this line from the Rolling Stones demonstrates.
c) Last week I had a party. Native speakers do not usually make past tense mistakes.
d) She was a friend of Jack's. Correct Saxon genitive constructions come easily to most native speakers!
e) I'll do it on my own. 'Me' for 'my' is common in spoken English in many parts of the British Isles.
f) If I were/was rich, I wouldn't bother to work. This form is considered grammatically incorrect but often heard in North America.
g) I see/saw the policeman comin', and I run/ran down the road and disappear/disappeared as fast as I can. This use of the 'dramatic present' with the third person 's' used for the first person is considered grammatically incorrect but often heard in many regions of the British Isles. Most native speakers would probably use the simple past to tell this kind of anecdote.

UNIT 9

Guidelines: *Can* and *be able to* for ability

1 In the future *can* may be used to talk about possibility, usually when it is to do with planning. For example:
*I **can** come on Friday.*
However, if we want to talk about probable ability in the future we must use *to be able to*. For example:
*Next year I'**ll be able to** run even faster.*

2 *Could* is used to talk about general ability in the past. For example:
*My grandmother **could sing** like a bird.*

3 *Could* cannot be used to talk about ability on a particular occasion in the past, when it means 'managed to'. You must use *be able to*. For example:
*The doctor arrived quickly and **was able to** save the accident victim.*

4 *Could* + *have* + past participle is used to say that it was possible for something to happen in the past, but that something did not in fact happen. For example:
*You **could have bought** that house ten years ago when you had the money in the bank.*

5 *Can/could* are not possible in other tense combinations, for example the present and past perfect, or with the infinitive.

Answers

1 b) Correct c) In two months' time, you will be able to drive really well. d) Correct e) She was a very strong swimmer and was able to save the drowning man. f) I have not been able get any more information about the case so far, but I'll keep trying. g) The vet said afterwards that he could have given the dog an injection which would have saved his life.

2 b) in the future when talking about probable ability. c) when talking about particular ability on a particular occasion d) in combination tenses such as the present perfect (as in example f), etc.

3 a) was able to escape b) could have got c) could not swim d) cannot come e) will be able to walk

Key

Guidelines: *Can*, *could*, *may* and *might* for possibility

1 *May* or *might* are used to say that there is a possibility of something happening in the future. For example:
*It **may/might** rain*.
If *might* is contrasted with *may*, it expresses a weaker degree of possibility. For example:
*Well, I **may come** to the party*. (50% chance). *I **might come** to the party* (5% chance).
However, in most cases it does not make much difference if you use *may* or *might*.

2 *Could*, *may* and *might* are used to say that something is possibly true at the time of speaking. For example:
*Sarah **could/might/may be** home by now*.

3 *Can* is used to talk about events that are theoretically possible without talking about any particular chance of their happening. For example:
*It **can rain** a lot in England, but it **can also be** very sunny*.
Could is used to talk about the past in the same way. For example:
*School **could be** a lot of fun, but it wasn't all the time*.
Can in this sense is near to the meaning of 'sometimes'.

Answers

1 b) Almost the same, though some people might argue that with *might* there is less of a possibility of the person being right.
c) Almost the same. When contrasted with each other, there is less possibility in *might* than in *may*.
d) Completely different. Sentence i) means that it is sometimes warm in Scotland in September, whereas sentence ii) means that there is a chance of it being warm this coming September.
e) Completely different. i) means that the person is capable on some occasions of being a nuisance. ii) means that on a particular occasion that is envisaged there is a chance that the person will be a nuisance.
f) Completely different. In i), there is a distinct possibility that a group of people will swim across the river on a forthcoming occasion. Sentence ii) simply refers to the fact that the river is not too wide or dangerous for people to swim across.

2 b) i) RC ii) RC c) i) RC ii) RC d) i) T ii) RC e) i) T ii) RC
f) i) RC ii) T

UNIT 10

Guidelines: Expressing contrast

1 Different ways of expressing contrast

Conjunctions linking two parts of a sentence both with a main verb	Preposition and a noun	Adverbs (or adverbials) contrasting the ideas in one sentence with the ideas in another
although though but whereas while yet	despite in spite of	however nevertheless but (informal) all the same

2 In spoken English, contrast is very often expressed by *but* and contrasting intonation patterns. Complex sentences with conjunctions are used more often in written English. However, note the following distinctions:
a) Contrast words which are mostly used in written English: *despite, nevertheless*
b) Contrast words used mostly in spoken English or informal written English: *but* (as an adverb), *all the same*

Answers

1 <u>Although</u> Bill and Bob were not identical twins, they looked almost exactly alike. When you studied them closely, <u>however</u>, it was possible to tell them apart, for there were quite a few tiny differences. Bill had a minute scar over his left eye <u>whereas</u> Bob did not. Bob had neat flat ears but Bill's struck out a little. <u>Despite</u> these distinctive marks, people often mistook one for the other. <u>Though</u> Bill and Bob were very serious-minded young men, they did enjoy confusing people. So Bob would sometimes go on a date with Bill's girlfriend, <u>while</u> Bill would sometimes go into Bob's office. Friends knew that the terrible twins were likely to get up to tricks, <u>yet</u> they were often taken in all the same. One day, Bob fell desperately in love with Anna. <u>In spite of</u> the fact that he was sure it was 'the real thing' and he wanted to marry her, he couldn't resist having a bet with Bill. Bill was to win the bet if he went on a date with Anna without her realising that he wasn't Bob. Bob was fairly certain he would win. <u>Nevertheless</u>, he waited apprehensively. <u>But</u> Anna was taken in like everybody else, and had a wonderful evening with Bill, thinking that he was Bob. When she found out what happened, she was not amused. <u>However</u>, she soon got her sense of humour back – and sent her own identical twin on the next date with Bob.

4 Possible answers
b) Although I know her well, there are many things about her that I don't understand. or I know her well, but there are many things about her that I don't understand. or I know her well. However, there are many things about her that I don't understand.
c) Although your offer is very generous, I can't accept it. Your offer is very generous. I can't accept it, all the same.
d) In spite of the fact that she didn't have much money, she decorated her home beautifully.
e) He left school at sixteen. Nevertheless, he was extremely well read.
f) Despite the risk of another explosion, the rescue workers continued to look for survivors.

UNIT 11

Guidelines: *It*

1 *It* as a pronoun cannot usually be left out as the subject of a clause. For example, you must say:
It is raining. and not *Is raining*., *I drove the car home and put **it** in garage*. and not *I drove the car home and put in garage*. and *I painted my room green because **it's** my favourite colour*. and not *I painted my room green because is my favourite colour*.

2 *It*, like other personal pronouns, is not normally used if there is already a subject in the sentence. For example, you must say:
The accident was terrible. and not *The accident it was terrible*.

150

3 *It* must usually be used to refer back to an object already mentioned. For example, you must say:
*Do you like this picture? Yes, I love **it**.* and not ~~*Do you like this picture? Yes, I love.*~~

4 *It* is not usually used in the expression 'I know'.

5 *It* is used as an 'empty subject', that is, it does not refer to anything specific which has already been said, to talk about time, weather, temperature and distance. For example:
*It's hot today, isn't **it**?*

Guidelines: *There*

1 *There* is used with the verb *to be* to talk about something that exists. It is also used with verbs which express states such as *remain*, *exist* and *live*.

2 *There* is often used to introduce sentences of which the subject is *some, any/somebody, no one, anything*, etc.

3 Idiomatic expressions: *There's no point, There's no use, There's no sense, There's no need*.

Answers

1
b) i) 'Joe Cocker is giving a concert at the end of the month.' 'I know.'
  ii) Correct
  iii) 'It'll be a good concert.' 'I know.'
c) i) Correct
  ii) My aunt is coming to visit next week.
  iii) The film is very funny.
d) i) It rained for three days.
  ii) It's a long way to the nearest garage.
  iii) Correct
e) i) There remains nothing more to be said.
  ii) Correct
  iii) There is someone at the door.

3 a) ii) It iii) It or There iv) There v) It vi) It vii) There viii) It ix) It x) There

b)
A	B
It's no use . . .	There's no use . . .
It's a shame . . .	There's someone . . .
It takes . . .	There's no point . . .
It doesn't matter . . .	There's no need . . .
It's a pity . . .	

UNIT 12

Guidelines: Nouns in groups; the link with *'s* and *s'*

1 *'s* or *s'* structures are nearly always used to express a relationship between a person or a living creature and another person, living creature or thing. For example: *Jane's accident, Bob's aunt, Jenny's cat*.

2 *'s* or *s'* structures are often used to express a relationship between nouns that refer to groups of people, to places where people live, to human institutions and so on. For example:
The government's policy, Africa's resources, London's traffic, the tennis club's championship, the Earth's surface.

3 *'s* or *s'* structures are nearly always used with nouns referring to the duration of an event or a specific time in expressions such as: *a day's work, a moment's notice, a week's holiday, tomorrow's programme*.

4 *'s* or *s'* structures are not normally used with objects or abstract nouns. You may hear expressions like *the raincoat's belt*, or *the train's arrival* but some speakers of English consider this to be incorrect. In any case, other solutions such as noun groups, for example: *door knob, table leg*, are usually preferred.
NOTE
Common mistakes of form:
1 A proper name with an *'s* is not usually used with a definitive article. For example you cannot say:
~~*The Shell's sports club.*~~
You must say: *The Shell sports club.* or *Shell's sports club*.

2 Note the place of the apostrophe in plurals: *Boys' clothes*

Answers

1 b) normal c) normal d) not normal: door is a thing and you would be more likely to find *door knob* or, in some specific contexts, *the knob of the door.* e) not normal: *Mountain top* or *top of the mountain* f) normal g) normal h) not normal i) normal

2 people, animals, organisations, names of countries and towns, expressions of time.

3 i) iii) v) are true

4 a) The car factory workers . . . b) The prisoner's escape . . . c) war films d) Correct e) Hitchcock's films, or the films of Hitchcock f) spider's webs or spiders' webs g) hero's welcome h) river banks i) Correct

Nouns in groups: understanding relationships

Answers

1 a) ii) b) i) c) ii) d) ii)

2 It is comparatively easy to work out meaning relationships in noun groups if you begin with the last one in the group, and almost impossible if you begin with the first one.

3 a) a system for the management of traffic b) an event at which the championship for basketball for the world is played c) a breakthrough in research to do with surgery on the heart. d) a plan to develop a road with a toll e) a network of information about software for computers

UNIT 13

Guidelines: Linking words

1 Ideas can be linked together in different ways, and the exact words and expressions used will depend on the choice of the individual speaker and on criteria of concision and elegance. Examples:
a) In one of the following examples the speaker has chosen to focus on reason, and in the other on result.
  i) *I had to walk because the car broke down.*
  ii) *The car broke down, so I had to walk.*
b) In one of the following sentences the speaker has linked two ideas with a conjunction, and in the other the speaker

has preferred the concision and impersonality of a prepositional phrase.
i) *Since we did not have enough funds, we were unable to go ahead with the project.*
ii) *Owing to lack of funds, we were unable to go ahead with the project.*

2 In the table below, the main conjunctions and prepositional phrases for expressing cause and reason, purpose, and result and consequence are listed.

	Conjunction	Prepositional phrase
Reason, cause	because, as, since	on account of, owing to, because of
Purpose	in order to, so as to, to, so that	for
Result, consequence	so that, with the result that	as a result of, as a consequence of

Answers

1 ii) so, result iii) as, reason iv) so that, purpose v) since, reason vi) with the result that, result vii) (so as) to, purpose

2 ii) owing to, reason iii) as a result of, result iv) for, purpose v) as a consequence of, result vi) on account of, reason vii) because of, reason

4 Possible answers
i) I bought a giant TV screen because I wanted to watch documentaries / in order to watch documentaries.
ii) I didn't visit my aunt, owing to lack of time / I didn't visit my aunt because I didn't have time.
iii) We didn't go out on account of the bad weather. / The weather was too bad, so we didn't go out.
iv) I lost my money so I had to walk home. / Because I lost my money I had to walk home. / I had to walk home on account of losing my money.
v) Since we're going past your house anyway, it's no trouble to give you a lift. / We're going past your house anyway, so it's no trouble to give you a lift.
vi) As more people than expected came to the party, there was nothing left to eat for latecomers. / More people than expected came to the party, so there was nothing left to eat for latecomers.

UNIT 14

Key: Vocabulary

Entries from the *Longman Dictionary of English Language and Culture*

> **independent school** /ˌ··· ·/ *n BrE* (in Britain) a private school which does not receive money from the government. Only a MINORITY of children go to independent schools but some of these, esp. the PUBLIC SCHOOLS, are considered very important and influential.
>
> **sixth form** /ˈ·· ·/ *n* [C + *sing./pl. v*] the highest level in a British SECONDARY (1) school. Students usu. go into the sixth form at the age of about 16 and stay there for two years. preparing to take their A LEVELS. Sixth-form students usu. have more freedom in what they wear, in their choice of activities, etc., than students lower down the school – see also LOWER SIXTH, UPPER SIXTH – **sixth-former** *n* : *I'll be a sixth-former next year.*
>
> **high school** /ˈ·· ·/ *n* [C;U] **1** (in Britain) a SECONDARY SCHOOL for children, often for girls, aged between 11 and 18; used esp. in names: *Manchester High School* | *She's still at high school.* **2** (in the US) a school for children aged between 15 and 18 – see also extra information on page 408
>
> **ex·tra·cur·ric·u·lar** /ˌekstrəkəˈrɪkjʊlərˈ/ *adj* (esp. of activities such as sports, music, or acting) outside the regular course work (CURRICULUM) in a school or college. These activities are usu. free, and allow students to follow their own interests while using the facilities (FACILITY) of their place of study: *extracurricular activities*
>
> **A level** /ˈeɪ ˌlevəl/ also **advanced level**– *n* **1** [U] the higher standard of examination in the British education system, necessary for entrance to a university **2** [C] an examination of this standard in a particular subject, usually taken at the age of 18. Students usually take 3 or 4 A levels: *She took A levels in physics, chemistry, and mathematics.* - compare O LEVEL, GCSE see also extra information on page 408
>
> **GCSE** /ˌdʒiː siː es ˈiː/ *n* General Certificate of Secondary Education; a school examination in any of a range of subjects which took the place of O LEVELS and CSEs in Britain in 1988, and involves not only final examinations but also work done on a two-year course. GCSEs are taken by pupils of all abilities: *She's taking seven GCSEs* – see also CONTINUOUS ASSESSMENT; compare O LEVEL and see also extra information on page 408
>
> **Ox·bridge** /ˈɒksˌbrɪdʒ||ˈɑːks-/ (of, from, or typical of) the universities of Oxford and/or Cambridge: *Oxbridge students* – compare REDBRICK
>
> ▶ CULTURAL NOTE Oxford and Cambridge are the two oldest and most highly-regarded universities in Britain. Although both have tried in recent years to take more students from state schools, many Oxbridge students come from private or PUBLIC SCHOOLS, and Oxbridge GRADUATES often go on to become influential and powerful in British society. Because of this, people regard the two universities as being part of the British ESTABLISHMENT and class system, and use the word Oxbridge to refer to values and beliefs which they consider EXCLUSIVE, ELITIST, and out of touch with ordinary people. Others use the word to refer to TRADITIONAL values and high standards in learning and teaching. ◀
>
> **first²** *n, pron* **1** [(the) S] the person, thing, or group before all others: *"Are we the first?" he asked, as their host opened the door.* | *The minister's television appearance – his first since taking office – was a great success.* [+to-v] *He was the first/one of the first to collect Picasso's paintings.* | *Whoever is (the) first to finish will get a prize.* | *the first of a series of programmes on life in Russia* –compare LAST² **2** [C (**in**)] the highest class of British university degree: *He got a first in history.* –see also DEGREE (CULTURAL NOTE)

Guidelines: Ellipsis

Sometimes we only need to repeat part of a sentence and can leave out the rest in order to avoid repetition.

1 Auxiliary verbs can stand for verbs or whole clauses. Examples:
Have you finished? Yes, I ***have***. (*finished*)
I thought I'd have a nightmare, but I ***didn't***. (*have a nightmare*)

2 To can stand for a complete infinitive, or a phrase. Examples:
Are you going to win the race? We hope ***to***. (*win the race*)
Shall I help you carry that pile of rubbish over to the dump? I'd love you ***to***. (*help me carry that pile of rubbish over to the dump*)

Guidelines: Substitution

Sometimes we avoid repetition by using substitute words.

1 Pronouns replace nouns. Example:
The gremlins invaded the earth. ***They*** *arrived in hundreds of space ships.* (*The gremlins*)

2 Auxiliaries replace verbs and other parts of the sentence. Examples:

*The word processor works well. The printer **does** too.* (works)
*We enjoyed the holiday. My parents **did** too.* (enjoyed the holiday)

3 *So* replaces a whole sentence with the meaning 'also'. Example:
*We are leaving on Friday. **So** are we.* (we are leaving on Friday also)
Neither or *nor* replaces negative sentences: Example:
*I'm not leaving on Friday. **Neither/nor** am I.*

4 *So* can replace a *that* clause after certain verbs such as *hope, think, believe, suppose* and *expect*. Example:
*Is Susie coming this evening? I think **so**.* (she is coming this evening)
or *I don't think **so**.* (I don't think she's coming.)
Not can be used in *that* clauses with a negative meaning. Example:
*Have you lost your wallet? I hope **not**.*

Answers

1 b) Make up your mind. Are you coming on Monday or *not*? (or aren't you?)
c) A: Why are you painting that cupboard? B: My father told me *to*.
d) A: I'm tired. B: *So am I*.
e) A: I'm not hungry. B: *Neither/Nor* am I.
f) He said he'd phone but he *didn't*.
g) A: Is Barbara a doctor? B: I think *so/not*.
h) B: No, I *didn't*. It was my parents who wanted me *to*.
i) A: Where is Ben? Do you think he's got lost? B: I expect *so*. He often *does*.

2 a) 1 Ø 2 you 3 you 4 Ø 5 Ø 6 he 7 we
8 I 9 Ø 10 Ø 11 Ø 12 Ø 13 you 14 Ø
b) 1 we 4 I 5 we 9 They 10 it 11 there 12 I 14 that
c) You would have to add the following:
3 What did you see? 10 it's 11 there are 12 I'll come... 14 that would be great

UNIT 15

Guidelines: Conditional sentences

1 The basic rules about which tense to use in conditional sentences are often described as follows:
a) Type 1 Talking about something that is quite possible.
  If + present + *will, can*, etc.
  If it rains   we'll stay at home.
b) Type 2 Talking about imagined situations in the present which are less likely than 1.
  If + past   + *would*
  If it rained   we would say at home.
c) Type 3 Talking about an imagined situation in the past.
  If + past perfect + *would have*
  If it had rained   we would have stayed at home.

2 Other tense sequences do occur. (see *Development*)

3 *If* and *when* have almost the same meaning in conditional sentences only when used to talk about things that really happened in the past or in generalisations about things that happen repeatedly. Examples:
***If/when** Grandma came to visit we played Monopoly.*

***If/when** you leave the bottle open, the liquid evaporates.*
When cannot be used instead of *if* to talk about things that are not certain. Example:
~~*We'll play tennis when it doesn't rain this evening.*~~

Possible answers

1 b) If I had time, I would help you. or If I have time, I'll help you.
c) If it's fine tomorrow, we can play tennis.
d) If you came to the party, you'd meet Susanna. or If you come to the party, you'll meet Susanna.
e) If you had asked me for some money, I would have lent you some. In spoken English in North America you may have here: If you would have asked me for some money, I would have lent you some. However, it is considered incorrect in British English.
f) We would go to the seaside if the weather was fine.
g) Correct.
h) I would enjoy the dinner more if those people over there weren't making so much noise.

2 a) f) We could easily say 'We would go to the seaside when the weather was fine.'

3 b) If we have enough money, we'll go on holiday.
c) If he didn't eat so much, he wouldn't be so overweight.
d) We wouldn't have cancelled the picnic if it hadn't looked like rain.
e) If we don't buy some petrol soon, we'll run out.
f) The house wouldn't have been burgled if we had installed a burglar alarm.

UNIT 16

Guidelines: Preferences

1 Preferences in general
a) *Prefer* can be followed by a noun, a form in *-ing* or an infinitive to talk about preferences in general. Examples:
*I **prefer** black coffee.*
*I **prefer** swimming.*
*I **prefer** to swim.*
NOTE: *Prefer* is similar to verbs like *love, like, hate* which can also be used either with the infinitive or the *-ing* form.
b) When you state one preference over another, the following structures are used:
*I **prefer** black coffee **to** white coffee.*
*I **prefer** swimming **to** playing tennis.*
*I **prefer** to swim **rather than** to play tennis.*

2 Preferences in particular situations
a) *Would prefer* or *'d prefer* can be used to talk about a preference in a particular situation. Example:
*I **would prefer** to visit the cathedral.*
v) When you state one particular preference over another, the following structure is used:
*I **would / I'd prefer to** visit the cathedral **rather than** (visit) the museum.*

3 *Would rather* (*'d rather*) can be used in the same way as *prefer* to express a particular preference. Note the absence of *to* with the base form of the verb. Examples:
*I **would rather** go on a safari than read about one.*
*I'**d rather** be an astronaut than a chemist.*

4 *Would prefer* and *would rather* are often used in

discussing plans and making arrangements. Examples:
'How shall we go home? On foot or by bus?' 'I'**d rather go** by bus.'
'Where would you like to go to this afternoon?' 'I'**d prefer to go** to the cinema.'

5 Stating preferences about what you would like other people to do. Note the different structures of *prefer to* and *would rather*:
a) in the present
i) (*would/'d*) *prefer* + object + *to* + base form
I **would prefer** *you to pick me up at 8 o'clock.*
ii) *would/'d rather* + subject + past tense
I **would rather** *you picked me up at 8 o'clock.*
b) in the past
i) (*would/'d*) *have preferred* + object + *to* + base form
I **would have preferred** *you to pick me up at 8 o'clock.*
ii) *would/'d rather* + subject + past perfect tense
I **would rather** *you had picked me up at 8 o'clock.*

Answers

1 b) Correct c) Rob prefers to go out to eat rather than cook at home. d) A: Can I give you a lift? B: No, I'd prefer to walk. e) Correct f) Correct g) On Sunday I'd prefer to stay at home rather than drive all that way to the seaside. h) Correct i) I'd rather we stayed at home this evening.

UNIT 17

Guidelines: Comparisons

1 Comparative forms deal with two elements only. When there are more than two a superlative form is needed.

2 a) One-syllable adjective and adverbs, and some common two-syllable ones nearly always form the comparative by adding *-er*.
b) Longer adjectives and adverbs, some two-syllable ones and all three-, four- and five-syllable ones, form the comparative with *more* or *less*.

3 Comparisons of equal elements
There are several alternative structures:
a) *so/as* + adverb or adjective + *as*
Meals are **as** *good in New York* **as** *they are in Paris.*
b) *The same as . . . The same* is always followed by *as*, never by *like* or *than*.
Meals in New York are **the same as** *in Paris.*
c) *as* + adjective + indefinite article + singular noun + *as*
   as + adjective + ...   plural noun   + *as*
You can have **as** *good a meal in Paris* **as** *in New York.*
You can have **as** *good meals in Paris* **as** *in New York.*

4 Comparisons of unequal elements
a) *more/less* + two- or three-syllable adjective/adverb/noun + *than*
short adjective/adverb + *-er* + *than*. Examples:
She is **more/less** *fortunate than her sister.*
That box is **bigger than** *this one.*
We worked **harder than** *you did.*
She ate **more** *spaghetti* **than** *I did.*
b) You can also use the structures of comparison for equal elements with *not*. Example:
She is **not as** *fortunate* **as** *her sister.*

5 Superlatives
a) Superlatives need a definite article. Examples:
The **best tennis player**/*the* **most interesting film**
b) After a superlative form, *in* is more common than *of* with singular nouns. Examples:
***The tallest person in** the class.*
*He was **the tallest of** the people there.*

Answers

1 b) Inflation in Italy is higher *than* in Germany.
c) It was *hotter* today than yesterday.
d) Of all the movies I have ever seen that one really is *the worst*.
e) I'll have the same pudding *as* her.
f) You can have as good *a* meal in New York as in Paris.
g) The situation is bad enough, but it would be *worse* if it was raining.
h) It's the biggest diamond *in* the world.
i) My kitchen is not so well planned *as* yours.

2 The complete structures are:
a) the *same as*
b shorter *than*
c) *more/less* expensive *than*
d) *as* good *as*
e) *so* good *as*
f) *as* good *a* result *as* any
g) *the* best *in* the world/*of* the bunch

3 Possible answers
b) French men do more ironing than Spanish men.
c) Italian men do less cooking than Swiss men.
d) Spanish men do not do as much cleaning as Italian men.
e) Italian men do not do so much dishwashing as British men.
f) Italian men do more shopping than German men.

4 b) Almost, Nearly c) Far, A lot, A great deal d) Slightly e) far, much, etc. f) Half g) far

UNIT 18

Guidelines: Question tags

1 We form question tags in the following ways:
a) with the auxiliaries *be* and *have* if they are already present in the sentence. Examples:
He is here, **isn't he?**
You have got a pen, **haven't you?**
b) with a modal auxiliary if one is already present. Examples:
You can do it, **can't you?**
She might come, **mightn't she?**
c) with the auxiliary *do* in the simple present or the simple past. Examples:
He lives here, **doesn't he?**
You arrived early, **didn't you?**

2 To ask if a person agrees with a statement we use a) a negative tag after a positive statement and b) a positive tag after a negative statement. Examples.
She can come, **can't she?**
She can't come, **can she?**

3 In suggestions, with *let's* we use *shall*. Example:
Let's go to the cinema, **shall we?**

4 a) After imperative forms we use a tag with *will*, *would*, *can* or *could*.
b) After the imperative form in an invitation, we usually use the negative form. Example:
Come again soon, **won't you?**
c) After the imperative form used in requests, we can use positive or negative tags. Examples:
Open the window, **will you/would you/could you?**
Phone again soon, **won't you?**
d) After the imperative form used in orders, we use negative tags. Example:
Put that down, **will you?**

5 After a positive statement we can use a positive tag to express interest. Example:
So you're learning to drive, **are you?**

6 a) We use falling intonation patterns when we are fairly certain that the person we are speaking to will agree with us.
b) We use rising intonation patterns when we are not certain that the person we are talking to is going to agree with us.

Answers

1 a) i) Let's go, shall we? ii) Correct iii) She isn't coming, is she? iv) You are taking your exam next week, aren't you? v) Bob arrives at 8 o'clock, doesn't he? vi) Correct vii) Open the door, would/will/can/could you? viii) Correct ix) She can leave now, can't she?
b) i) a suggestion ii) an invitation iii) a request for confirmation or agreement iv) showing an interest v), vi) a request for confirmation or agreement vii) a request viii) an order ix) a request for confirmation or agreement.

2 a) i) R ii) R iii) F iv) R v) F vi) R vii) R viii) F ix) R
c) ii) an invitation R
iii) a suggestion R
iv) an order F
v) a request for confirmation or agreement R or F (Rising if you are not certain of the answer, falling if you are.)
vi) a way of showing interest R

3 b) Phone me next week, will you? R if a request, and F if an order.
c) You had spent too much money, hadn't you? R or F
d) Let's have a look, shall we? R
e) I'm coming with you, aren't I? R or F
f) She usually has three lumps of sugar, doesn't she? R or F
g) Shut up, won't you? R
h) You'd like a cup of coffee, wouldn't you? R or F
i) We haven't been here before, have we? R or F
j) Come to dinner next Friday, won't you? R

Tapescripts

UNIT 1

RECORDING 1
O - four - five - six - seven - one - nine - two

RECORDING 2

1: I learnt Russian at school. I never expected to sound like a Russian, but I wanted to get it more or less right, especially for passing oral exams – I actually loved those wonderful long complicated consonant sounds but I found them extraordinarily difficult. I could hear the difference, but I just couldn't get my tongue round them. There's also a completely different rhythm, that I just couldn't get. The teacher just used to laugh and shrug her shoulders.

2: You know, I'm a Spanish teacher, so I really wanted to sound like the Spanish do! It's quite difficult, because there are several sounds that don't exist in English, the [j] sound, and it's a bit gutteral. But I worked on it and found out exactly what they did with their tongues and their lips and so on – and I managed to sound fairly Spanish in the end!

3: I went to live in China for six months, and I took Chinese lessons all the time I was there. It was really just to get by, you know, I wanted people to understand me for the basics in the shops and while I was travelling. But I found the tone system so difficult. You know, in Chinese, the same word said in just a slightly different way – it sounds virtually the same to you or me – means two things that are completely different. Sometimes they used to collapse into giggles, because I thought I'd said something very serious, and it turned out I'd said something very rude.

4: I learnt Italian at evening classes, just for something to do, really. I like opera, and love going on holiday in Italy. But then, I got to love that sing-song pattern in the language, and really wanted to get it, you know, because it was so much part of the pleasure of learning the language, the essence of it, if you like.

5: When I was learning Arabic, I began to feel happy when people stopped asking me to repeat myself when I was having a conversation, over a dinner table or something. I had never felt the need to sound like a native speaker – but I did get frustrated when my pronunciation was obviously so bad that people just couldn't understand what I was saying, although I knew my grammar was right and I had already acquired an enormous vocabulary, so was able to follow quite complicated conversations.

UNIT 2

RECORDING 1

INTERVIEWER: Let's start with Aries? What are they supposed to be like?
EXPERT: Well, traditionally they're said to be fiery in temperament. And this makes some of them warm and generous, but in others it can come out as an authoritarian streak.
I: And Taurus? People say they're very direct.
E: Well, it's more a question of being hardworking and steady, I think. Taureans are usually quite level-headed too, and friendly.
I: And Gemini is the sign of people who are proud, isn't it? But they're also changeable, aren't they?
E: Yes that's right. Some people say versatile rather than changeable! Leo is the sign of proud people too. Leo is very independent as well, and can occasionally be rather bossy.
I: And Cancer?
E: Ah, that's the anxious sign. They tend to be conservative and shy as well. A bit sensitive.
I: Pisces people are sensitive too, aren't they?
E: Yes, very similar to Cancer, but Pisces are also very imaginative and creative.
I: And what about Virgo?
E: They're usually a bit obsessive – you know, they like things neat and tidy, no loose ends.
I: Mmm, sort of perfectionist.
E: Yes, that's right. They're also hardworking and practical. The opposite of Sagittarians, who are great talkers. They are a bit up-in-the-clouds, full of

Tapescripts

self-confidence, very independent, but don't ask them to put a bookshelf up! The other talking sign is Libra, but they are on the argumentative side. They're very pleasant, but you never know quite where you are because they are always changing their minds.

I: What's left? Erm, Scorpio, what about them?
E: Extremist, possessive, passionate, they're not the easiest sign to live with. But life is never dull with them!
I: And Capricorn – they're supposed to be conservative, aren't they?
E: Yes, that's true, and polite and shy too. But when you get to know them, Capricorns can be incredibly generous, not just with money, but with time and everything else too.
I: What are we left with – oh yes, Aquarians. What about them?
E: Well, Aquarius is the thinking sign, the intellectual. Maybe that's what makes Aquarians the most tolerant as well. They are independent in their judgements and in the way they live – but sometimes they tend to be a bit unstable, and, dare I say it, a little mad.

UNIT 3

RECORDING 1

1: To me nostalgia means something which reminds me of something in my childhood and it's usually pleasurable and sad.
2: Nostalgia for me is, er, well I actually looked it up in the dictionary and it means to return home plus pain and I would say it is this mixture of pain and pleasure ... from my childhood, I agree with you.
3: Spring is a time of nostalgia for me, when I walk in the country and see the green of the grass and little flowers growing up like a Walt Disney film. It reminds me of the time at nursery school, when we used to hunt for Easter eggs.
4: Nostalgia for me is a memory often conjured up by a smell and often taking me back to my grandparents' house when I was a child.
5: Wind is nostalgia for me. That's because I grew up in northern Canada where you have very fierce winds. And within this nostalgia is a missing. I miss the wildness of those winds.
6: Places are nostalgic for me – old hotels, old concert halls that make me think of a lifestyle which doesn't exist now.
7: Music is nostalgia for me – uhm music which takes you back to a time which probably didn't exist, an age of innocence, in the 1930s with Fred Astaire films with lots of tap dancing and blond women.
8: Toffee
9: Plasticine
10: Nostalgia for me is nearly always painful because it's remembering something that I can never go back to.
11: The strange thing about my nostalgia is that even though it's painful, the memories are somehow good. I grew up very near a very busy road, near a busy railway. Yet when I think back to my childhood everything was always peaceful and quiet.

RECORDING 2

Dialogue 1

1: I think we should do an article on the Twenties, don't you?
2: That's a very interesting idea, but I think our readers would prefer something more recent, nearer to their own time, don't you?

Dialogue 2:

1: The Wild West would be an excellent topic, wouldn't it?
2: I like that idea a lot. However, we did do a feature on 19th century America only last month, so I think it'd be better if we did something really historical, don't you? You know about chivalry in the Middle Ages or something.

Dialogue 3

1: Couldn't we go for something exotic? You know, explorers in 19th century Africa, the great adventure and so on.
2: That's a very original angle, though it might be better to stick to something domestic, don't you think? Something about life in the great mansions of the past.

RECORDING 3

BOB: What's this weird-looking, oblong contraption here?
SARAH: Yes, exhibit 1, a peculiar-looking thing indeed! It's a bread cutter. You can see the space to place the bread here towards the right, and the metal blade on the left is pushed across – this is the handle on the end here – slightly decorative, don't you think?
B: It seems a lot of fuss for nothing to me. Why didn't they just use a knife?
S: Not ceremonious enough, I suppose! Now, you must be wondering what on earth exhibit 2 is. Well, it's a coffee roaster. You put the beans in this cylindrical drum in the middle, and the heat came from this sort of box on the left – but you had to keep turning the handle here on the right. Exhausting work!
B: Yes, quite a few pairs of hands needed in the kitchen! I prefer to buy my coffee beans ready-roasted! Now, number 3 is more familiar. You still sometimes see things like this that people chase the crumbs from the dinner table with when they're too lazy to get the hoover out, don't you?
S: Yes, it's the ancestor of the carpet sweeper, and it hasn't changed that much. It still has the rollers and brushes and the stick handle, but of course nowadays it's not made of wood, but of plastic.
B: Number 4, too, isn't that old, is it? I can still remember seeing things like this used for wringing out clothes.
S: Yes, it's our old laundry friend, the mangle. You put the clothes between the rollers and turn the handle and the water gets squeezed out. Again, quite hard work and good for developing the biceps! Give me a modern spin-dryer any day!
B: Now number 5, I haven't got a clue! It's a very attractive object but what on earth is it? And what can you do with it?
S: Well, as you can see, it's a kind of wheel, and inside there's a stone, and it's a knife sharpener. Those are the knives sticking out from round the edges. As you turn the handle, the blades of the knives grind against the stone. It's quite neat, you can do a whole set of knives in one go! This was quite common in the nineteenth century, and I'm not sure we do much better at knife-sharpening today . . .

RECORDING 7

Excerpt 1

INTERVIEWER: Now you belong to an organisation that spends time reenacting battles and also providing living history about the Vikings. Why did you find the Vikings so interesting?

YOLLY KUTTER: It's such a, an interesting period of upheaval and yet they were capable of such incredible things at the same time. Most people still have this idea of the Vikings as being people who did nothing but rape and pillage and burn, whereas, they valued art highly, they must have valued their family life as well. They had a very sophisticated culture and they were capable of turning out the most exquisite works of art, whether they were practical things or purely ornamental. They were quite keen on music and telling riddles, sagas, singing – obviously a lot of carving, I mean anything that's wood virtually has got something carved on it. You see a lot of the doors and the boxes have got incredibly intricate carvings on them ...

The average man in the street erm, would have had a virtually vegetarian diet, you'd have had meat on feast days, high days, holidays. If your chicken got too old to lay you'd kill it and have, have that then.... At a show, all the ingredients that we use would have been available to people of the period depending on their rank, for example, for breakfast we'll have bread and honey, er, for lunch we'll normally have either a vegetarian stew, something like buttered worts which is made up of cabbage and leeks and any other green vegetables which you boil in a little water. Then you add butter and if you can afford to then you also add salt and pepper for flavouring, and you have that with bread or you have, er a meat stew or soup of some kind, garlic soup which is wonderful.

The clothes that they wore are very comfortable and they're far less restrictive than the sort of things you wear now. You've got er, if you're dressed in female clothing you've got the underdress and an overdress which, its basic shape is an A-line. It's a straight tube with side panels, and then long sleeves ... so you have lots of freedom. You can move about, you can do what you want.

Compared to the sort of houses we live in now, certainly the houses that the Saxons and the Vikings lived in would seem pretty basic, erm, but then again you didn't need as much. We're a very materialistic society and all you needed was some, some clothes to wear, a pair of shoes, something to sleep in at a most basic level.

There's definitely a special kind of atmosphere about it. Er, and I suspect that in the past when you were living in such a small community, erm, you do quickly learn to rely on each other. I like the fact that they were obviously such hard-working people and living in very very difficult times and yet they were capable of such, of making such beautiful things. Even something as simple as a wooden handled bowl has an incredible symmetry to it.

Excerpt 2

Well, if I could go back in history and live when I liked, I wouldn't go back very far. In fact I'd quite like to relive a period I've already lived, the 60s. Really because I think it changed everything, it was very exciting to be young. I was in my twenties, you know, and everything was being renewed. People were coming out of a stiff, formal and almost Victorian attitude. And you really felt anything was possible.

Meeting people was the thing, and you went to coffee bars, where you met friends, and people, and spent the evening. There were jive evenings in coffee bars, and if you couldn't get up to dance there was this hand jive that you could actually do at the counter, the music was on the juke box and everybody was moving around.

156

The cinema, the theatre – all that was very exciting with new things coming out, the French *Nouvelle Vague* but British cinema and theatre too. In fact we seemed to be out all the time. I don't really remember working – of course I was a student – or sitting around at home very much. That just wasn't where the scene was.

Even eating – it was the first time ordinary people started going out to eat – mainly fish and chips, of course, but curries were the thing too, Indian curries were taking off, and we'd go out in a crowd. We were beginning to be more adventurous about food. But we were more interested in meeting people, in being with people than in eating or drinking.

But dress, yes, that was the revolution. I mean girls went around in really short skirts and wore flowers in their hair, and men were in jeans and could wear their hair long too.

It was a wonderful period – it was like living in an age you could never have imagined, and that never has come back. We didn't have much money and it didn't matter, and there was plenty of opportunity to do whatever you felt like.

Excerpt 3

I'd like to go back to the 18th century, and perhaps in colonial America, in Yankee New England, or Long Island where one of my ancestors was ... because it was the beginning of something, it wasn't really the beginning, but the 17th century would have been too tough, too hard ...

By the 18th century, there was a feeling of community that had grown, there was prosperity in many places, there was a lot of intellectual excitement, I think. My ancestor was an itinerant preacher galloping around the countryside. People lived in small communities. There were fishermen and farmers who provided fresh food that tasted and looked like food – none of your unrecognisable wrapped monstrosities of today's supermarkets – and there were small towns and New York wasn't that far away. There must have been a feeling of building something, a new society, something very genuine.

I'm deeply attached to the Puritan tradition, not in a religious sense, but they believed in working for something, working for goals and I like that. They worked hard at whatever they did, but they had a sense of achievement. They believed in goodness, in community, in helping one another, I think.

I love the colonial fabrics, all the gold silver work, the furnishings, the combination of elegance and simplicity, I love it. The printing, the books, the embroidery, I'm very attached to all that kind of thing. It may not all be very entertaining in the modern sense of the word, but I would've enjoyed spending my evenings in that environment, discussing new ideas, building a new world. And I can see myself sitting on a small chair by the fire embroidering a sampler.

UNIT 4

RECORDING 1

INTERVIEWER: Brian, how do lexicographers decide when to put a new word into a dictionary?
BRIAN O'KILL: Well, that really is quite a problem because even in our largest dictionaries we can't possibly include every word in the language. Uhm, nobody really knows how many words there are in English, but at a rough guess, I'd say there were probably about half a million words in English and we probably get about 2000 new ones every year, so it is very difficult for us to make this decision. And what we do to help ourselves a bit, we read a lot of newspapers, magazines and books and from them we collect examples of words and the way in which they're used. Now it's these examples, which we call citations, which we analyse afterwards so we can make a decision about whether to include a word and how to describe it. Uhm, when we look at these citations and decide whether to include a new word we don't have any absolutely rigid rules but I'd say that as a rule of thumb we want at least three examples of a new word before we would include it in a dictionary.
I: Right. Three examples, three citations.
BO: Yes.
I: Would you exclude slang words or words that are very new?
BO: No, certainly not. Uhm, because we think that our main task in compiling a dictionary is to record the language that people actually use and not to make any judgement about whether words are good, proper, well-established or likely to last. So in effect, the dictionary should be a register and not a rule book.
I: Right. Can you give some examples?
BO: Well, yes. Sometimes new words become established very quickly. Er, for instance, *perestroika* came into English in 1987, I think it was, uhm, and originally it was just used to refer to reform in the Soviet Union, but very soon, within only a couple of months, a lot of people were using it to refer to reorganisations in British Institutions. Uhm, or the other sort of word, the slangy word, one that recently, uhm, soon became very popular was *couch potato*, a lovely term that came over from America, to mean a lazy, unimaginative person, you know the sort of person who sits in front of a television all evening and doesn't move.
I: Now, turning to Wordwatch, what is the purpose of the Wordwatch scheme, and how does it work?
BO: Well, the Wordwatch scheme is something that gives the public a chance to contribute to the recording of the language, uhm, by sending us examples of any kind of new or unfamiliar words which they come across either in writing or in speech. And now, we've got hundreds of people in all walks of life, policemen, plumbers, professors, the whole lot, who send us material which we then add to our collection of examples. Uhm and of course it helps us a lot by giving us more examples of words and from a greater variety of sources. So that it really does help us to feel that we are keeping our finger on the pulse of the language.
I: And what sort of words have people sent in?
BO: Oh, an incredible variety of words collected from all over the place. Words that people have seen in reading newspapers, books, letters, words from conversations, broadcasts, signs and shops. People have found interesting words everywhere.
I: Can you think of one off the top of your head?
BO: Well, I think some of the ones that I find particularly interesting are the kind of words that don't often appear in print and so tend to be overlooked by people who write dictionaries. Uhm, it's the kind of words that are used mainly in speech or by a particular group of people. Uhm, for instance, a lot of people have sent us words that are used by children or teenagers, like, like, apparently children nowadays use *derbrain* as a term of abuse and teenagers use words like *wicked* and *rand* to mean 'great' or 'very good'. Uhm, we also get quite a few words that come from the dialect spoken in particular parts of the country. A lovely one we got was the word *gongoozler* which apparently is a word used for somebody who stands beside the canal doing nothing all day. And we also get some very nice words that are used by people in a particular job. Uhm, a policeman told us about this word *polac* which is used by the police to mean an accident involving a police car.

UNIT 5

RECORDING 2

SIMON: I don't know if you can call it a coincidence but my older brother Kevin always phones me as I'm holding the phone and dialling him. Every time. And it's very rarely, I must say but every time I'm phoning him, he phones me.
PHILIP: .....mine's about meeting someone. This is a number of years ago. I was in Florence in Italy on holiday. And I was bored and tired and it was raining and I was walking around the streets with my umbrella trying to look at sights with difficulty because it was raining and I couldn't see anything with the umbrella and a woman carrying an umbrella walked into me. And she started shouting and screaming in Italian, and I thought 'these excitable Italians' so I shouted back at her in English. And then we both lifted our umbrellas up and I realised that she wasn't Italian at all. But she was one of my closest childhood friends.
KAREN: It was really very strange. My daughter and my daughter-in-law both had a baby in the same hospital the same day and it was the day of another daughter's birthday.
TIM: Right, no. The coincidence is this. Not planned in any way at all. At the moment I live in Bayswater, which is near the centre of London. Immediately before coming back to London, I lived in Bilbao in the north of Spain. Immediately before living in Bilbao, I lived in Brussels in Belgium. Immediately before that I lived in Brighton in the south of England, and immediately before that I was living in Morocco, in Casablanca, but the name of the street began with a B – two Bs in fact because it was Boulevard and then the name afterwards. So my coincidence is the letter B.
JAMES: And that makes me think of – I was born in All Saints' Road. When I was eighteen I left home and I moved to another town and I lived in St. Mary's Road. And then I moved to Bristol and I lived in St. John's Road. And then I moved to London and I lived in St. Alban's Road. And that's purely by coincidence.
TIM: Maybe there's something saintly in your personality!
JAMES: I doubt it!

UNIT 6

RECORDING 1

INTERVIEWER: I think it's probably quite a well-known fact by now that the distinguished actress Susan Hampshire is a dyslexic and Susan's just written an autobiography which is at the same time an exploration of this, uhm, this what? And I am stuck for a word straight away, Susan. What is it?

157

Tapescripts

SUSAN HAMPSHIRE: Well, it's a specific reading and writing difficulty which means that we find it difficult to spell correctly, and in one sentence we may spell the same word in three different ways, all with a logical reason but none of them correct. And we may be able to spell it today and we can't spell it tomorrow. Uhm, with our reading we find it very difficult to read aloud because we jumble the words. We sometimes miss out a word. We sometimes reverse the sentences and sometimes . . . so if the word is *thorough*, we'll read *through* and so that completely changes the sense of the sentence.

I: Yes.

S: And the reason for this is that, uhm, that the right side of the brain governs the left and the left the right, and there's a section that governs language and our section which governs language is you could say is asleep. It's malformed, it hasn't ever been opened up. And the first time that they got proof of this was about 18 months ago. They did an autopsy on a very severely dyslexic boy in Boston. He had a motor cycle accident and the parents agreed that they could do this autopsy and they discovered the whole of the section of the brain that was governing language had never been used and in a way – this was a complete revelation because people had always said either that dyslexia is a middle-class disease and it's made up you know - parents that've got children that aren't as bright as others are saying: 'Oh, this is the excuse.' But now they really have — uhm, it was very difficult to get dyslexia medically recognised, very difficult for the government, for the education authorities to get involved with it. But now one actually has positive proof that it is a real disability and it's actually in the brain and you can see the bit that doesn't work, I think it's going to be a lot easier. Probably, – have I explained clearly what it is?

I: Yes, well I think you have, indeed, but what I'm not quite clear about is whether in learning to live with it, learning to cope with it, as you have yourself, in fact the disability recedes somewhat.

S: Er, it only recedes - if you haven't had remedial help, if you say are diagnosed dyslexic at five and you have remedial help, within two years you've pretty well overcome the basic problems. That means that you've relearnt the concept of spelling, which we don't learn in the 'look and say' method, because we just don't absorb it as other children do - naturally learn to read and to spell. We just can't. It doesn't go in and it doesn't come out.

I: And yet you've chosen as a profession one in which it's absolutely essential for you both to read and to learn and for it to stay in.

S: Yes, well, I've learnt only – I've developed a tremendous amount of tricks to get me over it. But if I'd had remedial help I wouldn't be using tricks. I'd be using a sort of positive method and a much more sort of sound way of doing it. When I started to be an actress, I had no idea that it would involve so much reading. I hadn't any idea that in order to find one part that you wanted to do or to be au fait with what was going on in the theatre, you had to read so many scripts. I thought you just stood up on the stage and said the words.

UNIT 7

RECORDING 1

PAUL: You know, Ben's given up making those terrible faces he used to make. The other day, came home from school almost in tears. Teacher said if he went on like that his face would get stuck when the wind changed!

JEFF: And he believed her? A tough little lad like that?

P: Yeah, but don't forget, he *is* only little. Don't you remember all those things we used to believe when we were little. I remember my Aunt Mary. She always used to say if you swallow a cherry stone, a tree will grow out of your mouth – and I'm still terrified today if I swallow one by mistake – you know, sort of unconsciously.

J: Yeah, I suppose you're right. The one that used to get me was that swans could break your leg with a blow of the wing.

P: They can, can't they? I always thought they could.

J: Pretty feeble leg! No, they're not nearly strong enough. But what about the one, you know, if you put a postage stamp on upside down, you'll go to prison.

P: No, never heard that, but my grandmother was a terror for that kind of thing. You know, you'll get a spot on your tongue if you tell a lie. If you eat crusts of bread your hair will curl – as if I wanted curly hair – that was probably for my sister. And the other one was, you can see in the dark if you eat raw carrots.

J: Any sort of carrots isn't it? There was a good one though, it was my Uncle Sam, who was a bit of a tease, he always said that there was a reward if you went to Madam Tussaud's, the waxworks, you know, and spent the night in the Chamber of Horrors – with all the torture gear and hangmen and stuff. I was terrified – I'd never have done it, not even for a thousand quid.

P: We went on this camping trip once in Italy, and my wife spent the whole time worrying about bats – in case she got a bat in her hair. She said her grandmother reckoned you had to shave your head to get it out. Terrified she was.

J: Daft, isn't it. And we expect our kids to tell the truth when they grow up!

UNIT 8

RECORDING 1

SUE LAWLEY: Richard, tell me just a little bit more about your family life before we hear about making the first million. Where were you brought up?

RICHARD BRANSON: Well, I was brought up in a very small village called Shamley Green which was south of Guildford in Surrey. I was brought up by two very loving parents who are still two very loving parents and so was very fortunate in having a very stable background. My father would never tell me off for, you know, anything I ever did and somebody I can always turn to, and is always interested, and my mother is very much, you know, getting up and going, pushing you forward – nobody's allowed to sit and watch the telly – you know, you've got to be doing all the time.

SL: And you have two sisters, so you were a very spoilt boy.

RB: Yes, very spoilt, I suppose.

SL: Quite a legal family, though, I gather – your father was a stipendiary magistrate.

RB: That's right.

SL: And your grandfather was a high court judge.

RB: That's right. I've got, I think, seven generations of judges behind me.

SL: So you left school Richard, you said, at fifteen and you were a millionaire by the age of 19?

RB: It's very difficult to know because I would never sell any large chunks of my company, so it's only on paper. I think perhaps it was the – you know, sometime in the early days of the mail-order company or the record retailing that one became a paper millionaire.

SL: But just going back a bit, I mean how does a young boy of fifteen, sixteen, leaving school, how does he set up a magazine? Where did you begin?

RB: Well, I didn't have uhm outside finance, uhm, so I had to sell enough advertising to cover the printing and the paper costs. And set myself a rule that I wouldn't launch the magazine until I'd had £5000 worth of advertising sold, and I actually worked out of the telephone box of the school and I used to put on a false voice to pretend that I had a secretary because I didn't feel that advertisers would accept a schoolboy in a telephone box at school otherwise. And, er, and then I put on my real voice as Richard Branson and anyway somehow managed to blather my way into getting £5000 of advertising.

SL: What, you did the female ...

RB: No, no, I was a male assistant. I couldn't quite do that ... Although sometimes I'd use the switchboard operator.

SL: So there was a lot of conning of people, in the sense of fast talk?

RB: I think you had to believe in what you were putting out, so I mean I was putting out a magazine that was going to go to fifty thousand young people and I had to act more grown up than I really was. I didn't want to let on that I was fifteen and once I'd got £5000 worth of advertising committed I then had to persuade them to wait until I'd actually got the first edition together.

SL: At which point you then had to persuade people to contribute to this magazine and you persuaded people like Gerald Scarfe, David Hockney, John Le Carré, the Dean of Liverpool, I mean how did you do that on the public telephone from school?

RB: Most of it on the public telephone, uhm occasionally writing them letters from the school library. The idea of a magazine run by young people appealed to most of these people. And once you got one or two, you could name-drop a bit so it was easier, uhm ...

SL: So it worked and you started to sell the magazine and then as you said you started to sell cut price records through the magazine but it was all done by mail order and the money was rolling in, but then, in 1971, the man with the handle-bar moustache, Tom Jackson, stepped in and led a postal strike. What happened?

RB: Yes, well that was a bit disturbing because all our income was then coming from the mail order company and an eight-week postal strike was – we, you know, we faced going out of business, so we headed off down Oxford Street one day and went into various shops and finally ended up in a shoe-shop and I walked upstairs and saw they had an empty space and went up to the manager and said how about letting us have that space for a record shop, you'll sell lots of shoes and we'll sell lots of records. And, er, he said yes and about a week or two later we opened our first record shop. And we sold lots of records but I think a lot of his shoes walked out of the shop without being paid for.

158

RECORDING 5

1: Well, I'll be taking my 'A' levels in June, and by mid-August I hope I'll have been offered a place in a university. As soon as I get the results, I'll know what my chances are. In three years time I'll have got my degree. Then I have to work for three years as an articled clerk in a lawyer's office before taking my final Law exams. After that I'll be able to get a job and start earning real money and being successful!

2: Well, an amateur tennis player's life is a hard life, you know! So I'll be training hard for the next three weeks, right up until the Forest Hills tournament, which is next month. After that there are several other tournaments so I won't be getting much rest for a few months. By the time it's all over, I'll be really exhausted and I'll be taking a month or two off. But not before I've won a couple of tournaments, I hope! And next year I'll be turning professional. Well, that's the plan anyway.

3: I'll have finished school in a couple of month's time. I won't go to university. I'll be going straight to drama school for two years. Although I'll be studying full time, I hope I'll be getting the occasional part in a play or a film. I'll probably be doing a few ads just to earn a bit of money to keep going. But I won't accept just anything. For example I'd never make an ad for a company which uses live animals in its research.

RECORDING 6

1: I think my mum's very successful because she's managed to bring up three children – excellently – in such a horrible society that we live in today. She's taught us to be kind and loving, she taught us to share, she taught us to love our family – be very family-orientated – and I think that's really important.

2: The person that I can think of within my life, well, I probably can think of several but the one that instantly came to mind when you popped this question to me was somebody who lives in Harpenden and who has overcome physical difficulty of arthritis remarkably well, and not allowed it to hold her back any more than is obviously necessary because of her physical disabilities. So I think she's made a very good – a great success of overcoming a difficulty.

3: I think, uhm, Mable Davies, here who's very successful. She's a deaf lady who's now the headmistress and I think that must have been hard, so I've got a lot of respect for her, because my parents are also deaf so I know how difficult it is to work your way up having a handicap so I've got quite a lot of admiration for her.

4: Well, I think in professional terms Kenneth Branagh, the actor, has been very successful and I think the reason for this more than anything else is that he's a very good self-publicist. He is undoubtedly a very good actor. Er, I've not seen him on stage, I've seen him on film and he's got an enormous amount of energy and as I say, he's a very good self-publicist.

UNIT 9

RECORDING 4

1: People want a film that says something, that makes a point, that makes them think a little, and that's just what we've got here.
2: We can make an action-packed film which will make the audience's hair stand on end from beginning to end.
3: The characters are psychologically complex and will grip the audience's imagination.
4: We can create a torrid atmosphere that will reach the audience's deepest feelings.
5: This fascinating book has a wonderfully exciting story-line.

UNIT 12

RECORDING 1

ANNOUNCER: Seven MPs are calling upon the government to ban the import of *pâté de foie gras* (goose liver pâté). Its production they say is unkind to geese. Two million suffer. But not everybody agrees that the method of production is cruel, as our reporter Norman Smith discovered. He spoke first to one of the MPs, Jerry Steinberg, the member for Durham.

JERRY STEINBERG: What actually happens is the geese are placed into restraining braces which hold their wings tightly to their bodies and their necks are stretched up and raised up and then a funnel, a tube funnel is forced down the throat of the geese and spring clips are attached behind the skull of the bird so that they can't move, and then 6 lbs of salted maize is forced down the throat of the geese; and this happens for about 8 weeks. It means the geese actually put on something like 60% weight but their livers are enlarged by something like 400%. They're kept in boxes of ten inches by fifteen inches, and they just go through purgatory.

A: So does the production of *pâté de foie gras* cause misery to two million geese? Newcastle University farming expert, Bill Weekes:

BILL WEEKES: We are not being cruel to two million geese and the French are not being cruel to two million geese. More and more you find people who literally don't know the backside of a badger from that of an Aylesbury duck getting up and condemning farming practices about which they know absolutely nothing.

NORMAN SMITH: But geese are forced-fed to produce *pâté de foie gras*....

BW: Yes but are they force-fed? Alright in the old days you'd get a mixture of Sussex ground oats literally funnelled down the goose's neck. Now, that is not cruel, it's force-feeding, it's the type of force-feeding that you may do to someone who is suffering from a blockage in their oesophagus and can't take food any other way. But that type of feeding geese is now going out. The geese are kept in comfortable environmental surroundings and all they are subject to is a certain restriction of their liberty and they have this fattening food fed to them ad lib.

NS: Isn't that unnatural?

BW: Well there again, what on earth is natural these days? People working in department stores, in air-conditioned department stores, that isn't natural, and the French and the EEC people are in many instances ahead of us in implementing the regulations which ensure that the animals that are kept for human food consumption do not suffer any deleterious or bad effect whatsoever.

NS: But is a force-fed goose a happy goose?

BW: If they were not, in inverted commas, 'happy', they certainly would not thrive, they certainly would not put on weight and they certainly would not produce healthy livers which can be transformed into healthy *pâté de foie gras*. Animal psychology is such that if the animal is not happy, it will not eat and it will waste away and this seems to be a fact which has escaped the attention of this no doubt very keen MP for Durham.

RECORDING 3

SALLY: I've got hold of some of the stuff the animal rights people are putting out. It's got some amazing photos in it. They should make the public sit up and think all right. Look at this one. It's incredible! Surely they don't need to kill all those elephants just for their ivory tusks.

DAVID: Why are they burning the ivory anyway? I can't see why people don't understand that it's in everyone's interest to use plastic instead of ivory. Even the experts can't tell the difference most of the time.

S: And look at this one. It's disgusting. The man with the syringe looks so threatening and the baby rats so helpless.

D: Yes, okay, it's disgusting, but let's not forget we do need some medical research.

S: Yes, but most of it is unnecessary and you must admit that doing it like that is very cruel. It makes me feel sick just to look at those little creatures.

D: Yes, you're right. There must be other ways of doing it.... And look at this one. It's terrible! The poor seal! Wouldn't it be better to outlaw seal hunting altogether?

S: Yes, I think so. There are hardly any seals left – everyone knows that we must protect them. But nothing's being done.... We've got to help the animal rights people to get this campaign moving somehow...

UNIT 13

RECORDING 3

DEFENCE LAWYER: Mr Stern, may I ask you - do you think it was necessary and fair to arrest Steve Brill?

HENRY STERN: I don't know whether you realise that this man has been eating up our parks for five years? And he is encouraging other people to do the same thing, every single day. Hoards of people. He has been organising groups to destroy our urban wildlife.

DL: But Mr Stern – this situation has been going on happily for five years. Why did you suddenly decide to do something about it?

HS: Well, at first we just thought he was a crank, a bit odd, you know. But over the years we came to realise that he's a dangerous crank. He's ruining our city environment. Parks are to look at, not to eat. It's just as if you were going to allow people to walk through a zoo and eat the bear cubs.

DL: But surely you or your park keepers, Mr Stern, could have discouraged Mr Brill from his activity without going to such drastic measures, without arresting him?

HS: Steve's a nice fellow. But what he's doing is illegal. He knows an awful lot about wild weeds. We'd be very happy to let him organise tours if he just wouldn't eat the plants, and wouldn't encourage other people to do so too. You never know what this could lead to – all sorts of people ruining our parks in all sorts of ways. This kind of thing is very definitely criminal behaviour and must be stopped.

PROSECUTION LAWYER: Mr Brill, can you tell us how you organise your plant-eating tours?

STEVE BRILL: Well, if you talk about plant-eating tours, it rather gives the wrong impression. We pick maybe one dandelion weed out of hundreds

and thousands that are mown down by the gardeners – that's something the park keepers don't mention. And as everyone knows, the more dandelions you pick, the more they grow back.
PL: Yes, Mr Brill, but what about the actual tours?
SB: Yes, people get to know about me and come and find me around two o'clock near the fountain.
PL: I believe you take money for the tours, Mr Brill?
SB: Yes, of course. I'm offering a service. The Parks Commissioner is trying to say that I am getting paid for weeds that are public property. But it's not that at all. I'm paid for passing on my knowledge and expertise. What people actually do, whether they take the weeds or not is none of my business.
PL: But you must realise, Mr Brill, that what you have been doing is illegal.
SB: People are so out of contact with nature in cities these days, I think the parks should be paying me. I'm offering a public service.
PL: What actually happened on September 5th, Mr Brill?
SB: Well, there were these two strange characters in the group, a man and a woman. They were taking photos and asking a lot of questions, but they didn't mingle like people usually do. Then all of a sudden things got nasty. I couldn't believe it when they started to arrest me. They handcuffed me, hustled me into a police car and took me down to the police station. They fingerprinted me and charged me. It's ridiculous. They surely have better things to do with their time.
PL: Can you tell us exactly what happened on September 5th, Ms Stokes?
SARAH STOKES: Yes, I'd been asked to gather evidence about the ways in which Mr Brill was damaging our parks. Everybody knows Mr Brill. He's been doing this for so long – his white helmet is a landmark. So it was easy to join a group of tourists – they meet at 2 pm most afternoons at the fountain, a fairly out-of-the-way spot, anyone in the park can tell you where to find him.
PL: Were you alone, Ms Stokes?
SS: No, my colleague, Tony O'Brien was with me. He was taking the photos.
PL: Photos, Ms Stokes?
SS: Yes, it wouldn't have been right to pick weeds ourselves and eat them in front of everybody, even if we wanted to. But we needed the evidence. Mr Brill was very cooperative. He showed us all sorts of plants, explained what their nutritive value was, how to cook them and so on. Some of our photos show him plucking and eating dandelions.
PL: What other evidence do you have?
SS: Well, we know he charges for his tours. We paid him our 13 dollars with marked notes. He's actually making a lot of money out of vandalising our parks.
DEFENCE LAWYER: Can you tell us something about yourself, Ms Brown, and what you know about Mr Brill?
ALEXANDRA BROWN: Well, I'm a botany student at City University, and I often go on Steve's escorted tours – he knows so much about the wildlife in the parks.
DL: Ms Brown, would you say that Mr Brill's activity is destroying the parks?
AB: It's silly to say he's destroying the parks. First of all, most of the people who come just want to know about plants, it's a scientific interest, that sort of thing. Of course some of them do take plants home, you know Steve knows what you can eat and what you can't. He's good on nutrition and how to cook things and all that. But they only take things that would be killed by weed-killer or by the lawn-mower anyway. We never go near the proper flower beds, you know the things the gardeners look after. The stuff Steve is interested in, you know, water mint, day lily shoots, wild black cherries, carrots, mustard blueberries and so on grow in really out of the way places where people don't normally go.
DL: Were you with Mr Brill on September 5th, Ms Brown?
AB: Yes I was. I thought those two people were a bit strange. They didn't talk to anyone. They kept taking photos. But I couldn't believe it at the end when they started to search him for weapons. What did they think he'd have – insect repellent to spray them with?

UNIT 14

RECORDING 1

INTERVIEWER: You're the headmistress of Oxford High School for Girls. How many girls do you have here?
MRS TOWNSEND: We have 650 girls because we start from the age of 9, just under 100 girls age 9 and 10, 400 then from 11 to 16, and between 150 and 160 usually in the sixth form each year.
I: In your experience, do girls do better academically, and later professionally in single sex schools?
MRS T: Yes, I think they do better academically, and you can measure that very crudely from examination results. I also think they do better academically because they have more opportunities to take the leading roles in discussion and in managerial responsibilities. I think they see the role models of the chief positions in the school being held by women and I think that they see that as something they can then aspire to, and I think that they're not disadvantaged at all later on because as soon as they leave school they go into a mixed environment, but they go out with far more confidence, having managed things within school for themselves.
I: Do boys and girls react in the same way to single sex education?
MRS T: No, I don't think they react in the same way to single sex education. I think that boys don't notice one way or the other as much as girls do. So I think if you were to ask boys whether they thought it was a good idea to be in a boys' school or a co-educational school, many of them would have no opinion on it whatsoever. But I think that the - when you actually go on beyond school it doesn't make very much difference I think once you've reached the higher education level or you go out into employment. The difference that it does make for the girls is that they are more confident because they've had more experiences than they would have otherwise.
INTERVIEWER: I wonder if you could say then in a few words what the advantages are for a girl at a single sex school.
MRS T: Well, I think within the classroom she is going to have full opportunity to express her own opinions. She isn't going to be shouted down by over-confident young gentlemen. There are going to be no distractions about her appearance and so on, nobody is going to be commenting on that within the classroom. It's very cutting to have your spots and so on noted by somebody of the opposite sex when you are actually engaged upon your Latin verbs and so on. I think that for mathematicians and scientists, there is within society a view that the girls are not going to be as good as the boys and this can be reinforced in laboratories, for instance when boys can monopolise the apparatus and the teacher's time. Within a girls' school, they are given all the opportunities to use the computers and so on, and so they are the most important people, and they can show that they are just as good as the boys.
I: Do the girls like these schools?
MRS T: They love them at the beginning, at the age of nine, ten and eleven, and twelve. In the middle school doldrums - thirteen, fourteen and fifteen, they might be looking for other things but as we are a nine to eighteen school I think to get the true flavour, you have to ask the sixth form what they think, and if you talk to the sixth form then it comes through very loud and clear that they enjoy being in a girls' school and they can see the advantages.
I: Are teenagers in particular, do you think, sheltered too much from contact with the opposite sex? Does this cause them difficulties when they find themselves in mixed groups?
MRS T: Well, I would like to find the parents who could shelter girls from the opposite sex if they live in Oxford - or the environs of Oxford. They encounter boys all the time socially out of school, and through debating societies and things like that, some school activities as well.
I: So, no disadvantages at all?
MRS T: I don't think there are any disadvantages. I think that it's grossly overstated that one needs to have contact with the opposite sex right through the whole of life, in the classroom and outside the classroom and at all ages.

UNIT 15

RECORDING 1

As the chart shows, the coming decade will see a significant decrease of the working population who are in their twenties. 9.2 million today, there will be two million fewer in the year 2001. On the other hand, the number of retired people in the community will be roughly stationary, rising from 11.8 million to only 11.9 million. The number of people between thirty and fifty-nine in paid employment will rise from its current level by about 900 000 to reach a figure of 24.2 million. There will be a slight increase in the number of children in school - forecasts say the figure will rise to about 15.8 million. However, thirty years later in the year 2031, the scene will be somewhat different with 16.3 million people enjoying retirement. Whereas 22.2 million mature adults and 7.4 million young adults, that is a total of 29.6 million, will be in employment, there will be 15.3 million schoolchildren. This means that with a total population of over 60 million the ratio of people working will be less than two to one.

UNIT 16

RECORDING 1

INTERVIEWER: When you write a novel, do you know where you're going?
P. D. JAMES: Yes, you must really if you're writing the classical detective story because it must be so carefully plotted and so carefully clued. I have schemes, I have charts, I have diagrams. It doesn't mean to say I always